THE DEV SHASTRA III

THE DEV SHASTRA III

PHILOSOPHY OF MAN

SHREE SATYANAND AGNIHOTRI

Translated by

SATYAVAN P. KANAL
Dept. of Philosophy
University of Delhi

DEVATMA

To order additional copies of this book, contact:
Xlibris
800-056-3182
www.Xlibrispublishing.co.uk
Orders@Xlibrispublishing.co.uk
777672

Devatma (1850-1929), the most worshipful founder of Dev Samaj Society and the discoverer and teacher of the one, true science-based, universal system of soul culture for all mankind, lived an ideal life.

This ideal life, possessed of the highest sense of obsessive love for truth and goodness, and complete repulsion for untruth and evil was unique in personal life and conduct, in his aim of life, in his teachings and in his life mission and work. His ideal life, as Herbert Spencer had predicted is incomprehensible to millions of men even now. The life of highest psychic senses and the ideal standard of conduct, with the evolution of his love for truth and goodness, He developed a unique psychic light and power and became a future luminary of the soul world.

Spiritual Name: Devatma
Birth place: Shri Akbarpur, Distt-Kanpur U.P. India

A NOTE FROM DEVATMA ORGANISATION

Devatma Organisation presents the philosophy of Devatma where one finds a philosophical response to the scientific climate. In Devatma Organisation one finds a frank admission, that the philosophical reflections based on the bedrock of scientific discoveries and on the critical on Nature, man and society.

Devatma brought a naturalistic, scientific, altruistic, rational and evolutionary point of view to bear upon all problems concerning the nature of the universe, theory of knowledge, nature of human personality, and the nature of human bondage and freedom. The goal of Devatma philosophy is a life-service in which low-loves and low-hates are held to a lower-point, while the individual endeavours in high loves and high hates to remove the presence of evil in life, wherever he may find it. The philosophy of Devatma is not founded on science alone; its religious teachings are characterized by consistency and continuity with scientific knowledge in other fields. The scientific method must be employed in the field of religion and religion can be made into a science, like other sciences.

We need a philosophy of life that is scientific by nature. It is through Devatma that the Science of Religion replaces mythological religion, just as the scientific mind needs a non-theistic and non-absolutist scientific religion. As Julian Huxley, the great biologist stated: "The beliefs of this religion — are not revelations in the supernatural sense, but are the revelations that science and learning have given us about humans and the universe."

The universal philosophy of Devatma can open up new vistas of truth. Devatma asserts that values, which can be studied by the empirical method and human ideal, are part of the empirical life of humans and can well be accommodated in the naturalistic worldview.

Devatma interprets the origin and nature of the human soul in both evolutionary and biological terms, while it also raises many interesting points regarding the evolutionary origin of the human entity. The human entity is a new entry, an emergent entity, from the ovum of a female and the sperm of a male, and its characteristics are the result of the interaction between these two cells and environments. Therefore, to understand the human entity-soul body organism, we first need to understand the laws of heredity-environments.

Humans are part of nature. Hence, the human ideal is to seek and realize true harmony with existence in nature. However, harmony with others does not merely concern refraining from doing harm to them — humans must be serviceable to others to achieve the ideal of harmony. This is possible if they develop higher feelings of disinterested service of others. This is the evolution of humankind, and these are some of the truths about soul-life which differentiate Devatma from the world Religions.

Since these truths are founded on scientific verification, there is a moral obligation to accept a number of truths, as detailed in the following summary:

- Humans are evolute from the animal world – not a special creation.
- Each human soul is a new entity unknown to the previous history of the universe. Hence, transmigration is false. The human soul is neither a substance nor a pure cognition – it is a nutritive organism, a motor and a sensory instrument with affective, conative and cognitive functions. As such, it is the doer, affecting change and changing itself. Thus, the human soul is under the law of change and subject to growth, decay and death under certain conditions.
- The origin and condition of the continued existence of each human entity is in nature. He is inseparable from Nature – his first and last home. His destiny is to establish harmony with other existences in nature on an evolutionary basis (i.e. Truth, Goodness and Beauty).
- A religion that develops a scientific mode of thinking in religious matters is a true religion. Moreover, true religion delivers humans from evil and forms the complete embodiment of truth and goodness for love.
- An ideal society needs ideal men as well as ideal institutions – neither can bring about the ideal society alone. Humanism has played a noble part in changing the institutions of society, and true religion specializes in encouraging humans to be more altruistic.

Thus, humanism and true religion need to work together to create a society of altruistic love and justice for all; a society void of untruth and evil, and where altruistic loves are capable of walking the path of Truth, goodness and Beauty.

In Devatma, humanism will find its best companion, its highest guide and its noblest fulfillment.

- Devatma can enlighten a disciple to see his duties in relation to all the four orders of existences and to discharge them according to his capacity. Devatma offers the greatest blessings to a devotee by offering his sublime life as an object of love. The feeling of devotional love helps the devotee to realize its dream of becoming a perfect being in Devatma, and, in turn, finds the complete satisfaction of its love in this embodiment of Truth, Goodness and Beauty.
- We live an altruistic life when:
  - we know how to control the evil motivations that threaten the very existence of our life and the life of others.
  - we know our aptitude and abilities and engage ourselves in their development.
  - we utilize our development aptitude and abilities in the service of the family of man.
  - we develop a vision and love for the sublime life, a complete love of Truth, Goodness & Beauty and a complete hatred of untruth and evil.
- An ideal human soul is one who:
  - is illumined with the scientific truth of the philosophy of Devatma;
  - rises above his low loves and low hates;
  - cultivates higher loves and higher hates; and through them lives a dedicated life of innocence and service of the four orders of existences; and who
  - is in complete rapport with Devatma through the redevelopment of the feelings of faith, reverence, gratitude and love for him, to the extent a person achieves this ideal four-fold life.
- The universal religion of Devatma is the only complete humanistic religion which places the origin of the human personality, both the body and soul, in human society. It also places the human ideal in human society by developing a system of meditation to reshape and refine the interpersonal relationships through the development of appreciation, gratitude, compassion, altruistic love and service in various interpersonal relationships. Its founder's life has been illumined with ideal interpersonal relationships, and in its uniqueness, Devatma's philosophy and the founder has the permanent capacity to help us build interpersonal relationships on the basis of altruism of appreciation, gratitude, love and service. In this way, Devatma is the religion for a civilization of sweetness and light in interpersonal relationships. It is too great in its excellences and achievements in human relations to justify

despair about its future service in interpersonal relationships. As long as Devatma lives, the future of humanity will be preserved through maintaining ideal interpersonal and infra-personal relationships.

- Devatma is the highest form of altruism in relation to the four kingdoms of nature. There is no religious leader in the history of the world who has sung of his connection to humans, animals, plants and the physical worlds with the same intensity as a mystic sings in praise of a deity. His contemplation is not on a supernatural power, but on his gratitude towards the four kingdoms and how best he can serve them. His life gives inspiration to those seeking the all-out altruism of understanding, as well as the appreciation of, gratitude for, and service to the four kingdoms. When education unites under the philosophy of Devatma in a close and warm embrace, a new, golden future beckons for this industrialized society – a future where we can recognize our interpersonal and infra-personal relations on the basis of altruism, and thus enjoy the best intellectual and emotional satisfactions open to human life.
- The direction of evolution is towards individual health and social and cosmic harmony, and accordingly, towards a reduced state of suffering. Much of the suffering in this world arises through an unjust social structure. In addition, unjust social discrimination has condemned large sections of humanity to a life of ignorance, poverty, disease, denial and deprivation, and consequently, immeasurable suffering. The law of evolution is the name for the processes of changes in entities, which are conducive in bringing about the reign of Truth, Goodness and Beauty for complete harmony on earth.
- Evolution is the key concept of Devatma.

This universe of embodied existences in ceaseless change, for better or worse, which perpetually develops higher and higher life on earth, is the only self-existent, self-explanatory reality. Hence, evolution is reality, for change is real, time is real, and the history of the planet is real. What is the highest is the product of time, change, and evolution. Dev Dharma provides the highest evolute in Devatma to grow in humans.

- Scientific attitude to seek and accept facts;
- To develop society-centred, altruistic feelings of justice and benevolence as decisive values;
- To awaken man to his soul welfare;
- To create faith in the reality and inevitability of evolution and make humankind fit to be the managing directors of evolution, and thus, to usher in world peace.

This religious perspective can be possible in an evolutionary religion, because only an evolutionary religion can give this paramount importance and respect to the physical, biological and social environments of man.

I feel very much at home in the philosophy of Devatma and thanks to evolution for the emergence of Devatma where humankind leaps forward in evolution and obtains the meaning of life under the light and power — the embodiment of truth, goodness and beauty.

If Devatma Organisation is able to convince to readers that a new system of philosophy was born in contemporary Indian thought which offers ontology (theory of Nature), epistemology (theory of knowledge), ethics & spirituality which does and can challenge in its truth, the ancient Eastern and Western schools and that in this system, this naturalistic thought has sought new horizons, it has performed its service.

Author of The Highest Meaning of Life

TRANSLATOR'S NOTE

The title of the book *'The Dev Shastra'* by itself is liable to opposite responses by readers according to their mental attitudes. In case of reader's attitude is pro-traditional, he may be tempted to think that the Shastra deals with super-sensible reality of God and eternal soul. If his attitude is pro-scientific, he may dismiss the book as another superstitious talk about Atma and Paramatma. These negative and positive responses to the first look at the title are liable due to equivocal character of the word 'Dev'. The popular meaning of 'Dev' is that it refers to a divine or heavenly being or to a deity. It points to a super-terrestrial being, a being outside the natural order of things as studied by science. In this super-sensible sense 'Dev' also stands both for a being of good and evil character, a god or an evil demon,(A.V. 111, 15, 15). However, the word 'Dev' also stands for things of existence(R.V.,A.V., S. Br). It has also a neutral sense of anything shining or brilliant. In short, the word 'Dev' has both super naturalistic and naturalistic connotation in Vedic literature. There is thus, no reason to protest if the word 'Dev' is given a naturalistic meaning. In this book the word 'Dev' is used in naturalistic connotation. It is used as an adjective for excellences which have their origin and development in natural conditions explicable through natural evolution.

The word 'Shastra' is today contrasted in popular thought with 'vigyan'. 'Vigyan' stands *particular method* of investigation of truth. It is a method of observation, construction of a hypothesis, deducation from the hypothesis and verification, in contrast to the method of speculation or dialect. However, modern economics books, for example, are called 'Arth Shastra' though modern studies in economics use the scientific method. In this book the word 'Shastra' is used to stand for a study of the nature of human soul and its destiny undertaken within the bonds of the scientific method. It could as well be called 'Dev Vigyan'.

2

Let us return to the word 'Dev'. What is its connotation in this book. The author entitles the excellence of his soul as 'Dev'.

It is best to explain the excellence of 'Dev' as applied to Devatma for the word repeatedly occurs in the book. 'Dev' in Devatma has a specific connotation. It stands for the excellence of complete love of truth and goodness and complete hatred of untruth and evil. The author of this book is 'Devatma' which means that he developed his potentiality of the love of truth and goodness and hatred of untruth and evil inherited from his parents as a spurt development of the evolutionary process.

What is the psychology of a soul who has complete love of truth and goodness? It does not mean that he stands loyal even at the point of death and with what believes to be true and good? A man of very strong will can exhibit this character. A Hitler can stay loyal to what he believes to be true and good. Such character of staying loyal can be found both in a godly man as in a devilish man. Love of truth and goodness in the author of this book stands for a *new psychology*. His psychology is that all his thoughts and conduct are determined by the principle of truth and goodness in contrast to human soul which gravitates to love of pleasure in the determination of his thoughts and actions. Even the best of altruistic men finds in him certain weakness of the flesh or ego, and absence of certain virtues. Even the sages have been found to deviate from the path of purity. This is due to the fact that the hedonistic psychology of sages have deviated them into untruth and evil. But a Devatma has no weakness of the flesh or ego, no lack of virtues. He is above all weaknesses and is complete in his virtues. Further, there is no disposition in him to entertain untruth or evil conduct, much less to do it. His is a soul which is clean of any trace of temptation, for, his soul has complete hatred for all temptations. He has no lack of virtues for his love of goodness leaves out no virtue undeveloped. Devatma thus defines his 'Dev-anuraaga'(sublime love of truth and goodness and his hatred of untruth and evil) in his autobiography, chapter 1:

"Psychic Forces of Love of Truth"

"When a soul evolves all-sided psychic forces of love of truth,
   (1) he develops deep concern to explore, discover and assimilate truths through developing contact with different kingdoms of Nature which is inexhaustible source of useful knowledge. Through such light of truth, his soul gets more and more illuminated and acquires greater and greater capacity for evolving truth consciousness; and
   (2) he reaches out to others the light of truth which has dawned on him and thereby establishes prestige and dignity of truth.

"Psychic Forces of Complete Hatred for Untruth"

"When a soul evolves complete hatred for untruth,
   (1) he develops deepest concern and strength to give up all that appears mythical or false to him and which stands in the way of discovery of truth in different kingdoms of Nature. He does not in any way and at any time entertain or support whatever he knows to be mythical or false, and thus does not want to dim or betray the soul-illuminating light and the high ideal of life; and

(2) he exerts to the limit of his capacity to deliver myth-ridden souls with the true light of the soul life."

"Psychic Forces of Complete Love of Goodness"

"When a soul evolves complete love of good,
   (1) he develops complete concern and strength to know whatever is good in any department of Nature and to uphold it; and
   (2) he exerts to the limit of his capacity to bring into being whatever good can be actualized in any department in Nature.

"Complete Hatred for Evil"

"A soul which has evolved complete hatred for evil,
   (1) is above indulging in any evil activity in relation to any of the kingdoms of Nature or universe and thus does not un-necessarily harm any existence in Nature; and
   (2) he exerts to the limit of his capacity and understanding to abstain from evil activity or harm to any existent."

The whole of the autobiography is inspiring presentation of his sublime love of truth and goodness and sublime hatred of untruth and evil.

How the excellence of Devatma is different from that of human How souls is concisely and precisely detailed in chapter 10 of this book.

All this presentation is highly abstract and technical for the new reader. If a reader wants a companion to help him to understand and appreciate the differential excellence of Devatma from 'manushya-atma' (human soul) in simple language, he is invited to read "Devatma ka Parichey" (Hindi), perusal whereof can give easy appreciation of the spiritual genius of Devatma.

Devatma points out that he alone can give scientific knowledge of soul-life who satisfies the following condition. He writes thus in the same autobiography, chapter 29:

"To see higher truths about soul, there is imperative need of sublime life besides keen intellect. Without the sublime life there can be no light to see higher truths about soul. This invaluable and supreme light was increasing in me day by day. Now,

(1) this sublime life (of love of truth and goodness and hatred for untruth and evil);

(2) the invaluable light produced by the sublime life:

(3) the complete love for scientific method; and

(4) the most essential knowledge of the processes of evolution and devolution, were my total equipment for study and research of soul-life." It is this genius of his psychology that makes him most competent to study the origin, nature and destiny of human soul with the use of the scientific method.

3

The basic foundation of Devatma's study of human soul is that all human soul is a part of Nature. It has biological origin. It is product of the evolutionary process. This view makes a complete break from all other religious studies of human soul.

Human soul is product of changes in the natural world and therefore is in ceaseless change for better and for worse. It can stay alive under certain physical and psychological conditions. It can die under certain physical and psychological conditions. It has a dependent origination. This philosophic perspective makes a complete departure from all other religious studies of human soul.

This human soul of biological origin has the power of construction in it to build, sustain, repair and re-produce its own kind. This constructive power of evolution is inherited from the process of evolution for the process of evolution is the process of bringing into being of newer species which have resulted in man. The emergence of man through the evolutionary process reveals the character of the evolutionary process. Man has the capacity to discover some truths, to actualize some elements of justice and compassion in its social life, to appreciate and create beauty.

Devatma holds that truth and goodness are the conditions for the preservation and strengthening of the constitution of the soul. If a human soul indulges in falsehoods and evil conduct, he harms the constructive power of his soul which sustains his being and if he persists in falsehoods and evil conduct, the constructive power of his soul is completely lost and since there is no power of the soul left to sustain the body, both the soul and the body get extinct.

4

Devatma makes a painstaking study of why human soul is deviated in untruth and evils which destroy the constructive power of his soul and bring about its death. According to him, when a man's desire is satisfied, it is accompanied by pleasure. This pleasure fascinates man. He succumbs to its attraction. He seeks the pleasure of the desire, at the cost of what is true and good for him. An intemperate man goes in for tasty things at the cost of his health and strength and if he persists in it, he brings about his premature death. He indulges in falsehood when he makes light of the harms that come to him, and when he holds that his suffering and death are matter of his fate. The love of pleasure derived from our ego satisfaction makes us over-estimate our own character. We attribute excellences to ourselves which are not possessed by us and it makes us harm even those who wish to help us to proper estimate of our worth.

Devatma thus lists the various groups of loves of pleasure:
1. Love for various pleasures pertaining to body;
2. Love for various pleasures pertaining to 'self' or ego;
3. Love for various pleasure resulting from affection of off-springs;
4. Love for pleasures pertaining to wealth and property;
5. Love for various pleasures derived from traditional beliefs; social connections and various habits;
6. Love for pleasure derived from violence ('himsa');
7. Love for various pleasures derived from false beliefs; and
8. Love for pleasures arising out of various altruistic feelings.

He offers in chapters 9 to 18, a detailed study of the ruins brought about by the love of the pleasure derived from bodily and ego urges and desires for money, children, group-life, violence and false beliefs. Even Pleasure derived from such altruistic feelings, as compassion, deviates us into untruth and evil.

After study of the particular evils brought about by each of the pleasure-dominated desires, Devatma draws common characteristics of the love of pleasure in human psychology in chapter 21 thus:
1. The dominance of love of pleasure of a desire makes soul insensitive to the values and makes him incapable to see truths of soul welfare.
2. The dominance of the love of pleasure of a desire perverts vision to see facts in their true character. The soul takes false as true and true as false, good as bad and bad as good.
3. The dominance of the love of pleasure leads to avoidable suffering in the form of diseases, dejections, misadventures of life and death.

4. The dominance of the love of pleasure of a desire saps the strength of the constructive power of soul ultimately leading to complete extinction of both the soul and the body.

Devatma offers a new interpretation of moksha and new 'sadhana' for obtaining moksha in chapter 25.

5

In the popular division made between morality and religion the life of truthful thought and right action in the inter-personal life is considered as the stage of morality. Dev Dharma is generally accused of being an ethics and not a religion, for worship of a worshipful being is regarded as the core of religious life.

Devatma also holds the higher religious life is possible through worship of a savior. However, he differs with regard to the kind of worshipful being worthy for worship. All worship is not worthy. Even worship of the best of altruistic beings is not best worship, for even at its best the altruist is not free from weaknesses of the flesh and ego and lacks some virtues. True worship is of Devatma as defined earlier. The author claims that his soul is Devatma. Devatma deals in chapters 27 to 35, with the feelings and beliefs and actions which a 'sadhak' must develop to worship Devatma. These chapters present at par excellence the psychology of a true religious 'sadhak'.

6

In view of the popular interpretation of 'Dev' as 'Divine' which means supernatural excellence, we have translated 'Dev' as 'sublime'. The development of the love of truth and goodness, into maturity illumines the soul with the light to see truths about soul life, about its origin, nature and destiny. It is a light that dispels untruthful beliefs about soul, as created, un-created, eternal and unchanging. It shows the truth pleasure, of the biological origin of soul, its weakness for love of pleasure, which leads it to a life of untruth and evil. This light show's evil feelings, in all their ugliness. The light is called Dev Jyoti and it is translated as 'sublime light'.

When the love of truth and goodness and hatred for untruths and evil matured in Devatma, they produced power in his soul which is called 'Dev Tej' and 'Dev Tej' is translated as 'sublime power'. This sublime power helps a receptive sadhak to get strength to reduce or remove the evil feelings in him as well as past impurities. The combination of Dev Jyoti (sublime light) and Dev Tej (sublime power) is called `Dev Prabhavas, and is translated as 'sublime influences'. `Atma-andhkaar' is translated as 'soul-darkness'. Soul darkness includes not only absence of true knowledge of soul but also false beliefs about soul. A person is suffering from soul darkness if he believes that his soul is created or uncreated, eternal and unchanging; if he believes that his evil conduct does not touch the character of his soul and if he believes in transmigration. Further, in a state of soul-darkness a person is not in the know of the laws of evolution and degradation of soul. 'Atma kathorta' it translated as 'soul-insensitiveness' or 'hardness of heart'. It means that soul becomes incapable to receive truths about his soul life.

'Atma-bodh' is translated as 'soul-consciousness'. Here consciousness means the same as in the context of heath consciousness. A man with health consciousness is anxious to know the principles of the hygiene of his body and observes them. A man with soul consciousness is anxious to know how evil thoughts and evil conduct injure his soul as man with health consciousness knows how smoking harms his throat or hot food harms his digestion. He knows how altruistic feelings right actions strengthen one's soul as nutritious food strengthens one's body. In the light of this knowledge, he avoids evil thoughts and actions and cultivates altruistic feelings. Above all, he knows that he is not sufficient unto himself for this task. He needs to have regular rapport with Devatma to keep him in the light of truth about his soul and to give him strength to reduce or remove the influence of evil thoughts and actions and cultivate altruistic thought and right action.

We offer this translation as the first attempt at English presentation of the third volume of The Dev Shastra which is Devatma's opus magnum in philosophy of Ethics and Religion. The reader will find at places the translation to be awkward, clumsy and involved in expression. This is partly due to the fact that we have stuck to the literal translation in contrast to free translation for it has the advantage that nothing is left out. However, the reader can find book entitled `Dev Atma'. It offers an inspired and inspiring summary of the whole book in its part vii, chapter vi, pp. 542-593. This can help the reader to experience the flow and the spirit of Devatma's writings in word and thought. The two versions, literal and free translations, will give advantage to the readers of both forms of translation. If the reader is interested and anxious to avail of commentary on this philosophy of soul, he is invited to read the book entitled 'The Ethics of Devatma' by the translator.

S.P. KANAL

DEV SHASTRA VOL. 3
PHILOSOPHY OF MAN

The Sublime Utterances of Devatma concerning the Need of Soul-Consciousness and Soul-knowledge

1. Who could be more pitiable than a man born a human soul, who feels no concern to get true knowledge about his own personality!
2. There is no greater privilege for a man as man then to feel concerned to get knowledge about his own person - especially his soul - for no animal lower to him has the privilege to get such knowledge about his being.
3. It is an extremely pitiable condition to feel soul, to feel concern to get true knowledge about his soul but be incapable to gain such knowledge or be benefit of such concern to get knowledge and thus live a life of complete ignorance and darkness about his soul.
4. It is the highest privilege for man as a human soul to be capable and to get opportunity to develop soul-consciousness and gain soul-knowledge.

MANUSHYA-JAGAT KE SAMBANDH MEIN DEVATMA KI DEV-ANURAAGA-MOOLAK SHUBH-KAAMNAAYEN

Aatma-prakaashak Devjyoti mam;
Aatma-timir-har Devjyoti mam;
   Chaaron-dig yeh parkeeran ho!
Timar se niklen jan adhikaari,
Aatma-rup dekhen adhikaari,
    Atma-gyan un mein utpan ho,
    Satya-dharam ka gyan utpann ho,
Uchch-ghrinaa-prad Dev Tej mam,
Uchch-dukha-prad Dev Tej mam,
    Chaaron-dig weh parkeeran ho!
Uchch-ghrinaa paaven adhikaari,
Uchch-dukha paaven adhikaari,
Neech-raaga tyagen adhikaari,
Neech –ghrinaa tyagen adhikaari,
    Aatma-rog se nistaaran ho!
    Aatma-paat se nistaaran ho!
    Neech-gati se nistaaran ho!
    Aatma-naash se nistaaran ho!
Uchch-bhaava-prad Dev Tej mam,
Uchch-raaga-prad Dev Tej mam
Uchch-anga-prad Dev Tej mam,
Uchch-gati-prad Dev Tej mam,
    Chaaron dig weh parkeeran ho!
Uchch-bhaava paaven adhikaari
Uchch-raaga paaven adhikaari
Uchch-anga paaven adhikaari
Uchch-gati paaven adhikaari
    Uchch-roop un mein utpann ho!
    Shreshth-roop un mein utpann ho!
    Atam-bal un mein utpann ho!
    Jeewan-bal un mein utpann ho!

(English rendering on the next page).

SUBLIME-LOVE-INSPIRED BEST WISHES OF DEVATMA FOR THE HUMAN WORLD

Soul-illuminating sublime-light mine;
Soul-darkness-dispelling sublime-light mine;
    May that radiate in quarters four.
From darkness be out deserving beings;
Soul's real form be seen by the deserving ones;
     Soul's knowledge be in them awakened,
     True Religion's knowledge be awakened,
High-hate-awakening power-sublime mine;
High-pain-awakening power-sublime mine;
      May that radiate in quarters four.
High-hate be gained by the fit;
High-pain be gained by the fit;
Low-love be renounced by the fit;
Low-hatred be renounced by the fit;
     They be free from the illness of soul;
     They be free from the fall of soul;
They be free from the low-activity;
They be free from the soul's extinction.
High-feeling-imparting power-sublime mine;
High-love-imparting power-sublime mine;
High-capacity-imparting, power-sublime mine;
High-activity-imparting power-sublime mine;
     May that radiate in quarters four.
High-feelings be developed by the fit;
High-love be developed by the fit;
High-capacity be developed by the fit;
High activity be developed by the fit;
      High-form in them be awakened;
      Beautitude in them be awakened;
      Vigour of soul in them be developed;
      Vigour of life in them be developed.

CONTENTS

THE MOST DEPLORABLE IGNORANCE OF MAN ABOUT HIS OWN BEING

It is true that in the evolutionary course of Nature, man has come to be endowed with certain special mental powers, which are absent in the animal world. By the gradual evolution of these mental powers, under various suitable conditions, for thousands of years, man has been able to discern and get knowledge of the various truths about different departments of Nature, which truths the beings of the animal world have not been able to discern and are not thus cognizant or in the know of them. In spite of all this, it is also true that in millions among mankind even the desire to acquaint themselves and to get knowledge of those various kinds of truths of utmost importance, which pertain to their very being, has not as yet awakened. They are, therefore, not as desirous of getting knowledge about their own being as they are about getting knowledge with regard to existences other than them.

Of all other departments of knowledge and learning, the most essential for man is the true knowledge relating to his own being, because no other knowledge is, and nor can it be, so valuable as the true knowledge about his own being.

Even as regards his own being, the knowledge about his own soul is far more essential for him than the knowledge of his body. But alas! How sad it is that not to speak about soul, even so far as the body is concerned, millions of men are at such an elementary stage of development that no desire is awakened in them even to get knowledge about the various necessary truths based on Nature about such subjects as the physiology of their body, the causes of its ordinary diseases, the harmful effects of those diseases, its protection from such harmful effects and its development into a symmetrical, beautiful and strong one.

On the contrary they are so very ignorant about their body and so deeply dominated and enslaved by various pleasures that, as compared to different kinds of animals, they are in a very inferior degraded state so far the growth, health and immunity from disease of the body are concerned. That is, million upon millions of men neither possess such well-formed and beautiful bodies, nor do they enjoy such good bodily health and freedom from different kinds of diseases, as we find among the various undomesticated birds like crow, pigeon, parrot, mayna and undomesticated mammalia like monkey, deer, stag, antelope, rabbit etc. Why is it so? This is because in contravention to the beneficial laws of Nature, man has become a lover of and slave to such of the pleasures from which all these existences of the animal world are free.

Besides this, these millions among men have developed low loves for different other pleasures connected with their body and ego. Hence they are so deeply engrossed in ways and means for the attainment and gratification of those pleasures and are so immersed in the thoughts and activities relating thereto, that in their most deplorable state of unconcern about their being, they do not pay any attention to the most essential part of their being i.e., soul (the prime source of all activities of this life) and remain totally unconscious ('be-sudh'), insensible ('aboddhi') and ignorant (agiani), about it.

Again, the persons who in the name of religion cherish one or another kind of faith relating to soul and also preach, propagate and do religious exercises in conformity therewith, remain totally blind to and ignorant about the true knowledge concerning the soul and its life as all their fundamental beliefs are against the true laws and facts of Nature. In consequence of all this, we find unrelieved darkness, blindness and ignorance about soul-life prevailing among the people of all countries all over the world.

What is meant by 'aatmik aboddhita' or ignorance about soul in men?' It means that, on the one hand, they do not possess any desire at all to get true knowledge about their soul and, on the other hand, their own various pleasure-seeking low-loves produce in their souls intense soul darkness. On account of being enveloped in such deep soul-darkness, they are incapable of perceiving the highly-essential truths about the nature and organism of their soul, its diseases, its degradation, its dissolution and its evolution. They do not possess any awareness even about their such Incapacity i.e., they are totally devoid of all cognitions of such kind. It is the absence of all such cognitions in a person which is called ignorance about soul ('aatma-abodhitaa') in man.

LOVE OF LOW PLEASURE IN MAN IS THE ROOT CAUSE OF HIS MOST DEPLORABLE IGNORANCE ABOUT HIS SOUL

The utter blindness about his soul that prevails in mankind is due primarily to man's consciousness of various low pleasures and his deep attachment to or love for them. This love of low pleasures in man is most harmful to him. He is inevitably led by this love of pleasures not only to desert goodness on several occasions but also to prove unfaithful or inimical to it and throttle it and join hands with evil. It is also inevitable for every such lover of pleasures to harm not only his soul but also the constitution of his body. Hence by growing love or attachment for the pleasures of taste, sex, intoxicants, sloth, etc., man commits those excesses and acts of intemperance in relation to the organism of his body which excesses and intemperances are not found in the animal world.

Therefore, the various kinds of diseases and the unnecessary pains and weaknesses caused by them which man develops in the constitution of his body by his such excesses are absent in the animal world. Hence animals do not need all those professional doctors and hakims and curative medicines which have come to be considered essential for man.

Now, every living person in spite of his love for pleasures, has a strong biological urge to live and a strong repulsion for death and so led by this strong urge of self-preservation, he naturally wishes to prolong his existence and avoid death, yet he feels no uneasiness in living in ignorance about the most necessary laws of life and death of his being. Being in such mental state, he is found not only unconcerned about and blind to the laws of life and death relating to his soul but even indifferent to the knowledge relating to the well-being and degeneration of his body. This is not all, but the worse follows.

Even when he comes to know that due to gratification of one or another love of pleasure, his body is being adversely affected, his health is being impaired, his vitality is going low and one or another physical malady is developing in him, even then due to dominance of or slavery to that pleasure, he feels on several occasions utterly helpless and feels compelled to harm his being and thus become his own enemy. Oh! What a sad and degraded state of man incontrast to the animal world!

THE EMERGENCE OF THE SPIRITUAL EVOLUTE, THE DEVATMA, IN FULFILMENT OF THE LAWS OF NATURE, IN ORDER TO REMOVE THE MOST INJURIOUS SOUL IGNORANCE OF FIT ('ADHIKARI') PERSONS AND TO BRING ABOUT HIGHER CHANGES IN THEM

Whenever any man becomes a slave to the love of pleasure—the pleasure may be of any kind—or when pleasure enslaves him, it becomes inevitable for him to take the path of various kinds of untruths, and evil practices. It is for this reason that the number and variety of falsehoods and evils or sinful practices which flourish in the human world are not found in such diversity and to such an extent in the entire animal world.

By loving and following the path of evils and untruths every man according to the immutable devolutionary laws of Nature, harms the organism of his soul in the same way as he harms his bodily organism by intemperance. This deterioration of the soul-organism is called soul-degradation ('aatmik patan').

This soul-degradation is manifested in various ways. One of its forms is perversion of soul-vision ('ulti drishti'). Due to this perverted vision whatever affords pleasure to man—however harmful that pleasure may be to him and to others—is viewed by him, on account of his prejudice for it, as something good, beautiful and profitable; and whatever affords him no pleasure or gives him pain—however beneficial it may be for him and for others—is considered by him as evil and harmful. In such a mental state, not only he does not like to accept goodness or truth when they are antagonistic to his pleasure but, on the contrary, he cherishes hatred for them. Led by this hatred he, as far as possible, gives a wide berth to truth and goodness. What a deplorable state of man is this!

For millions of years this state of affairs reigned in the human world. In order to bring about a change for the better in this most degrading and harmful condition of man, it was inevitable that there should be the emergence of such a soul who should be endowed with absolutely new powers, i.e., who should evolve in himself complete love of goodness instead of love of pleasure and complete hatred for all forms of falsehoods and evils which are born of the love of pleasure, and also complete love of every kind of truth concerning all departments of Nature. And in accordance with the immutable laws of the spiritual world in Nature, he should evolve in himself in all such thoughts, sayings, beliefs, utterances, talks, sermons, writings, and undergo all such sacrifices, etc., which are the natural result of the gradual evolution of these highest psychic forces of the love of truth and goodness. Then by the gradual development of these highest psychic forces of the love of goodness and truth, this soul should evolve in himself the Dev Jyoti—that unique light which reveals the nature of soul— and Dev Tej—that unique power that helps to destroy evil and to promote goodness in different relations in Nature. And on account of possessing the complete love for goodness and truth, this unique emergence should become the spiritual sun for the perverted-visioned, benighted, ignorant and degarded fit-souls (adhikaari atma') of the human world and bestow on them his Dev Jyoti and his Dev Tej according to their individual capacities and prove true worshipful being, true deliverer, true guide and guru and complete and all-sided benefactor for them. Without such a unique spiritual sun, there could be no hope for the most blessed changes of this kind in the fit human souls. Such unique manifestation, who has appeared on this earth endowed with the above unique powers in the course of the evolutionary process of Nature as working in the human world, is called the Devatma.

This Devatma endowed as he is, with the unique Dev Joyti and Dev Tej, is as true and completely blissful spiritual sun for every fit human soul, as our grand luminary is for the physical benefits of all human and sub-human living kingdoms.

The various highly profound, most essential, most wonderful and most precious truths which this spiritual Sun or the Devatma has seen in his own Dev Jyoti or highest psychic light about the following subjects, are dealt with in detail in the subsequent chapters of this volume of The Dev Shastra:

1. The origin of human soul.

2. The relation of soul with its body.

3. The organism of soul comprised of the different kinds of powers.

4. The loves of different kinds of pleasures in the organism of human soul.

5. The prevalence of various kinds of falsehoods and evil practices resulting from these loves of various pleasures.

6. The most deplorable soul-degradation of man through them.

7. The deliverance of man from such a degradation.

8. The necessity and the methods of the development various life-giving higher forces in him, etc.

MAN, HIS SOUL AND HIS BODY

Q. What is meant by Man?

A. The individual comprising of two specially organized existences—body and soul is called man.

Q. How did man come into existence on this planet?

A. After the evolution of the animal kingdom on this planet, human being appeared in the evolutionary course of one of the various kinds of subsections of the mammalian branch of the animal kingdom.

But, although, this living being called man, has evolved from the animal world, yet there have developed in him certain special powers by virtue of which he has distinguished himself from the rest of the animal kingdom, which is devoid of these special powers and which cannot develop in any of them.

Q. What is human soul?

A. The organized life-force, comprising of different kinds of powers, inhabiting the living human body, is called the human soul.

Q. How is the human soul born?

A. According to Nature's immutable law, when man and woman copulate, their two special living cells (known as sperm and ovum) sometimes unite by their mutual attraction to form one new living cell and the life forces of both of these cells also combine into one life-force. It is only through the process of such union that this new life-force, exhibits in itself the power of constructing an organized living human body. This very body-building life-power is the absolutely new tiny soul in the womb of that woman. Thus by this process of Nature an absolutely new soul, which did not at all exist before, comes into being.

This new tiny soul by and by, constructs for itself an organized living body of the human type in the womb of that woman.

Q. How does the human soul construct for itself an organized human body?

A. A brief and cursory summary of what the various able embryologists have come to know in this respect, through their investigations, is given below:

When a new soul comes into being in this united cell (zygote) of man and woman, it, at first, utilizes the material already present in that cell for body building and develops into a very very tiny worm-like embryo of three layers. Then this embryo establishes somewhere in the thin membrane of the womb by attaching itself to it and prepares from this membrane a soft sponge-like substance known as placenta connecting it to that membrane. Three blood vessels, coiled in the form of a rope, branch off from this placenta and connect the embryo with the blood vessels of the pregnant woman. This coiled up rope-like substance is called the cord. One of these three blood vessels carries the pure blood of the pregnant woman to the embryo and the soul utilizes it for developing this new embryo. Then the impure blood which remains behind, finds its exit through the remaining two vessels which are connected with the veins of the pregnant woman and thus it reaches her heart and lungs to be purified.

At first, this embryo in the uterus of the women is just like an awl pin, i.e. at the upper end it has a small head-like sign which tapers down like a tail. It is connected by this tail with the placenta through the cord.

For the protection and further development of this embryo, the soul covers it up with a membranous sac which is filled up with an aqueous substance and the embryo floats in that closed sac.

In the first month the weight of this embryo, is about 1.25 to 1.5 grams only. In a month and a half, very very small grooves indicating eyes, ears and face appear on it and the head and the trunk are seen distinctively. At this time, its weight increases to about 1.75 grams. In two months, the embryo becomes about one inch in length and weighs about four grams, and the organs of head and heart are formed and the development of hands and feet begins. After three months, its length increases to about 3.5 inches and the weight to about an ounce. At this time, the fingers of the hands and the feet appear, and the bones begin to be formed and the placenta is completed. After four months, the length of this embryo rises to about five inches and the weight to about a quarter of a pound. At this time, the openings of mouth and anus appear and the sex organs also become distinguishable. In five months the length increases to about seven or eight inches and the weight to about 5/8th of a pound. At this time, the hair begin to grow. After six months, its length grows to about twelve inches, the weight becomes a pound and a half. At this time the eye-lids are formed but the eyes are closed. On completion of the seventh month, its length becomes about fifteen inches and the weight about two and a half pounds. After eight months, its length reaches about sixteen inches and the weight comes to about five pounds. After nine months, its length is about eighteen or twenty inches and the weight about six to seven pounds. Thus, in about forty weeks, this embryo develops into a complete child and under favourable circumstances leaves its mother's uterus in accordance with the natural process. On its coming out in the external world, the upbringing of both its soul and body begins by another process in with the law of Nature.

Q. By what process of Nature, the nourishment and further development of the child's body is carried on after its coming out of the womb in a complete form?

A. When the body of the child comes out of the womb of its mother, in the normal and living form after it has constructed all the necessary organs there, it begins to breathe in the air. The various under mentioned senses then appear in it through the working of its nervous system for its physical well-being and further growth:

(i) Sense of hunger; (ii) Sense of thirst; (iii) Sense of defecation;

(iv) Sense of urinating; (v) Sense of sleep; (vi) Sense of rest;

(vii) Sense of pain; and (viii) Sense of comfort.

The process of Nature, by which the nourishment and growth of the child's body, goes on after the appearance of these senses is as follows:

The preparation of blood for the nourishment of the body

There is a very long canal in the human body commencing from the mouth, passing on to the stomach and then from the stomach to small and large intestines. This canal throughout its length i.e., in the mouth, in the stomach and further on in the intestines has attached a great number of large and small glands. These glands secrete and give different kinds of juices for it. When the child feels hungry and takes milk or in due course of time, some other kind of food, these glands send their various kinds of specific juices in order to digest and bring required chemical changes in that food. When this food changes by their chemical action, enters the small intestines, the part of it which can be converted into blood is sucked up by the blood vessels and the remaining portion passes on into the large intestines as faeces.

The work of blood circulation in the body

The food essence which the small intestines convert into blood is taken by the blood vessels to a vital organ called the heart. The heart sends the blood through its vessels to the lungs. Again, the lungs, which breathe air day and night, purify the blue venous blood into red arterial blood by means of the oxygen inhaled and return it back to the heart through other vessels. Again, the heart, sends the blood to all the organs of the body through the arteries. When the blood in the course of its circulation passes by different organs, each of them takes up sufficient nourishment out of it and passes on its waste matter to the blood, thus converting it into blue venous blood. The venous blood comes back again, through the veins to the heart and then to the lungs to be purified. It again comes back to the heart and then goes through the arteries to the various organs of the body for their nourishment. In this manner, the circulation of blood goes on throughout the body, day and night and by means of this vital organ i.e., heart, the circulation of blood is carried on in the whole body.

Again, the blood vessels, come out of the heart for the circulation of blood in the whole body. There are also at several places several other kinds of small glands which pour their different sorts of juices into the blood stream. One of such glands (thyroid) lies on both sides of the wind-pipe in the throat and two more small glands lie a little below it.

Similarly, pituitary gland lies in the fossa of the sphenoid bone at the base of the skull and two supra-renal glands just on the top of both the kidneys. There are some glands in the pancreas which lie behind the stomach three or four inches above the navel.

Until now it is thought, that these glands play great part in the growth, metabolism and health of the body and the development of its different organs; and if any of these glands fail to work properly, for some reason or another, the body becomes very weak, exhausted and a prey to many diseases.

The system for removal of several kinds of poisonous and harmful matter from the body

That portion of the food which cannot be converted into blood, passes on from the small intestines to the large one. This is called faecal matter. This faecal matter passes out through the large intestine which ends with the anus. Besides this, many other minute, unnecessary and in some cases, poisonous particles of food get mixed up with the blood.

If they do not get a chance to collect in some muscle of the body, they remain circulating in the blood vessels and thus when the), pass by the kidneys, they are absorbed by them along with the dirty water of the blood. This dirty water is passed through the urethra to a small bag known as bladder. This dirty water goes on collecting in this bladder and is called urine. The urine passes out of the bladder through the Uthera from the opening in the head of the penis.

Again, while the blood is circulating and traversing the whole body, much of its waste and poisonous element finds its exit through millions of very minute holes or pores in the skin. It is this very poisonous and waste matter which is known in ordinary language as perspiration. Similarly, when the lungs take in atmospheric air and redden the blood by its oxygen, the carbon of the blood corpuscles mixes up with this oxygen and produces a poisonous gas called "carbonic acid gas", It is this combustion of carbon by oxygen which produces the necessary heat and keeps the body warm and alive. This poisonous carbon acid gas is expired out by the lungs. By this process, these four kinds of organs viz., intestines, kidneys, skin pores and lungs throw out of the body, various kinds of waste and harmful matter.

The work of directing the various organs and evolution of several kinds of consciousnesses

Starting from the most important organ i.e., the head, passing through the spinal cord, there spreads to all the organs and sub-organs of the body, a very vast and most precious network for its protection and maintenance. This network is called the nervous system. It comprises of lakhs of living threads inter-linked with one another. It is only through this nervous system that human soul can move one or other organ of his body. It is through this system that he feels the sensation of any pain or distress, pleasure or comfort, heat or cold, weight or pressure & c. in any organ of his body. It is again, through this nervous system that the working of various digestive organs goes on and food is changed in one or other form and conveyed to one or other organ. It is due to this that lungs inhale and exhale air, that heart works continuously and various kinds of poisonous matters are driven out of the body. Through this very nervous system all the other organs i.e. hands, feet, head, neck, tongue, etc., are moved and all the organs of the body are directed and several kinds of sense consciousness are obtained.

The framework of the human body in which all these organs are arranged is roughly described as under:

From head to both the feet, this framework is made up of a bony structure. These bones are of various shapes and forms, e.g., some long, some cylindrical, some flat and some of other forms. There are about 250 bones in the whole human skeleton. Except the exposed parts of the nails and the teeth, the whole of this Skelton is covered with muscles which in ordinary parlance are called flesh. These muscles are made up of thread-like tissues of flesh. Some of these muscles are long, others flat or some of other shapes. There are in all about 500 such muscles in the whole human body. There is a good deal of elasticity in them, therefore, they can expand and contract when in motion. Many of these muscles are voluntary i.e., they are under human volition and the others are involuntary i.e., they work by themselves without the aid of human will.

There is a layer of fat over these muscles for their protection and then the whole is covered by the skin. There are two parts of the skin, which are called the inner and the outer epidermis. One can see the outer epidermis distinctly in the cover of a blister when it rises on any part of the body. The outer epidermis is very thin but the inner one is much thicker than the outer. Under the outer epidermis, there are millions of white, black, yellow or red coloured cells, due to which some people appear white, some black, some yellow or red skinned. The hair that appear on the outer skin have their roots in the inner skin. The hair are of many colours e.g., golden, silvery, black, brown etc. There are hundreds of small glands in the inner skin, which secrete a kind of oil for the protection of hair. Besides these, there are hundreds of other small glands in the skin, which draw the impurities of the body. They are then excreted in the form of perspiration through millions of small pores which open on the outer epidermis.

The human skeleton is like the case of a watch. As there are component parts and sub-parts in a watch, so there are many organs in the human body like brain, heart, lungs, stomach, liver, intestines, kidneys, etc., which work for the maintenance of the body.

The nervous system in human body has its roots in the head. The head or brain of man is the most important organ of his body. The brain is well protected by several membranes within the cranium and is a kind of whitish grey matter. The whole of the nervous system is made up of similar matter, and issuing forth from the head spreads in the whole body in the shape of threadlike ducts sheathed in a cover.

In the front part of the head are situated the eyes, the ears, the nose, the mouth &c. The human nervous system has two kinds of nerves i.e., motor nerves and sensory nerves. By means of motor nerves, man can move the various muscles etc., of his body according to his will. The sensory nerves enable him to receive various kinds of sensations. Both these kinds of nerves are absolutely essential for his good. If the nerves of the first kind be cut off, the muscles which are controlled by them will fail to move; for instance, if the motor nerves which control the eyes be cut off, man will not be able to close his eyes at his will, and his eyes shall always remain open. In the same way, if the sensory nerves that reach the eyes be cut off, man shall not be able to see the form of anything inspite of the eyes. Same is the case with every other organ.

Q. What is meant by man's physical development?

A. The different organs of the human body which the soul constructs in the mother's womb gradually grow and develop by the nourishment it receives and thus the body of small structure grows into a big one. The body gains in weight and grows in strength. At first the digestive organs which are not able to digest any solid food except very light and liquid diet, gradually grow in strength and are able to take solid food and digest it. In the beginning the child is not able to sit up by himself owing to the want of strength in his muscles, but gradually the muscles grow so strong that he is able to sit up by himself. Even on becoming able to sit up, he is too weak to stand up, and to walk even a few steps by himself. After some time as his muscles gain more strength, he is able to stand and walk and by and by even to run. At first he is not able to lift anything with his hands but as the hands grow stronger, he gradually gains the power at first of lifting light things, and then comparatively heavier ones. All such changes for the better mean the development of his human body.

Q. How can the bodily constitution of man be kept free from disease and in a state of health?

A. In order to keep human body free from disease and in a state of health, and still more to keep it alive, it is necessary that:

(1) All the digestive organs in it whose function is to transform food into blood should, on the one hand, be complete in their structure and on the other hand perform their allotted work properly.

(2) All the organs in it whose function is to purify and circulate blood should, on the one hand, have proper structure and on the other hand, do their function properly.

(3) All the above organs and besides them all of the bones and muscles in the body should have the power to absorb and assimilate the necessary nutrition from the blood stream which passes by them by the working of the above mentioned two systems.

(4) All its organs should have the capacity to completely eliminate all the refuse and other harmful and poisonous matters which remain there after all the organs have assimilated for their maintenance and proper nutrition from the blood stream.

Then again, the four kinds of organs which have developed in the human body for eliminating the unnecessary and harmful matters from the system should have the vitality to perform their functions properly and do so successfully. These organs are (1) the intestines, (2) the kidneys, (3) the lungs, and (4) millions of pores in the skin.

Now, if any one of all these physical organs is defective in its structure or it fails to perform its function properly due to its weakness, or the body fails to receive, in proper condition and sufficient quantity, the necessary materials for its nutrition from outside, as well as the other special things such as water, air, light and heat &c., which are essential for its life, the body would not remain in proper health. In other words there will appear one or other kind of disease or diseases and also weakness etc., which follow in the wake of such diseases; and thus its health will deteriorate. And if its health continues to deteriorate body will cease to live and it shall completely die.

In this way the immutable laws of Nature about the life, degeneration disease and death or destruction in the case of every living being shall inevitably operate.

The organism of human soul is also subject to similar immutable laws of Nature.

Q. What are the laws for the proper maintenance and protection of the human body?

A. Nature alone is responsible for man to have living organized body having various organs, and it is Nature alone which has ordained beneficial laws for its maintenance and protection. Therefore, it is absolutely necessary for man to know these laws and be able to follow them faithfully.

But alas! Man has turned a deaf ear to these laws on account of the fact that moved by the instincts of hunger, thirst, taste, lust and sloth etc., he has become habituated exclusively to the pleasures obtained through their satisfactions. Being a lover of happiness, he certainly does not like pain and, therefore, he hates all such diseases that cause him any kind of pain. But inspite of this instinctive response, millions of men do not know and have no desire to know even as to what their bodily organism is, and what are those organs in it, especially the vital organs—by means of which the work of its living is carried on. Neither do they feel the need of having the true knowledge of the things which exist in Nature and which are helpful in the maintenance of their bodily organism in proper health. Generally people of all sorts wish to get pleasure by satisfying their various pleasure-giving desires which have developed in them, and nothing more. Thus during thousands of years of life human species have formed habits and love for various kinds of bodily pleasures and have thus reached such a degraded stage that they fall prey to various kinds of diseases which the beings of the animal kingdom are not heir to. By such diseases man harms his bodily constitution in a manner which animals do not do, because the animals have not developed so much the love of physical pleasures as man has done. Man does not follow the laws of Nature as much as animals do by following their natural instincts. Hence the latter enjoy physical health to an extent which human beings do not do.

Q. What are the useful laws of Nature conducive to health which man violates under the sway of his love for various pleasures '?

A. Besides going against other laws of Nature, man badly violates those major laws which specially relate to the following matters:

(1) About diet.

(2) About breathing fresh air.

(3) About the use of light and heat of the sun in the required quantity.

(4) About the proper and sufficient exercise of the various physical organs.

I. On becoming slave and habituated to the pleasures of palate, man takes several things which Nature has not made to be beneficial for his living organism but which are distinctly harmful to him.

Under the dominance of the love for delicious things, he takes edibles out of all proportion to his needs and at improper times and thus further harms his health.

2. Millions of men do not breath in open and fresh air by which they could take sufficient amount of oxygen so as to keep their blood in a healthy tone as the deer, the antelope, the wild cow and various kinds of birds &c. of the jungle do, nor do they build their houses in such a way that free and sufficient air may have access to them.

3. Lakhs of people do not make proper use of the light of the sun. Especially the civilized men keep their body over-dressed in all seasons and at all times and thus their skin which is full of thousands of pores, does not get sufficient rays of the sun and contact with cold air in a proper way, by which it may get sufficient power to enable it to perform its allotted functions properly and thus be able to eliminate different kinds of waste and poisonous matters from the body. The work of the skin is hampered, in this way, and therefore, physical health suffers.

Then, again, lakhs of people do not want to know much less do they like to practice the exercises necessary for the preservation of their health and the methods by which and the extent to which the various organs should be exercised, so that the muscles can maintain their elasticity and the blood can circulate properly.

Therefore, the amount of work which millions of the beings of the animal kingdom, motivated by their various instinctive necessities, put in and the quantity of activity which they thereby produce in their organisms is not done by millions of men. By remaining in such an indolent condition they become so dull and so lazy that they do not do and do not even desire to go through the trouble of taking sufficient exercise of any kind.

Therefore, being a lover of pleasure and acting against the beneficial laws of Nature in these respects, man falls a prey to such diseases— sometimes to such incurable and fatal diseases and suffers various kinds of such excruciating pains and aches of various kinds that sometimes he is even obliged to commit suicide when such pains become unbearable. All such diseases, all such terrible pains and unbearable tortures are neither suffered by the animal world, nor are suicides committed by them.

Q. What scheme of diet has Nature ordained for the proper maintenance of the human body and the preservation of its health?

A. In accordance with the laws of Nature, man can take such articles of diet of the animal kingdom procured by proper methods such as milk and milk products, like butter, clarified butter (ghee), curd, buttermilk etc., and nothing besides them from the animal kingdom. Besides these, it is desirable and necessary to take

17

such things of the vegetable kingdom which each man by personal experience has found to be useful to him, such as all kinds of dry and fresh fruits, green leaves, roots and flowers of various plants, and grains. Again, considering things of the vegetable kingdom, the skin of wheat should not be discarded, but the whole wheat grain should be grounded and whole meal (unsieved) bread be taken because the skin contains ingredients which are useful for the building of muscles and therefore removal whereof makes the food deficient. In the same way, Nature has developed various kinds of salts etc. in the vegetables which are necessary for the maintenance and protection of the human body, therefore, as far as possible, they should not be cooked, but be cleaned properly and taken raw. In case it is necessary to cook any one of them, it should be cooked by steam in such a way that the necessary salts etc., contained in them are not lost. In short, according to the laws of Nature, the preservation of the human body and its health requires milk and milk products, dry and fresh fruit, vegetables and grains of the vegetable kingdom as its proper food and nothing else. By the proper and systematic use of these things, human body can be preserved in health and fitness. There is no other way to secure health.

Q. What other functions the human soul discharges in relation to its organized body besides that of building it?

A. The human soul not only builds its organized living body according to the laws of Nature, but it also lives in that body and maintains and protects it. It further utilizes it in various ways for the fulfilment of its one or other purpose. It is able to keep it alive subject to the laws of Nature and keeps itself alive by remaining united with it.

HOW CAN IT BE PROVED THAT THE BODY OF EVERY HUMAN BEING IS BUILT BY ITS SOUL AND THAT THE SOUL IS NOT AN EXPRESSION OR A PHASE OF THE BODY

Q. How can it be verified that the body of every human being is built by its soul?

A. It is the organized constructive life-power that builds the body not only of every human being but also that of all the sub-human living beings, viz., the body of every big and small animal and of every big and small plant. It is this very constructive life-power of human being which is called soul. This fact can be truly and irrefutably verified by actual experimental test.

Q. What is that true experimental test?

A. If a woman gets abortion after four or five months' pregnancy, the life-force of that embryo which was busy in constructing its body in the mother's womb by assimilating the necessary elements from her blood, would completely cease to operate, and consequently the embryo would never under any conditions have its body completed i.e., it would never become a complete baby. No so-called God or any other deity would be able to develop that complete body of the baby into its complete form.

Q. Can this truth be verified by any other method?

A. Yes, it can be. If you put some living grains of wheat into boiling water, after some time the heat of the water will destroy their life-powers i.e., they will die. Thereafter you may sow these grains in the right season and in suitable and moist soil but you will find that days after days would pass, but none of those grains would sprout and grow into wheat plants. Why? It is because after the destruction of the body-constructing life-powers which existed in these grains, there is nothing left to construct their bodies. Therefore, this work of constructing plant bodies ceases forever. Although according to the belief of the theists, their real and living, omniscient, omnipotent, creator of the universe, God, is present in these grains (whose constructive life-powers have been destroyed by heat) as well as in the soil in which they are sown, yet it is impossible for such a being to produce by any of his powers, a living plant out of these dead or non-living grains.

Again, although it is true that the existence of any such God is a myth and, therefore, such a myth cannot grow a living plant out of these dead grains, yet even if any real living human being (whose being is not a myth) tries to produce a living plant out of these dead grains, he too would utterly fail to do so. This is so because such a feat is impossible according to the immutable laws of Nature and whatever is impossible in Nature can't be made possible by even a true living existence.

Again if you want to test this truth in the animal kingdom, take a boiled egg will see life-force has been destroyed. This egg will never hatch into a chicken by any method whatsoever whether you keep it under a hen or try to hatch it by any other artificial method. The reason underlying this is that the body constructing life-power of the egg which could hatch a chicken out of its material under favourable circumstances, is dead. None but this life-power of the egg can build a living chicken out of its material in it. Nay, even the God of the theists cannot build a living body of a chicken out of that dead egg. In accordance with the true and eternal laws of real Nature, no being, "divine", human or any other, can produce a living chicken out of that dead egg. The body-constructing life-power alone which was present in it and which was destroyed by heat alone could do so.

Q. Materialists hold that the human soul has no fundamental and distinct existence of its own but that it is an expression of the organized material living body of man and that the soul dies with the death of the body. How far is this view true?

A. This view of the materialists is absolutely false because since soul is, in fact, the builder and the manifestor of its living body, then how, in the nature of things, can it be the expression of it? It is the very soul of man that is the architect of its skeleton, flesh, circulatory system, and the nervous system. It is, again, the human soul that is the builder of all its various organs viz., brain, eyes, ears, nose, mouth, lungs, heart, stomach, liver, intestines, sexual organs, hands, feet, etc. It is the soul of man which preserves and keeps alive the body that it has built. If the soul or life-force of man had been non-existent, there would not have been any human body on the surface of this earth. Hence not only the human soul is not or cannot be an expression of its body but, on the contrary, it is the one true builder and manifestor of its body.

Consequently, the belief expressed by the materialists that human soul has no existence distinct from body but it is a sort of expression or manipulation of the organized living body is absolutely against truth and the fundamental laws of Nature and is nothing more than a fanciful imagination of their own. In fact, it is the soul which is the fundamental and most primary thing in the being of man. It is, therefore, the greatest misfortune of man to remain ignorant and unconcerned about it. And it is a great privilege of man to be capable of acquiring knowledge about its life and activities.

Q. Are there any life-forces in Nature which though alive, yet possess no capacity of building a living body for themselves?

A. Yes. Some living cells of different parts of the body of every living human being, animal and plant contain such life-forces which have absolutely no capacity of building a new body for themselves. For Example:

Such plants, the cuttings of which sown in a suitable soil in proper season and given proper cultivation grow into new plants or trees— possess a number of branches which no doubt possess life-forces in their living "cells" but are incapable of building a new tree or plant out of them. If these branches are planted in congenial soil and in proper season and given good gardening, even then none of them can grow into a tree or a plant.

Besides this, the life-forces which are found in some of the metals are also incapable of building up a living body.

Q. Are life-forces found even in some metals?

A. Yes. And these life-forces are known by their special reaction peculiar to all life-forces.

Q. What are these special reactions?

A. If we were to connect a metal possessing life-force to an electric apparatus and give it an electric shock, then the life-force in the metal will generate a certain reaction which would manifest itself in drawing special sort of lines on a paper attached to the electric apparatus. If some poison be introduced into the metal, then too it would respond to it by the same kind of reaction. If this process is continued, the metal would gradually lose its life-power till after some time the life-force becomes extinct altogether. When it becomes completely extinct, no electric shock or poison would have any of its erstwhile responses of drawing lines or of exhibiting any characteristic peculiar to life-forces.

Q. Are all life-forces identical in their nature in the small or big living bodies of men, animals and plants?

A. No. They are not identical. They differ in their character from each other in their capacity and various other qualities and functions. The organized life-forces in the trees have ordinarily the capacity of building living cells for the purpose of building their bodies from the non-living earth, water, air, sunlight and heat. But the life-forces of men and animals possess no such capacity i.e., they cannot build a living body from materials taken only from the non-living kingdom.

Again, the capacity which is ordinarily possessed by organized life-force of men and animals of locomotion i.e., moving their bodies from one place to another is not as a rule found in the life-force of plants.

Similarly, the life-forces of men are generally characterized by progressive intellectual powers which are not found in the life-forces of animals. But inspire of their differences, these life-forces share, certain fundamental characteristics in common.

Q. What are the fundamental characteristics common to all life-forces?

A. All of them, under favourable circumstances, are able:

1. To build one or other kind of living body;

2. To maintain or nurture that living body;

3. To keep that living body alive for longer or smaller period; and

4. To multiply itself.

These fundamental characteristics are present in the life-forces of plants, animals and human worlds.

PROPAGATION OF VARIOUS FALSE VIEWS ABOUT SOUL

Q. What do you think of the belief of those who consider the human soul to be unborn and self-existent'?

A. This belief of theirs is absolutely untrue. It has already been shown in the previous chapter as to when and how the human soul takes its birth in accordance with the eternal laws of Nature. In that chapter evidence has been adduced to show that the human soul or life-force is not self-existent or eternal but that it is brought into existence at one or another time and is the result of the coalescence of sex-cells of a human male and a female, and that it cannot come into existence without any such coalescence. Therefore, from the point of view of time, human soul has a beginning, and it is not eternal or ever-existent.

Q. Is the human soul sin-proof and absolutely spotless? Does it remain un-affected by its own evil thoughts and evil or sinful acts and does it continue to remain unchanged, a sinless and spotless being inspire of its committing all such evil thoughts and evil acts?

A. Not at all. Soul is constituted of various forces and all its good and bad thoughts and good and bad actions, are motivated by the activity of one or another of its forces or feelings. And in accordance with the immutable law of Nature, every such activity or its feelings brings about a corresponding change in its own organism, and every such change brings a change in itself too. That is, if one's inner thoughts and actions are evil or degenerating, his soul necessarily deteriorates through them. And if one's thoughts and actions are good or higher, one's soul undergoes a change for the better through them and it becomes higher and nobler than before. Therefore, those who believe soul to be changeless and sinless hold an absolutely false belief.

Q. Is the belief of those who hold that soul never dies and that it is immortal, true?

A. Such belief of theirs is absolutely untrue. There is no life-force existing in the body of any living being, whether it be of man, animal or plant, which cannot be destroyed under certain circumstances. As in accordance with the evolutionary or constructive laws of Nature any life-force with the living body of a man, animal or plant comes into being, so also in accordance with the dissolutionary or destructive laws of Nature, such a life-force dies or can die or become extinct. Under the operation of the dissolutionary law of Nature a human soul degrades or deteriorates, and besides undergoing various other evil effects, it begins to lose its constructive power by such degradation and when it loses its constructive power altogether, then, being unable to build a new living body and on having no living body to manifest itself, it dies altogether. Similarly, if a soul can become conscious of the evolutionary law of Nature and is, in accordance therewith, able to develop some kinds of higher loves or altruistic forces in its organism, it can gradually develop its constructive power too. By development of its constructive power, it not only becomes better and higher in its own nature but can also prolong the period of its existence day by day.

Q. Can the soul of a man come to a premature end just as his bodily existence does by some untoward event?

A. Yes. Just as heat destroys the life-forces of wheat or other grains of the vegetable world as well as the life-forces of eggs of different birds, and the life-force of a human child gets destroyed by abortion, in the same way the life-forces or souls of the grown up human beings are also destroyed by various kinds of accidents. Therefore, the belief of those who think that human soul never dies and that it is eternal or that though human soul has a beginning it does not die, is absolutely false.

Q. Is the belief of those people true who hold that the souls in different bodies of human beings have no individual and distinct existence from one another but all of them are parts of the one supreme soul or "Brahman" which is imminent not only in them but in all the various existences, i.e., Brahman in fact is all and everything distinct from it is a chimera?

A. No. This belief or creed too is absolutely false. As the face of a human being is recognized to be distinct from every other human face in virtue of its several specific distinguishing marks or physiognomy, so the soul of every human being too possesses some such differentiating innate dispositions or traits by which it can be recognized to be distinct from all other human souls. It is because of these

24

differentiating psychological traits that every human soul possesses an absolutely distinct existence. Besides this, when the soul develops consciousness of 'self' or 'I', it also comes to recognize itself to have absolutely distinct existence from others. On acquiring consciousness of his own individuality or ego a person clearly understands that when some other person says to him about his body, "I am suffering from tuberculosis and my lungs are affected by tuberculor germs and that they are eating into them; I get fever everyday due to toxins produced by the germs; I also get cough", then he, the person spoken to realizes and says to himself, "My body does not suffer from any such disease." Again, when a teacher is imparting a lesson to a boy in his school, he knows it very clearly that the soul of the boy who is receiving lessons from him, asking him questions or getting knowledge from him about other things, has an absolutely separate or distinct soul from that of his own.

Similarly, when a shop-keeper sells something to a customer, he knows it very well that he and the customer are not one and identical existences. Again, when a person accuses another of having beaten him or stolen his money or committed murder of his child or having kidnapped his wife, he knows but too well that he, the complainant, is not the same person whom he accuses but that the accused person is a separate individual existence quite distinct from him. In short, just as all human souls in the world, in view of various kinds of diversities in their feelings, their thoughts, their beliefs and their actions, are different and therefore they do not and cannot have one and the same individuality, so also they are not and can never be parts of any one individual entity or anyone intelligent being called "Brahman".

This belief in monism or Vedantism is not only absolutely false but it is also very harmful for mankind. Because if one gets the wrong belief that no being save and except that of Sat Chit Anand "Brahman" has any real existence and that the vast universe of countless living and non-living existences which are given in perception have no real existence but are purely fictitious and that they appear real only due to his illusion, ignorance or `maya' and that besides and outside the conscious "Brahman" there is no other existence, it is quite logical for him also to hold the false belief that he cannot commit any unjust or sinful act in relation to other beings as no other being save "Brahman" has any real existence, hence he cannot become guilty in relation to some other being. If along with this, he also comes to hold that being a spotless Brahman he cannot be soiled or degraded by doing any evil or wrong act, it would not be surprising in such a state of his mind for him to feel inclined to commit a sin or crime and actually commit it when possessed by the urge of pleasure of some strong evil passion. Hence various kinds of evil practices have come to be prevalent in the human world owing to this false belief also.

Again, those who are called materialists, believe that soul has no separate or distance existence and that it can neither get harmed by any falsehood, or any evil or unjust or sinful act, nor can it gain anything by an altruistic or noble act. In view of such a belief they cannot feel either for themselves or for their relatives and others any need whatsoever of getting freedom from any falsehood, or any evil or wicked act etc., which does not result in any pain to them or feel any need either for themselves or for their kith and kln and others to evolve such good-producing higher or altruistic powers, the absence of which causes them no pain.

In short, just as Vedantists and monists absolutely deny the reality of all material entities and consider the whole universe "Brahman" or indivisible universal consciousness, so the materialists altogether ignoring all the non-living forces and life-forces of all living beings and their body-building functions and believing all such forces to be only an expression of body, reduce the entire Nature into matter alone.

The truth is that matter and energy are both found in Nature and they among themselves constitute the true and complete reality of Nature.

Q. What is your view about the belief of those who assert that by means of the so-called yogic exercises man's soul can leave its material body at some place and can go to some other place in a disembodied state or fly into the skies like a bird and after travelling through the celestial regions can re-enter its original material body?

A. Such a belief is absolutely untrue. In this connection it is necessary to bear in mind two truths. The first truth is that if a human soul completely leaves its body, then according to the law of Nature that body cannot remain alive and it dies instantly and therefore, it can never be resuscitated or made alive by any means i.e., it dies forever.

The second truth is that without having a living material body, whether gross or refined, it is impossible for the human soul to see anything, to hear any sound, to speak any word, to understand or know anything, to conceive any thought, to feel any pain and pleasure, to express any feeling, to go to some place or return from there and to do any other form of activity. Thus, just as it is impossible according to the immutable law of Nature for a disembodied soul to travel from one place to another and return from there or to have a flight into heavens, so also it is impossible for it to re-enter the same body which it had once left.

Now, if it be argued that on leaving its gross material body, the soul builds a refined material body for itself and with such a body it becomes able to travel to another place or any etherial plane, then this position may certainly be acceded to as it conforms to the law of Nature. But after uniting itself with its refined body, the soul can never by virtue of any yogic exercises, re-enter and dwell in its previous dead gross body nor resuscitate it and perform or manifest any form of activity through or by means of it. Therefore, such belief is absolutely untrue.

Q. There are some people who believe that by virtue of yogic exercises or of a 'boon' bestowed by some exalted being or by recitation of some mantras or magic etc., a man can, by his will, transform his body into that of a goat, sheep, cow, bull, horse, camel, elephant, bear, wolf, lion, dog, crow, pigeon, serpent, scorpion, mosquito, bug, etc., and then again he can, at his will re-transform his such animal body into his original human body. Is this belief of such people true?

A. It is absolutely untrue. This kind of metamorphosis is entirely impossible according to the laws of Nature. Therefore, not only is such a belief utterly false but all such stories that have been coined and propagated about various persons are also entirely false.

Q. There are people who believe that someone among their divine beings or any of his incarnations ('avatars') or any of his special relatives or devotees, or messengers or some such 'sidha purusha' (one who attains some special powers) was gifted with such a power that when he grew angry with any being and cursed it, that curse had an immediate effect.

That is, if he cursed a tree by saying, "You living and green tree dry up at once", in an instant the tree dried up. If he said, "Let those dozens of sheep and goats which are grazing in that green field die, at once", they died instantly. When lie said, "Let that person die at once", he died instantly. Again, when he wished that a certain dead tree, or a certain dead sheep, or goat or a certain dead man should become alive again, they became alive there and then. If lie commanded a grown up man to change into an infant, immediately the metamorphosis took place. If he ordered a one day old baby to talk to him in a particular language, it would at once converse with him in that language. If he directed a certain tree to reply to a certain question put to it by him, the tree would reply to him in his language. Are such beliefs entertained by different persons about various kinds of animate bodies true?

A. No, absolutely not. All these beliefs are utterly untrue because they violate the laws of Nature. All stories of this kind current in any part of any land are absolutely untrue.

Q. Cannot even any so-called Omnipotent God, Ishwar, Parmatma, Allah, God, Vaheguru &c., make a completely dead human body come to life again? And can he not make any human soul migrate on the death of its body into the body of another human being, animal or plant?

A. Absolutely not. In the first place, no such being at all exists who is omnipotent. In the second place, even if we grant the existence of such a being for the sake of argument, it is impossible for any being to experimentally show to be true what militates against the laws of Nature.

Just as no so-called 'Deva' or supernatural being or any other being can make alive a completely dead man, animal or plant, so also no Devta can cause a new baby to be born by making the soul of a man who has left its body to migrate into the womb of a human or an animal mother.

Hence all such beliefs which are current in mankind and which violate the laws of Nature are utterly untrue.

ORGANISM OF HUMAN SOUL

Just as body of man has attained an organized existence by developing various bodily organs, in the same way soul has, by evolving several psychic powers, attained to a great extent an organized existence.

All the various organs which go to complete the organism of man's body, have gradually evolved in him in millions of years in the course of his evolution from the animal world in accordance with the evolutionary process of Nature. Again, in addition to the evolution in him of intellectual and affective-conative forces, he has progressed in various other ways as well.

Now, although the organism of human body has attained its completeness so far as all its essential organs are concerned, yet the human soul, so far the necessary psychic powers of its organism are concerned, is still in very much incomplete and rudimentary stage.

Q. What is meant by the incomplete organism of human soul?

A. Every human soul, in order to gratify his low pleasure derived from the satisfaction of his desires and urges is led into thoughts and actions which do great harm both to his body and soul organism. In order to save it against these harms, the human soul essentially requires according to the laws of Nature:

(1) That light which could show him the real ugly nature of each low love which has done harm to his being, and

(2) Those higher feelings of repulsion and pain which could help to remove or relieve him from such low loves. The human soul lacks such light and such higher feelings.

In the same way, it lacks all those various good-producing noble or altruistic forces, the evolution of which is, according to laws of Nature, essential for the promotion and prolongation of its life.

Again, millions of human souls possessing an incomplete, organism, have by the process of continual degradation, due to the various pleasure-seeking loves, have reached such a degraded stage that it has become practically impossible for them to evolve noble altruistic feelings. That is, there is now no possibility of any higher change taking place in their soul-organism. But, in spite of all this, there is certainly a class of fit and capable souls in humanity who can evolve the higher psychic forces to a certain extent which can deliver the soul and prolong its life and, therefore, the course of their progressive soul-life can go on to the extent of their capacity.

Q. Given the incomplete organism of the souls of the ordinary human beings of this world, to date, what are the groups of powers that go to constitute the incomplete organism of their souls?

A. Following are the various groups of powers that have developed in the incomplete souls of mankind:

(a) The four kinds of powers which go to build, maintain, keep alive and keep control over the body.

(b) Several kinds of knowledge-imparting mental powers.

(c) Several kinds of pleasure and pain imparting consciousness.

(d) Several kinds of loves for pleasures and hatred or repulsion for pain.

The nature of those various powers in the human soul which go to build the body has already been dealt with. The remaining three kinds of powers will be discussed in the following chapters.

VARIOUS KINDS OF KNOWLEDGE-IMPARTING MENTAL POWERS IN THE HUMAN SOUL

Q. What is meant by 'knowledge'?

A. Whatever direct awareness or cognition a man gets of the nature or the form or the qualities of some existence in Nature or of any phenomenon or its cause or of some law of Nature, that cognition of the true and direct truth is termed knowledge.

Q. What is meant by mental powers?

A. The various powers or senses of the human soul which impart some kind of knowledge to it are called its mental powers.

Q. How many kinds of mental powers are there?

A. These are of several kinds, but the four main groups into which they can be classified are as follows:

First group of mental powers

This group consists of the mental powers or senses given below:

(1) Sense of sight, giving consciousness of forms.

(2) Sense of hearing, giving consciousness of sounds.

(3) Sense of palate, giving consciousness of tastes.

(4) Sense of smell, giving consciousness of odours.

(5) Sense of touch, giving consciousness of heat and cold.

(6) Sense of touch, giving consciousness of weight of material objects.

(7) Sense of touch, giving consciousness of hardness and softness of material objects.

(8) Sense of touch, giving consciousness of roughness and smoothness of material objects.

A brief description of these senses has already been given in the Second Volume of The Dev Shastra. There is therefore, no need to repeat it here. Again, a further reference to these senses is made in this very chapter while dealing with the power of retention coming under the third group of mental powers. It is explained there that whatever kind of knowledge the human soul gets through these senses also stays in the mind by retention.

Second group of mental powers

Following are the mental powers of this group

(a) Consciousness of ego or 'I'.

(b) Consciousness of "my" and "me".

(c) Consciousness of "others".

(d) Consciousness of "his" or "her" pertaining to Others.

BRIEF EXPLANATION

After completing its bodily organism in its mother's womb when a human child comes in the outer world and begins to be reared by its mother, its tiny soul does not possess for some specific period any consciousness of 'ego' or 'I' or consciousness of its own separate individuality. Therefore, although it performs so many activities such as eating, drinking, sleeping, waking, passing stools and urine, feeling comfort or discomfort, seeing, hearing, weeping or crying, etc., yet it has no consciousness at all of these various activities as being done by its 'self' or by means of its own body. It possesses hands and feet but it does not know "This hand is mine", "This foot is mine". It also does not know: "This body is mine or this toy is mine, or this woman is my mother". It does not possess any consciousness of this kind. After some time, a stage comes in the growth of its body and soul when it develops the consciousness of 'I' or 'mine' or `me'. At this developed stage it comes to know and realize: "This particular woman is my mother";

"This is my toy"; "I have made water there"; "This sweet belongs to me"; "I don't feel hungry"; "I am feeling thirsty"; "I am feeling sleepy"; etc.

Although with the growth of the consciousness of 'I', 'mine', me' etc., a human child starts to refer some of his actions to his self, yet even till sometime after the appearance of this consciousness, he does not know and realize when somebody points out to him that a certain action of his is harmful to him or to anyone else, he is responsible for that action, or he does not say, "I am guilty or can be considered guilty and I can also be liable to be punished for it." It is because of this that up to a certain period of life children are not considered liable to any punishment by any civilized government for any of their misdemeanors.

Along with the growth of various consciousness of ego or 'I', the consciousness of "other" grows of itself. And with the growth of the consciousness of 'other', consciousness of 'him', 'his' or `her' also awakens.

Third group of mental powers

Q. How many kinds of mental powers belong to the third group?

A. These mental powers are of various kinds. But some of them which are common, in more or less degree, in all human beings are the following:

(1) Retention.

(2) Recall.

(3) Imitation.

(4) Imagination.

(5) Inquisitiveness.

(6) Thinking or discrimination.

(7) Logical Reasoning.

(8) Attention.

BRIEF EXPLANATION

1. Retention

Q. What is meant by Retention?

A. After the normal completion of all the necessary organs of its body when a human child comes out from the womb of its mother safe and sound, and opens its eyes, for the first time, and looks at the different forms of material objects around in the light of sun, lamp, or some other light, it becomes aware of the forms of those objects when the rays of light reaching its eyes bring the reflections of their illuminated forms to the visual centres in its brain through the optic nerve and excite a sensation therein. Similarly, when some sound waves carried by air strike the drums of his ears and through a special set of auditory nerves reach its brain, and produce an auditory sensation in it, it hears that sound.

Again; when it takes milk and the milk touches the taste buds in its mouth and the excitation thereof reaches its brain centre, it gets sensation of taste. In the same way, when at any time the particles of an odorous object stimulate its brain centre through the olfactory nerves of its nose, it experiences sensation of its smell. When the nervous system spreading underneath its skin comes in contact with one or another thing and the excitation thereof reaches the brain, it experiences sensation of heat or cold or pleasure or pain. Again, when any material thing having weight is placed on its muscles and its excitation reaches its brain, it experiences its weight. Similarly, out of its internal organs which are controlled by the nervous system, when its bladder is filled with urine and the nerves therein are pressed and its excitation is carried to the brain, the child experiences the need to pass the urine. When the pressure of faeces is felt by the colon and its excitation is communicated to the brain by the nerves, the child experiences the necessity of passing the stools. In the same way, the child experiences sensation or pain in any of its organs; and when that pain is gone, it feels relief. The power in the brain of the child that receives all such stimulations or excitations and on which gradually these sensations leave their imprint is called retention.

Besides the impressions of the forms etc., of the things around him, the human soul acquires through this power of retention, the different kinds of other impressions too. It is because of this, that the human child while learning the language of its guardians and others acquires all such beliefs as gospel truth whether they are true or false. All the opinions which are due to the exercise of this power of retention are called received or traditional beliefs.

2. Recall

Q. What is meant by Recall?

A. The impressions which a man receives from his very childhood through his sense organs or through the training given to him by his guardians are retained on the plate of his power of retention just like the impressions retained on the plate of a gramophone record. The mental power that at one time or another stimulates these retained impressions and reproduces them before him is called recall. If man had been devoid of the mental power of retention and reproduction or recall he would never have been able to know or learn anything from his very childhood nor could he become master of different kinds of knowledge.

3. Imitation

Q. What is meant by Imitation?

A. The word 'imitation' literary means copying. It is by the exercise of this mental power that a man is enabled in his infancy to imitate the sounds of the various words uttered by his guardians and begins to speak them and thus learns their language. He further learns by imitation the various kinds of letters of an alphabet etc., which have been invented to reduce any spoken language to writing. Similarly, through the power of imitation, he learns different kinds of sketch-making, map-drawing, embroidering various flowery and other designs on clothes and several other kinds of workmanship. It is by this mental power that a man imitates the fashions of other men in dress. It is by means of this power that he presents a play or drama by imitating the special language, the special bodily movements and other things of others. However, no one, with the help of this power can, except copying only the external form, sincerely exhibit in his life any higher virtue or virtues or qualities of anybody else merely by imitating him. It is because Nature has made it impossible for a man to manifest in his own life the true characteristics pertaining to any higher virtue or feeling, for which he possesses no inheritance or if at all he possessed the inheritance he could not develop or evolve it for some reason.

A crow cannot change itself into a peacock by sticking the peacock feathers on to its own and imitating its external form. Therefore, in accordance with this fundamental law of Nature, it is not possible for anyone to become himself or to make another to become on the basis of imitation, a distinguished person by application of predicate or predicates of virtue to himself or another. He cannot exhibit in himself or get the other person exhibit in actual life the true characteristics of that virtue. By such imitation he undoubtedly proves himself to be a rank hypocrite or pretender.

4. Imagination

Q. What is meant by Imagination?

A. Imagination is that mental power of man which presents to him one or another kind of mental picture or which helps him to visualize or draw to his capacity any mental picture of some description which some other person gives him. It is indeed a wonderful mental power. If this mental power had been non-existent in man, it would not have been possible for him to see the mental picture of any kind. The mental pictures which man's imagination draws are not all of them true, rather a lot of them are untrue. Though from among these mental pictures, many are absolutely false, yet they appear to be true and pleasant to some persons. There are lots of other mental pictures which though absolutely true, yet appear to be false and painful to some persons.

Besides the normal waking state of man, when imagination also draws the mental pictures during state of sleep, then these mental pictures are called dreams. The mental pictures of dreams are almost all false.

Those men whose powers of logical reasoning and critical reflection are, on the one hand, very poorly developed and who, on the other hand, are completely or almost devoid of the knowledge of what constitutes a true or an untrue belief about events or what is to be believed as possible or impossible phenomenon in Nature, are comparatively more swayed by imagination even in their wakeful state and so they are more inclined to accept false dogmas or creeds and get more deeply entangled in them than those who have by education developed better capacity of critical reflection and logical reasoning and possess more knowledge in relation to the real Nature.

5. Curiosity

Q. What is meant by Curiosity?

A. The word 'curiosity' means to inquire. When a man has no knowledge about a particular thing and feels the need to get information about it, the power that he exercises in such a state in order to get this information is called curiosity. The more the people of a country lack the spirit of curiosity about Nature, or are deficient in the spirit of investigation or study about the forms, qualities, characteristics and activities of the different existences of the various orders of Nature, and its manifold phenomena and laws, the poorer they are in the knowledge about Nature. The more the people of a country are actuated by the spirit of curiosity or investigation about Nature. and the more they acquire true or real (and not imaginary) knowledge about Nature, the more such people become able, by virtue of their true knowledge about the various forces of Nature, to harness these forces for the accomplishment of their various desired purposes. Such people are to the extent of their ability and knowledge, more enlightened and more powerful than the people of a land who have very scanty spirit of curiosity and investigation about Nature. The more the people of a country are deficient than the people of another country in their ability to utilize the true knowledge about Nature and its different forces, the more are they inferior to and weaker than the latter.

6. Thinking

Q. What is meant by the activity of thinking?

A. When a man becomes desirous to know as to how to remove any of his own or anybody else's felt need or to be successful in any of his undertakings or to be acquainted with the cause of any phenomenon of Nature or with regard to one or other of its orders of existence, and, moved by his such desire, engages himself in reflection over the solution of any of his problems, the mental activity through the exercise of which he is able to do such reflection, is called the activity of thinking.

This activity of thinking is found to a very limited extent in animals also. But in human beings ordinarily this activity of thinking is found in a progressive state.

This mental capacity develops more and more through continuous education, through increasing study of knowledge-promoting books, through investigation about various laws of Nature, and through mutual discussion and debate etc., on various useful topics.

Those countries where different kinds of educational institutions like schools and colleges exist in large number, where various sorts of illuminating books and periodicals are published in large number, where public libraries abound and where great number of lovers of scientific investigation for various truths about the different departments of Nature exist, are far more advanced both intellectually and financially than the countries which comparatively lack all these blessings.

7. Logical Reasoning

Q. What is meant by logical reasoning?

A. The admixture of various falsehoods in:

(1) Different kinds of beliefs and creeds assimilated by him from tradition from the time of infancy;

(2) Beliefs accepted by him as true in later life by hearsay;,

(3) Various kinds of thoughts or beliefs conceived by him under the influence of his low loves; and

(4) Various kinds of thoughts or beliefs formed under the influence or his low hates is present in man's mind and he remains lost in his falsehoods due to his ignorance. The mental power by the evolution of which man is able to see the element of falsehood in any of his above beliefs etc. and is further able to detect errors in one or other of his beliefs, creeds, thoughts, or conclusions, is called the activity of logical reasoning.

This mental activity can help a man to distinguish between what is true and what is false only to the extent that he is able to exercise it in an unbiased or impartial spirit. But if he loses the power of using it in an impartial spirit owing to his slavery to some low love or low hate, then neither does he remain desirous to use this power for distinguishing between what is true or false nor can he do so. This mental activity is called 'logic' in English' and 'mantiq' in Arabic.

The mental activity of logical reasoning renders great help to a man to be able to remove errors in various kinds of his thoughts and to draw right conclusions from different kinds of right premises.

8. Attention

Q. What is meant by attention?

A. The activity that enables a man to focus his mind or course of thinking continuously for the requisite length of time over the same subject is called the activity of attention. This attentive state of mind is called 'concentration of mind' in English and 'maraqba' in Persian.

It is through the development of this power that a man can acquire control over his thinking power and keeps it fixed on one and the same topic for a requisite length of time; otherwise one or other kind of his feelings of attraction and repulsion continue to drag his mind towards their own satisfaction and do not allow him to stay concentrated on the requisite topic or subject matter. This mental power of attention is intimately related to every form of man's activity. Without it none of his tasks can be completely done or properly accomplished. But so long a man has no interest or love for some subject, he does not naturally wish to concentrate over or devote his attention to that subject. Consequently, he can neither think over or study it, nor see or realize some truth about it. This is the reason why thousands and millions of persons who are, on the one hand, dominated by one or other low love, such as low love of wealth or property, of children or of any other relation, friend or comrade, or of one or other bodily pleasure etc., and on the other hand, do not possess in their heart any desire to get true knowledge about various problems connected with the most fundamental thing in their being i.e., soul, its true nature, its diseases and degradation and the most horrible consequences thereof and the necessity of its salvation from these diseases and of developing higher life in it etc., neither do not wish to engage themselves in regular study and contemplation on those problems nor seek good company. If they do or can get a true spiritual guide or seer of true knowledge about soul, they do not want to approach him in the spirit of humble inquirer in order to ask questions or make inquiries or get and accept any instructions from him about the problems of soul. They are content to keep themselves, their children, and their kith and kin in absolute darkness or in utter ignorance about these most essential and fundamental matters. They feel great satisfaction to remain in that most deplorable state of darkness and degradation as well as to keep their friends, relatives and others in that state. But those comparatively few noble souls who possess a reverential attitude of an inquirer for matters associated with religion, unfortunately approach such persons who, on the one hand, are devoid of the sublime light (Dev Jyoti) which imparts true soul-knowledge, and, on the other hand, are deeply committed to most harmful beliefs about soul. By listening to their sermons and assimilating their teachings, they do no real good to their own soul-life except to be misled and

39

lost. In this state of soul darkness they cannot get any true knowledge of soul by the study of and reflection over the contents of the so-called religious books, and so groping in their soul-darkness, they keep on ruining their invaluable soul life.

Q. Have these eight kinds of mental powers developed in the beings of the animal kingdom too?

A. Not all of them. But sonic of the mental powers such as that of sensory perception, recognition, thinking, memory, imitation and imagination are no doubt found in them to some extent. And in some animals these mental powers do or can develop also to a certain degree. But these mental powers in animals do not possess progressive character as is the case with man.

Q. Has man been able to establish gradually his sovereignty or domination over the beings of the animal kingdom on account of these progressive mental powers?

A. Yes, it is so. Man has become capable of establishing his dominance over various kinds of animals, partly on account of some of these mental powers of his and partly because of his superior bodily organism. Man is able to stand erect like a staff on his two legs alone and walk and run about freely in a manner which no animal is able to do. Again, due to the special construction of his palm and his fingers, man can twist and turn them for the accomplishment of various kinds of actions in a manner which no being of the animal kingdom can do at all.

Again, no being of the animal world has been able to develop, nor can it ever develop various kinds of conventional languages which man has been able to do as a result of his powers of imitation etc. Nay, it is not possible for any animal even to completely learn that language from man. By acquiring knowledge of various forces of Nature man has become able to establish his mastery over various animals who are physically far stronger than he. It is not possible for the beings of the animal world to acquire knowledge about these forces and through them get control over man.

Man has attained to excellence in various aspects over the beings of the animal world in virtue of these very progressive mental powers and the superiority of his bodily organism. By developing these progressive mental powers and by acquiring varied knowledge about other kingdoms of Nature, man has knowledge his dominance over them in several respects. Besides this, by extending the sphere of his knowledge about Nature by means of these mental powers, he has developed his civilization to a great extent.

The fourth group of mental powers

The mental powers of the fourth group which have appeared and developed in man's soul, are the following:

1. In relation to spatial forms:

(a) Consciousness of straightness or otherwise of a line, an edge or a boundary or any length or height etc.

(b) Consciousness of largeness, smallness, or equality.

(c) Consciousness of circular or globular forms.

(d) Consciousness of angles formed of two lines.

(e) Consciousness of various figures formed of several lines, such as a triangle, a rectangle, a heptagon, a hexagon, an octagon, etc.

(f) Consciousness of parallel lines.

(g) Consciousness of level surfaces.

(h) Consciousness of various kinds of arched figures.

2. Other consciousness regarding forms.

(a) General consciousness of beauty and ugliness of any form or shape.

(b) Consciousness of proportion or disproportion i.e., orderliness or disorderliness or harmony or disharmony in various organs or parts of a whole.

(c) Consciousness of cleanliness and dirtiness of any form.

(d) Consciousness of brilliance or dullness of any form.

3. Consciousness of harmony or rhythm in sounds waves.

4. Consciousness of space and time i.e., enumeration, extent, finiteness, infiniteness, limitedness, unlimitedness and time etc.

5. Consciousness of the ethereal, gaseous, liquid and solid states of material objects.

6. Consciousness of differentiation of material objects from each other.

7. Consciousness about the motion and energy of inanimate forces; consciousness of their transformation from one kind to another; consciousness of the various kinds of changes they produce in material objects; and the consciousness of the immutable laws of Nature according to which changes occur in matter and force.

8. Consciousness of the mutual differentiation of the various kinds of living forces; the consciousness of the constitution of organized living forms or of living bodies; consciousness of the health, diseases and death of the organized living bodies; consciousness about the physical development and degradation of organized living bodies or forms etc.

BRIEF EXPLANATION

The awakening of the consciousness of the beauty of various kinds of forms or figures has led to the growth and gradual development of different kinds of arts and crafts in the human world. By acquiring knowledge of material things and in relation thereto, man has attaine the power of melting different metals. He has made various kinds of useful articles out of them separately or by combining them.

Similarly, man has acquired the skill of making varied beautiful and useful things out of wood, leather, and bones, etc. By knowing the uses of cotton, wool, silk, etc., man has made various kinds of clothes, durries, carpets, floor covering ('jajams',) blankets, flannels, sheets and different kinds of beautiful dresses, etc. By the use of iron, man has been able to manufacture different things such as needles, nails, screws, rails, engines, cycles, motor cycles, cars, etc. By the use of concrete, stone, lime, earth, sand, etc., man has been able to build big houses, palaces, bridges, etc. By the growth similar knowledge, man has been able to construct roads and canals, etc.

By developing knowledge of the rhythm of sounds, man has been able to create poetry. It is due to such knowledge of art that songs, hymns, musical instruments and dancing etc., have originated and advanced.

Therefore, the people of a country who have, on the one hand, acquired and developed knowledge about these various arts, and crafts to a greater extent and, on the other hand, have grown and evolved beneficial Love for one or other of them, have attained to a very higher state of excellence than the inhabitants of a country who have developed knowledge of this kind and love for them to a lesser degree.

The former; therefore, have become in comparison to the latter more civilized, more healthy, more adventurous and more powerful.

Q. Have not all such arts and crafts consciousness evolved in the beings of the animal kingdom?

A. No. Some species of the animal world have certainly got to a certain extent the capacity of making nests for themselves, out of leaves, straws, wooden pieces etc., or hives consisting of small or big similar cells out of juices sucked from several plants; and some other kind of abodes out of earth etc. Then there are some birds who speak or sing something in some rhythm. Some of these beings also keep their bodies neat and clean. But beyond and apart from these things, the animals have not got and cannot develop these various arts and crafts which have developed in man.

Further, even the above-mentioned several do-how which some animals possess are not of the progressive character.

Therefore, in virtue of the above-mentioned capacities, man has been able to provide himself with various kinds of materials for his comforts and conveniences which animals have not been able to do nor can they do so.

ATTRACTION OR LOVE FOR VARIOUS KINDS OF PLEASURES AND AVERSION OR` HATRED FOR VARIOUS KINDS OF PAINS IN MAN CONSTITUTE THE ONLY TWO MOTIVE FORCES FOR ALL KINDS OF HIS INNER THOUGHTS AND OVERT ACTIONS

Man has descended from the animal kingdom and so he has inherited consciousness of various kinds of pleasures and pains from it. With time, these consciousness have gradually increased in number in him i.e., the number and variety of those completely new consciousness of pleasure and pain which have grown in different people of the human kingdom are non-existent in species of the animal kingdom and could not in the nature of things be evolved in them at all.

Examples: In the course of human evolution, several persons (not all) have developed, besides the various consciousness about the outer forms of different things, some consciousness, such as sense of cleanliness and uncleanliness, beauty and ugliness, order and disorder. Endowed with these consciousness they keep their bodies, their clothes, their houses, their shops, their factories and gardens etc., in a scrupulously clean and variedly decorated condition and in order. They prepare or manufacture various kinds of things or objects of beauty. They experience pleasure in the beauty of such objects and feel pain when they find them in an ugly state. All such consciousness are not found in any being of the animal world.

Again, in the same course of Nature's evolution, many persons have developed various consciousness about the harmony or disharmony in different, kinds of sound waves and this has enabled them to reproduce harmonious waves by composing various kinds of melodious songs and poems, inventing different kinds of musical instruments and developing different forms of dances. All such consciousness too are absent in animals. Men experience pleasure or joy in observing harmony in their arts and feel pain when there is disharmony in them. All such consciousnesses of pleasure and pain are not found in any being of the animal kingdom.

In the same evolutionary process, many persons develop various consciousnesses about beautiful combination of words in the structure of sentences. On account of such consciousness they feel pleasure or joy when they perceive harmony in their own composed speech or written article or in speeches or writings of others. They feel pain if the opposite is the case. All such pleasures and pains are not felt at all by the beings of the animal world.

Similarly, some persons (not all) develop consciousness about various kinds of sufferings of others even though the others may not in any way be connected with them by blood or other near ties. As a result of such consciousness, they possess the capacity of realizing the pain of another person due to disease or any other physical suffering or due to some want or mental shock, and, in virtue of and to the extent of depth of such consciousness they become helpful or serviceable in relieving such pain, want or suffering of another. They get pleasure by doing any such service to others and feel hurt on witnessing any act of cruelty done by anybody else. All these consciousness of pleasure and pain are also absent in the beings of the animal kingdom.

Besides the consciousness mentioned above, there are several other consciousness of pleasure and pain also which have evolved in several persons of the human kingdom, but have neither evolved nor could they evolve in the animal kingdom.

Man, having got in heritage the above different kinds of consciousness of pleasure and pain, has evolved, on the one hand, attraction for various pleasures, nay, love for several of them, and on the other hand, repulsion or worse than that, deep hatred for pain. Hence all his such feelings of attraction or love for pleasure and repulsion or hatred for pain have become the dominant motive forces of his life and, therefore, every person motivated by these feelings of love for pleasures and hatred for pains thinks all kinds of thoughts and does all kinds of actions.

In short, all the actions whether good or bad which are done by human beings all over the world viz. all kinds of deliberate falsehoods practiced in mutual dealings or behaviour; all kinds of fabricated false religious beliefs; all kinds of acts based on injustice or cruelty like cheating, treachery, breach of trust, stealing, deceit, bribe-taking, robbery, suppression of deposits, torture; all acts of intemperance dacoit temperance in eating and drinking; use of various intoxicants; all acts of sexual abuse such as adultery, sexual excesses, masturbation &c. all acts of brutality and slaughter of millions of animals for the purpose of diet, trade, hunting and sacrifice &c. and various kinds of evil and social customs and rites—are mainly due to their various loves of pleasure and hatred of pain.

Q. Is every man in this world motivated by his different consciousness of pleasure and pain in doing all and every kind of his actions?

A. Certainly. So long as man is man and continues to be man, he does all his actions (including his thinking) entirely under the motives of his love for different kinds of pleasures and hatred for different kinds of pains. Therefore, man wants to do and actually does all such actions, whether in relation to himself or to others, which afford him pleasure and which are not painful to him. But he does not want to do and hence does not do any such action which does not give him some pleasure or instead give him some pain, howsoever beneficial or good that action may be for him or for others.

Similarly, man does not want to and, therefore, does not reflect over that truth, or to speak that truth, or to accept that truth, or to propagate that truth, or to do any other action based on truth, if in doing so he gets no pleasure or instead gets pain or is distressed. Even for the sake of the good of his own being, if there is need to disengage himself from some relative or give up some money or property or dedicate his mental and physical powers, he does not want to do it and does not do it if in doing so he does not get any pleasure or instead, gets pain. And it is not even possible for him to do any such acts according to the immutable law of Nature. Therefore, in such a state of his soul he intentionally or unintentionally comes to believe in different kinds of falsehoods, indulges in various kinds of actions based on falsehood and evil in relation to himself and to other existences in Nature, and thus becomes lover of different kinds of falsehoods and evils.

Q. Is it the case that no man does any good to himself or to any other existence except when motivated by his love of pleasures and hatred for pains?

A. Man is primarily led by his one or other love of pleasure and hatred for pain in doing any of his actions. It is true that some actions of his also lead to one or another kind of good. That is to say, that while being led by his love for different kinds of pleasures and hatred for pains, man does various kinds of most degrading acts based on falsehood, intemperance and cruelty, etc., he is also led by them to do some such acts which are beneficial to various animate and inanimate existences in Nature. However, he does all these various good actions, primarily motivated by one or other kind of his love for pleasure.

Q. Is it also a fact that amongst those very persons who indulge in various acts of falsehood, intemperance, injustice and other wrongs or evils, there are some among them who's one or other happiness-motivated activity leads to one or other kind of good?

A. Indeed so. It is, therefore, that men, who are given to the use of various intoxicating and poisonous drugs such as wine, tobacco, bhang, charas, chandu, opium, cocaine, etc., and who are bribe-takers, adulterers, meat-eaters, liars, cheats, hypocrites and treacherous &c., do on occasions perform various acts which also prove to a smaller or greater degree beneficial for others. But here also they do them in order to get pleasure of satisfaction of their feeling of mercy or of name or fame; or if they are believers in some mythical god, they do so for appeasing that god to get the pleasure of one kind or another from him in return; or if they are bound with someone by ties of some low love, they do so for the sake of getting pleasure out of the satisfaction of that love.

Q. Does a man ever endure pain for the sake of getting one or other kind of pleasure?

A. Yes, he does. In order to get one or other kind of pleasure, man also accepts to endure several kinds of pain on many occasions and in some cases he bears very great and terrible pains and at times sacrifices even his life for its sake.

Q. Why is it so?

A. It is a law of Nature that when a force comes into conflict with another force, it is the stronger force that triumphs. When a man, has developed some very over-powering love of pleasure, he is knowingly but helplessly driven by it to do such actions for its satisfaction which are not only painful for his soul, but in several cases prove very harmful to his body also, and may even cause his death. In short, when a man, in love of some pleasure, becomes, in conformity to the law of Nature, a slave to it, he causes various kinds of physical and spiritual harm to himself and to others under the influence of this most degrading slavery.

Q. Do some men sacrifice their wealth, their property or endure one or other kind of pain in order to gratify some happiness-affording altruistic feeling?

A. Yes, it is so. As many persons, strongly addicted to various low pleasures such as drinking, adultery, etc., squander away the whole of their property in pursuit of them, in the same way, some rare persons, motivated by the strong love of pleasure emanating from the satisfaction of the feeling of mercy, devote their whole lives in the service of the sick. Some others make large contributions of their money for the establishment of big hospitals. There are many others who, being staunch believers or lovers of one or other so-called religion, sacrifice their entire lives or their entire properties for obtaining the pleasure of its propagation. Similarly, led or impelled by the love of one or other kind of intellectual education, different persons donate large amounts of money for one or other useful institution for the spread of that kind of knowledge. But while, on the one hand, different persons motivated by the pleasure of some intense altruistic feelings do various very commendable acts of public utility, on the other hand, they are led by their various pleasures of the low loves, to indulge in different kinds of acts also which are harmful to them and to others i.e., they do various kinds of unjust and sinful actions in different relations. They become intemperate in various ways so far their body is concerned. They support various evil social customs.

Many among them take meat, many are in the habit of using one or other kind of intoxicants, while many fabricate and propagate various kinds of falsehoods in order to spread their so-called religious creeds.

All such persons are completely devoid of and in utter darkness about the various absolutely necessary and most valuable truths relating to the nature and organism of their soul, its degradation and the most horrible consequences thereof, the true way of its freedom from such consequences and its evolution in higher life etc.

Q. Is it inevitable for every person enslaved to various loves for pleasure and hatred for various pains, to adopt even knowingly a course of falsehoods and evils in various ways in relation to himself and to various other animate and inanimate existences in Nature?

A. Yes. It is so. According to the immutable law of Nature, it is inevitable for every human being to follow such a course. Being possessed by love for pleasure and hatred for pain it is but inevitable for every man to indulge in various kinds of activities, both internal and external, which are based on evil and untruth.

Q. In view of this most deplorable psychic state of man, would it not be proper to define him thus:

"Man is a being who is lover of pleasure and hater of pain and because of these two feelings of love and hate he becomes a lover of various kinds of falsehoods and evils in relation to his own being and beings in the world around him".

A. It would be perfectly proper to do so and it is, therefore, a correct definition.

Q. Does a man helplessly resorts to a falsehood, or an evil, or a sin, or a crime because, on the one hand, his one or other strong love of pleasure clamours for its satisfaction and, on the other hand, he surely feels pleasure and feels no pain in the performance of such an act?

A. Yes. It is because of this that we find all kinds of acts based on various kinds of falsehood, injustice, intemperance or cruelty being indulged in by man all over the world, and it is inevitable for mankind to remain in this state of conduct.

Q. Does a man reject any creed or belief though based on truth or refuses to do some thinking, study or contemplation or give up some religious or other exercise, act or company even though based on goodness, because it does not afford him any pleasure?

A. Yes. It is so.

Q. Does a man give up some good work or some good religious exercise because its performance used at first to give him some pleasure but it has ceased to give him any pleasure any longer?.,

A. Yes. It is so.

Q. Is it due to this nature of man that he cuts off his relation with another, because for one reason or another he no more gets the pleasure which he used to get from him or he does get more pain from him than pleasure?

A. Yes. It is so. The truth is that all kinds of thoughts, all kinds of deliberations, all kinds of conduct or activities of mankind, are wholly and exclusively motivated by its various consciousness and loves for pleasures and their resultant feelings of hatred for pains and by nothing else.

THE EMERGENCE OF DEVATMA HAS THE PURPOSE OF RIDDING MANKIND OF ALL THOSE VARIOUS KINDS OF COMPLETELY FALSE AND MOST HARMFUL TEACHINGS ABOUT SOUL, PROPAGATED IN THE NAME OF RELIGION AND BASED ON THE IDEAL OF PLEASURE AND PAIN

Q. Is it a fact that all the various kinds of teachings which have been propagated among humanity in the name of religion too, are grounded solely on the ideal of attaining one or other kind of pleasure or of getting freedom from one or other kind of pain?

A. Yes. All the various kinds of teachings and practices which pass current even in the name of religion in every country and every creed of this world have without exception placed before mankind the ideal of attaining one or other kind of pleasure and getting freedom or salvation from one or other kind of pain. But as all such teachings and practices violate Nature's immutable laws of truth and goodness pertaining to the soul-world, they are not only completely false, but are in various ways most harmful and degrading for every person who believes in them.

Q. Is then, this love of pleasure in man alone responsible for all the creeds or beliefs which have been or are being propagated in this world in the name of religion but which are totally opposed to Nature's immutable laws of truth and goodness pertaining to soul-world, as also for all the various so-called gods and goddesses which have been or are being believed in, for all the various forms of worship which are in vogue in relation to these so-called deities, for all the various practices done in relation to them such as reading of scriptures, singing of hymns, repeating of 'mantras', performance of `yogas', burning of incenses, etc., or the slaughter of various animals in the name of sacrifice at their altar, or all the various kinds of surrenders ('Tyag'), austerities ('Tap') and vows, fasts, giving of alms and taking baths etc., for all the pilgrimages to various places considered as sacred, for all the various kinds of outward symbols, dresses or appearances etc. which, are adopted in various religions and for several kinds of other such practices?

A. Undoubtedly yes. Different kinds of religions and their sects prevalent in this world are, one and all, ultimately founded on these very loves for pleasure i.e., the basic motive of all of them is nothing besides and beyond the attainment of pleasure and freedom from pain.

In order, therefore, to give freedom to all fit human ('adhikari') souls from all kinds of false teachings, false religions, false spiritual exercises, false practices and ceremonials and all kinds of evil thoughts and actions and their consequent impurities resulting from the ideal of pleasure and pain and to impart to them the knowledge of the creed and faith of the true religion based on the immutable facts and laws of Nature pertaining to soul-world and further to develop in them soul-life- promoting various higher altruistic feelings, and thereby to do, in accordance with Nature's own laws, all-comprehensive good to mankind to the highest possible extent, after millions of years of the evolutionary process of Nature, this planet has been blessed with the emergence of the truly worshipful Devatma who is endowed with the consciousness and complete love of truth and goodness.

The fundamental distinction between human soul and the Devatma

Q. What are the fundamental excellences which the Devatma has evolved in his soul in virtue of his highest consciousness and complete love of all-sided truth and goodness which distinguish him from all human souls?

A. As a result of Devatma's 'Dev Bodhs' (sublime consciousness of truth and goodness) and 'Dev Anurag' (sublime love of truth and goodness) there have appeared the following fundamental distinctions between him and all other human souls for all time to come:

1. The entire human world was completely void of all those real highest sublime forces of complete love of truth and goodness and the necessary fruit of their evolution, the true unique ideal type of life which the Devatma has been able to evolve in his soul in virtue and by means of his various kinds of all the requisite surrenders and sacrifices and various other evolutionary cosmic forces. In fact

these highest sublime consciousnesses and sublime loves were absent in every human being including the so-called teachers or founders of the religions of the world.

2. The highest progressive sublime light called Dev Jyoti which the Devatma has been able to gradually generate in his soul in accordance with the law of the soul-world, side by side with the evolution of his highest forces of complete love of truth and goodness, was also absent, in all human souls including all the teachers and founders of the so-called prevalent religious denominations or faiths.

This sublime light can alone reveal those Nature-based various kinds of truths and principles about the organized being of that very subtle but real thing called soul, its organism, its diseases and degradation and their most horrible consequences, its freedom there from and its evolution in higher life, which truths alone constitute the knowledge of true religion. Hence in the absence of this sublime light all the human beings including all the teachers and founders of the so called religions prevailing in this world were devoid of the knowledge of these truths about religion.

3. The highest sublime power called Dev Tej which the Devatma has been able to develop in his soul, in accordance with the laws of Nature governing the soul world, in virtue of the evolution of his highest psychic forces of complete love of truth and goodness and which sublime power creates higher hatred and higher pain for all pleasure-affording low loves and low hates resulting there from as well as for all kinds of falsehoods and all kinds of evils, was also non-existent in all human beings including all founders and teachers of the so-called religions or faiths prevailing on this planet i.e. they were all devoid of this Dev Tej.

4. Devatma has in his sublime light discovered various truths about soul and has given the true philosophy of true religion based on the bed-rock of cosmic facts and laws of Nature. This true philosophy of true religion has been taught by no founder or teacher or guru (preceptor) of any so-called religion of this world, or by any devotee, incarnation, Nabi or messenger of any so called god or goddess by any muni, rishi, yogi (ascetic), saint, mahant, buddha, siddha, tirathanker or jin etc. for being devoid of this sublime light, none of them was competent to get at that true philosophy of true religion and hence none could teach it.

5. The unique supreme objective of his manifestation, which the Devatma proclaimed as a result of the evolution in his soul of the unique psychic forces of complete love for truth and goodness and being solely ruled and motivated by them, was never declared by any so-called founder or teacher of any religion, any

incarnation, prophet or messenger; any guru, devotee or yogi, any saint, mahant, rishi or muni, jin, siddha, buddha or tirthanker, etc. Being devoid of those sublime loves ('Dev Anurag') none of them could have such a unique supreme objective of life.

6. The unique example of life led in relation either with various human beings or with the sub-human existences, purely and exclusively on the basis of the highest psychic forces of the love of truth and goodness (and not on the basis of love of pleasure and hatred of pain) which the Devatma has set before the world by virtue of and as governed solely by his sublime love or 'Dev Anurags' and the highest and most beneficial ideal of life which he has thereby presented in all these relations, was neither set nor lived in the human world by any so called incarnation, prophet or messenger or any founder or teacher of any religion, guru, devotee, or yogi or any saint, mahant, rishi, muni, jin or any buddha, siddha, tirthanker etc. Being devoid of these sublime loves, it was impossible for any of them to have done so.

7. Various kinds of all necessary and complete surrenders and sacrifices which the Devatma made in virtue of his highest psychic loves, for the accomplishment of the supreme objective of his life based on those loves, were not made in the human world by any so-called incarnation, prophet, messenger or any founder or teacher of any religion or any guru, devotee, yogi, saint, mahant rishi, muni, jin or any buddha, siddha, tirthanker, etc. Being devoid of these sublime loves they did not and could not have such a supreme life objective and hence it was impossible for them to make the various kinds of necessary surrenders and sacrifices for its accomplishment.

8. The various kinds of most remarkable, changes which the Devatma being the spiritual sun of this darkness-ridden soul-world, has been able, by means of his sublime light (Dev Jyoti) and sublime power (Dev Tej) to bring about in the world—i.e., the higher changes which have been and are being brought about in fit souls through the alchemy of the rays of his unique psychic light and unique psychic power by creating in them true higher repulsion and above that true higher pain for their one or other pleasure-affording but absolutely false beliefs and creeds about soul-life in the name of religion and for their one or other pleasure-affording but unjust or evil deeds in relation to various existences in Nature—were not and could not be brought about in the human world by any founder or teacher of any so-called religion or any guru, messenger or any rishi, muni, or yogi or any saint, mahant, buddha, siddha, tirthanker or jin etc.

9. Unlike the human souls, the Devatma, being possessed of the highest psychic loves for truth and goodness, could not in accordance with the immutable law of Nature, develop love of some pleasure or make some pleasure as the goal of his life even -though he possessed various consciousness for pleasure and pain and hence he did not, like other human beings fall in love with some pleasure and did not make some pleasure as the goal of his life.

10. Unlike the human souls, the Devatma, in virtue of his unique and highest psychic loves of truth and goodness, could not establish his relation with any human being, animal, plant, or inanimate object on the basis of any pleasure-seeking feeling and, hence he did not form any such relation on that basis with any being.

11. The Devatma, in virtue of his unique highest psychic forces of love of truth and goodness did not form relationship with any animate or inanimate existence of Nature on the basis of pleasure, and hence like other human beings did not form any bias or prejudice for any of them and so he did not do so.

12. The Devatma, in virtue of his highest psychic loves of truth and goodness and his absolute freedom from every form of pleasure-seeking love, could not become a slave to any kind of pleasure and hence unlike men and women of this world he never became such a slave.

In short, just as in the evolutionary scale of Nature, the inorganic living objects possess superiority over non-living matter, the organic living plants and animals possess superiority over the inorganic living objects and the human beings are superior to all these existences, in the same way, in the human world the Devatma possesses superiority over all the human souls.

Hence as the Devatma, in virtue of his these true and unique highest psychic forces, is in the scale of the human evolution in this world, the most noble, the all-sided benefactor and the highest emergence. Having attained to the true and unique highest psychic forces and all their unique characteristics he possesses fundamental distinction from or superiority over every being of the human world, just as the human beings, on account of several kinds of special powers, have fundamental distinction from and superiority over every being of the animal world.

The Fundamental Distinction of the Devatma from all kinds of the so-called gods and goddesses and worshipful beings of the world.

Q. What is the fundamental distinction between the Devatma and all those beings which are called gods or are believed to be worshipful beings by various so-called religions of this world?

A. All the so-called gods, or the so-called goddesses or the so-called worshipful beings—whether they belonged to human species or came from animal or vegetable or inanimate worlds or were the creation of mere fancy--belief in whom has been propagated in this world, were, one and all, devoid of the true highest sublime forces ('Dev Shaktian') which have appeared and evolved in the Devatma.

Now, though the wholly imaginary gods and goddesses never had from the outset any real existence at all, yet even the real beings of the human, animal, vegetable and inanimate kingdoms which existed in fact and were called or accepted and propagated to be gods, goddesses or worshipful beings, were, one and all, inspite of real existence, devoid of the real sublime forces of the Devatma. Then, again, those from amongst the human beings who were called or believed to be gods, having human nature in them, were one and all lovers of pleasure alone, and were absolutely destitute of the real sublime forces which have emerged in the Devatma in the evolutionary course of Nature.

Therefore, the Devatma has and should be considered to have, the same distinction from all of them as he has from all other human souls.

LOVE FOR VARIOUS KINDS OF PLEASURES IN THE HUMAN WORLD

Q. What are the various kinds of loves for pleasures which have developed in mankind?

A. The following are the eight major groups into which these pleasures in mankind can be divided:

(1) Love for various pleasures pertaining to body.

(2) Love for various pleasures pertaining to 'self' or 'ego'.

(3) Love for various pleasures resulting from affection of off springs.

(4) Love for the pleasures pertaining to wealth and property.

(5) Love for the pleasures derived from traditional beliefs, social connections and various habits.

(6) Love for the pleasures derived from violence (hinsa).

(7) Love for various pleasures derived from false beliefs.

(8) Love for pleasures arising out of various altruistic feelings.

In the event of the occurrence of any phenomenon which may cause hindrance in the course of the satisfaction of any of these various kinds of loves of pleasure, the human soul receives a hurt which gives pain to it. It is such various pains which produce various kinds of repulsions or hates in it.

A detailed account of these topics will be given in the subsequent chapters.

LOVE FOR SEVERAL BODILY PLEASURES IN THE ORGANISM OF HUMAN SOUL

The earliest awareness which a human being develops concerns his various bodily pleasures and pains. With the appearance of these consciousness two distinct feelings of attraction for pleasures and repulsion for pains grow in him. Later on, he gradually develops love for pleasures for which his attraction grows. And he also experiences hatred for all such persons and things that cause obstruction or opposition to his such beloved pleasure no less for every one of his pain as opposed to his pleasure.

Q. What is meant by the growth of loves for bodily pleasures in the organism of human soul?

A. A human being gets consciousness of the various pleasures by means of one or another of his bodily organs. When he develops strong craving or longing for getting one or another of these bodily pleasures, such strong craving or such strong attraction for those pleasures is called love of bodily pleasures.

From the time of birth, every human being experiences various kinds of pleasures and pains through his sense organs. That is, when certain things are put in his mouth, he feels the different tastes of every one of them through the various kinds of taste buds lying in his tongue. He finds some of these things as pleasant or attractive and some others as painful and repulsive. In such a state, he likes to take in what affords him pleasure and to throw out what gives him pain. Again, he feels pain in the hot or cold atmosphere of a certain temperature and feels pleasure and comfort in a different temperature. Finding the atmospheric temperature in the former case to be painful, he feels aversion or hatred for it and finding the atmospheric temperature in the latter case to be pleasant, he feels attraction for it.

Then gradually various other kinds of consciousness evolve and develop in him through his nervous system.

On becoming conscious of different bodily pleasures and pains through his nervous system, a human being from his very childhood begins to crave for bodily pleasures and to hate bodily pains. He longs for pleasure—howsoever harmful and evil consequence it may produce for him. He does not want pain—howsoever useful and good results it may produce for him.

Again, when man's craving for some pleasure gradually develops into love for it, then naturally he loses his freedom and becomes a slave to it. On developing love of some pleasure he becomes a slave to it and this slavery in its turn leads him to harm both his bodily and soul organism in various ways. Thus by becoming a slave to some pleasure, he himself becomes an enemy of his own being and proves harmful for it.

Q. What are those various bodily pleasures, love of and slavery to which make a man harmful to and an enemy of his own being?

A. Such bodily pleasures are of several kinds, i.e.

(1) Love of pleasure derived from taste.

(2) Love of pleasure derived from intoxication.

(3) Love of pleasure derived from sex indulgence.

(4) Love of pleasure derived from idleness &c.

All these loves of pleasures are directly connected with the nervous system of man's body, therefore, they are all called loves of the bodily pleasures.

1. Love of pleasure derived from taste

By becoming possessed by or on becoming slave to this low love, a man does the following:

(i) He eats and drinks such things which, on being felt tasty, give him pleasure, yet they are such as are ruinous to his bodily health and which have never been meant by Nature to serve as wholesome food and drink for any human being and whose use for food and drink is never proper and is entirely opposed to its good laws.

(ii) He even wants to eat and drink such things which produce one or another disease in his body and cannot withhold himself from their temptation. In such a state, he becomes intemperate in various ways and ruins his bodily health and vitality and longevity of physical life.

(iii) He gets into the habit of over-eating or taking in excess not only inedible things but even things intended as food. This habit of gluttony puts a burden on the various organs of his digestive system which is beyond their capacity to deal with, so that they do not digest food properly and thus the necessary quantity of pure blood required for the maintenance of his body is not turned out. Along with this various kinds of poisonous and harmful elements get mixed up with his blood which cause various kinds of diseases.

(iv) On being a meat-eater, he himself slaughters or gets slaughtered by others, beings of the animal kingdom in order to eat their meat and thereby develops feeling of injustice in himself and abets others in such acts of injustice or oppression.

Besides this, he suffers from one or another kind of diseases by eating their flesh which contains various kinds of disease-producing matter.

(v) He gets into the habit of taking such salt which is either dug out from mines or manufactured from saltish water or saltish earth. Such salt is not constituted by Nature for human food.

Nature has given this capacity of converting mineral articles into living state to the vegetable kingdom alone i.e., the vegetables alone can transform the non-living things into living and organic state and thus make them assimilable into their bodies. Apart from them, no being of the animal or the human kingdom possesses this capacity. Therefore, the different kinds of salts which are necessary for the maintenance and nourishment of human body are produced for him in the plants of the vegetable world. In accordance with the beneficial laws of Nature, he ought to take all such different salts from the edible articles of the vegetable world and he should never take mineral salts. Swayed by love of taste, habit and custom, people take mineral salt in their food. The life-force of man cannot transform mineral salt into living blood corpuscles and cannot assimilate it into his living bodily organism. Therefore, a part of the mineral salt which people take, is ejected out of their system through urine &c., while some part of it lodges itself in one or other of their muscles, where it produces various kinds of diseases which is injurious to health.

(vi) He gets into the habits of taking tea, coffee and several other such things which are both unnecessary and undesirable for the human body.

The poisonous elements which these things contain make them unfit for human consumption.

Poisonous things produce various kinds of diseases in human body.

(vii) He gets into the habit of taking such condiments which are not food for him. By habitually taking these stuffs, he injures his health in various ways.

(viii) He produces various kinds of diseases in his body through various kinds of intemperance and in this state of disease he suffers various kinds of pains, sometime of the most severe and unbearable character. In some cases when he is no longer able to stand such pain, he even commits suicide.

2. Love of pleasure derived from intoxication

Q. What is meant by the love of pleasure derived from taking intoxicants?

A. The kind of pleasurable excitement that man feels when his nervous system is unduly stimulated by the use of poisonous things is called the state of intoxication. The strong craving or attraction for such pleasure of intoxication is called love of pleasure 'derived from intoxication.

Animals even when hungry, do not take bhang, poppy, tobacco or any other such poisonous thing. Even when thirsty they refuse to take spirituous liquors or water containing hemp and do not harm their body by their consumption. But man by becoming a slave to the low pleasures of intoxication takes, besides hemp and poppy, even such poisonous things as spirituous liquors, opium, morphia, charas, chandu, cocaine, tobacco, etc. Nature has never made desirable or proper, the use of any of the above-mentioned things for the sake of getting pleasure of intoxication. Their consumption greatly harms bodily health and impairs the vital organs of the body; as a result whereof it becomes prey to several diseases.

The kinds of diseases that are produced in the human body by the consumption of intoxicating things are the following:

(1) Diseases of the brain such as loss of memory or forgetfulness, insanity, trembling of the parts of the body, - coma, paralysis, etc.

(2) Diseases of the digestive system such as, constipation, dysentery, jaundice, dropsy, diabetes, etc.

(3) Diseases of the heart, such as, palpitation of heart, etc.

(4) Diseases of the kidneys, such as, rheumatism, gout, etc.

Besides these, various diseases of eyes, throat etc., are also caused by them.

3. Love of pleasure derived from sex-indulgence

Q. What is meant by love of pleasure derived from sex-indulgence?

A. The experience of pleasure felt by man and woman through their sex-organs is called the feeling of sex. A strong craving for the satisfaction of this feeling or over-powering attraction for such pleasure is called the love of sexual pleasure. By becoming lover of or slave to this sexual pleasure many persons do for its sake, such acts as under:

(1) They commit several acts which are against the beneficent laws of Nature, such as:

(a) Masturbation.

(b) Unnatural crime i.e., sodomy.

(c) Mating with an animal.

(d) Mating in excess with one's wedded partner.

(e) Mating with one's wife in her state of mensuration.

(f) Mating of wedded partners with each other when any one of them is suffering from some serious malady.

(g) Adultery.

(h) Rape.

(i) Casting lustful glances on some man or woman outside wedlock.

(j) Touching or kissing some part of the body of some woman, boy or girl outside wedlock in order to gratify sex instinct etc., (except on proper occasions of interchange of affection by husband and wife.)

2. They harm themselves in several ways by indulging in such thoughts and conversations, reading of such books, singing or listening to such songs, dancing or witnessing such dances, cutting such jokes, etc., which excite sexual desire.

3. Besides damaging their heart they very greatly ruin the vital organs of their body, especially their brain, by practicing masturbation and homo-sexuality. By such habits they deprive themselves of their capacity for becoming good thinkers or good scholars. By such evil acts they contract different kinds of diseases and thereby suffer pains of various kinds. On one or another occasion when a state of utter despondency and intense pain arises and they lack the requisite power to bear it, they even commit suicide.

4. Besides degrading their souls through the sin of adultery, they in many cases contract those peculiarly filthy venereal diseases of which they not only themselves suffer the most evil consequences but they also ruin others by spreading their infection to them. If after suffering from some such disease, they are able to procreate, then in many cases one or another of their children have also to suffer the dreadful consequences of such terrible diseases.

5. Even after marriage when they over-indulge in sex gratification for the sake of its pleasure, they gradually lose their nervous strength and in many cases become so weak that they are not able to protect their bodies from the attacks of various kinds of minute germs of such deadly diseases as tuberculosis etc. Hence it is that several people fall victim to some such deadly disease in the prime of their life and are slowly consumed by it to premature death.

6. Many men kidnap or abduct a daughter or a wife, a sister or a mother etc., of some other person by attracting her towards them or enticing her in some way by giving her some temptation and thus make her faithless to her relatives and in many cases abandon her on one pretext or another after committing adultery with her. Many a time in such a state of helplessness the abandoned woman finding no shelter anywhere, takes to prostitution and thus by selling her honour gradually becomes so low and degraded that she adopts prostitution as her profession. Through her very degraded character, she makes many other men and women adulterous like herself.

7. Lot of wealthy men do not limit themselves to gratifying their sexual, craving through professional prostitutes or spoiled women but many of them destroy the purity and honour of several wedded ladies and by degrading them into adultery, make them faithless to their relatives.

8. Those men who do not like to get sexual pleasure through adultery and who cannot get married by some right manner, purchase some girl by paying a heavy sum of money to her father, brother, mother or guardian and keep her with them for the purpose of their sexual gratification. In such places where the custom of selling unmarried girls or women prevails, they purchase them for sexual satisfaction and in their own turn sell such women for the same purpose to other males when they no longer feel the need of retaining them with themselves.

4. Love of pleasure derived from idleness, sloth or laziness

Q. What is meant by love of pleasure derived from idleness?

A. The feeling of doing absolutely nothing or doing as - little as possible for oneself or for another is called the feeling of idleness. Those who become addicted to the pleasures of this feeling, do not desire to do anything for themselves or for others. They are called lovers of the pleasure of idleness. And this low love of theirs is called the love of idleness.

Q. What are the various characteristics which are exhibited by idleness-loving persons due to their slavery to the pleasure of idleness?

A. By becoming slave to the pleasure of idleness many persons:

(1) 1 do not and cannot discharge their various kinds of duties or obligations towards others.

(2) In case they inherit an ancestral property which is sufficient for their livelihood, they wholly live on it and do not and cannot earn anything by their own effort or initiative and rust in idleness.

(3) Those idle persons who do not inherit any ancestral property and also possess no personal property, live by cheating others in one way or another or by taking money from others in, the name of loan.

(4) On being forced by circumstances to earn, even when they accept to do some work for others for some remuneration, they try to do as little work as possible;

and they base their such dishonest conduct on the following fundamental principle of theirs:

"Karoon bahut thora saa kaam, mujh ko miley bahut saa daam"

Translation "I should do very little work but I should have a very handsome remuneration."

(5) They take to the life of `sadhus' or `fakirs' and live by begging from others and thus put upon public the, absolutely undesirable and sinful burden of the various expenses of their living. Hundreds from amongst them cheat various people and thus endeavour to live on their earnings.

(6) Some do work for some years and lay by some money.

Afterwards they become idle for one or another reason and while away the rest of their lives.

(7) Lying idle, they waste their time in sex exciting jokes and jests or in slandering talk about the losses, or failings or defects of others or in hearing such talk from others. By all this they greatly degrade their soul-life also.

(8) What to say of helping or serving others, they even lose the capacity to act up to the principle of "self-help".

That is, they cannot do even the ordinary work of looking after their bodies, their houses and their other belongings &c. In case they are thirsty they would not, as far as possible, get up and take water or fetch it from any other place. They do not want to spread their own cots or spread their beds on them. They have no power left to protect their homes and things from clemency of weather and therefore cannot keep them safe. They do not take bath and do not wash their clothes and remain very dirty and ugly.

Lacs of persons of this type are also completely devoid of the feeling of self-respect and are very low and degraded as regards their state of soul-life.

THE LOVE OF PLEASURE IN THE ORGANISM OF HUMAN SOUL DERIVED FROM EGO

The love of pleasure in the organism of human soul derived from self-love or ego

Q. What is meant by the love of pleasure derived from self-love or ego?

A. When, with the growth of consciousness of 'self' or 'I' in man, he also grows the consciousness of 'my', 'Mine', and 'me' or 'myself', he establishes his relations with himself and various other living and non-living existences of Nature on the basis of this consciousness of 'I' or 'self'. His strong craving for the pleasure which he experiences due to this kind of relation based on self or 'I', is called the love of egoistic pleasure.

So long as a human child does not develop the consciousness that 'this is my head', 'these are the hair of my head', 'this is my mouth', 'these are my eyes', 'this is my nose', 'this is my tongue', 'these are my hands', 'these are my fingers', 'this is my chest', 'this is my stomach', 'these are my feet', 'this is my cap', 'these are my shoes', 'this is my toy', etc., he does not develop any love for any of these things.

Hence it is., that he experiences no pain nor any loss to himself, if the cap he wears, the shoes he puts on or the toy he plays with, gets spoiled or lost'-of stolen:. Even though these things are used by him and prove useful to him, yet so 'long as he does not develop consciousness of 'my' or 'mine' in relation to them, he feels absolutely no relation of his own with these things.

Besides this, so long as a human child does not develop consciousness of 'I' or 'self' and is not able to know and believe his own being or any other existence as his own, he would not experience any pain or hurt if, on seeing some defect in the structure of any of his eyes, his nose, any of his ears, his face, any of his hands or feet, etc., you were to make the defect known to him or point it out to him. But when he would develop the consciousness: of 'ego' or 'self' and would come to realize the organs of his body as 'his' or 'My' organ or any other thing as 'his' or 'my' thing, then if you would tell any of these things as bad or defective, he would not be pleased but would get hurt and pained. And if you praise—even if the praise be false—any of the organs of his body or something else which he thinks to be his own, he would feel happy and on being happier he would give a smile. By this expression, he would make evident to you that just as he feels displeased or pained at the condemnation of himself or any of the things connected with him, so also he feels pleasure or joy by the praise of himself or any of his things. After the awakening of the consciousness of 'ego' or 'self', man has developed, not only the pleasure-based love for self-praise, but also various other kinds of pleasures and loves related to self.

Q. What are all those various loves for pleasures of this kind in man?

A. All such loves of pleasure in man are

(1) Love of pleasure derived from praise.

(2) Love of pleasure derived from respect or honour.

(3) Love of pleasure derived from superiority or name and fame.

(4) Love of pleasure derived from selfishness.

1. Love of pleasure derived from praise.

Q. What is meant by love of pleasure derived from praise?

A. Praise means appreciation or warm approbation. Strong craving for the pleasure which one gets on hearing his praise from another, or on reading his praise in the writing of another or even on praising one's own self by tongue or pen, is called the love of pleasure derived from praise.

This desire grows in man from his very childhood after the awakening of the consciousness of 'ego' in him.

There is no individual in the human kingdom who does not feel pleasure or joy on hearing his praise from another or on knowing about his praise in some article. It is not only the case that a man gets pleasure or joy on hearing his praise from the spoken or written words of another, but he gets pleasure also by praising himself on one or another occasion through his own tongue or pen.

Just as every human being fond of praise gets pleasure on being praised, so also he experiences pleasure on hearing the praises of or giving praise to any person, animal, plant or anything else for which he feels some attraction or love. Just as he feels pain or hurt on hearing his own dispraise, so also he feels pain or, hurt when any person, animal or any other object with which he feels identified, is dispraised though such dispraise be entirely true.

Due to the love of this pleasure, every human being, in accordance with the laws of Nature, feels attraction towards that person also who praises him or any of his loved human being or animal or article. And due to this attraction, he feels him as his own friend and himself becomes his friend too.

Millions of people know that man is pleased on hearing his praise.

Hence, with the intention of winning his affection and getting some purpose served by him, they not only shower true praises on him in his presence but on many occasions even intentionally give him false praise. Hearing such praises he feels elated, gets drawn towards them and develops bias or partiality for them. Having reached this state of mind, he is ready not only to satisfy any of their desirable objectives, but on the contrary, even is ready to be helpful in fulfilling any of their wholly undesirable or unjust desired things.

Being conscious of this human weakness for love of pleasure of praise, thousands of men who are debauchees draw towards themselves some young virgin girl, or some married woman or some widow by singing false praises of the beauty of her person or bestowing false excellence on her. Besides employing other tactics, they use this method also to win her love and try to ruin her chastity.

Hundreds of lovers of the pleasure of praise pay money to others for singing their false praises and propagating them among others. Led by this love of pleasure of praise, various vicious persons, after their departure from this earth and on becoming evil spirits, have, in order to get the pleasure of false praise and false adoration from people of this world, created false beliefs in them by falsely declaring themselves as gods and being possessed of various extraordinary powers, which are absolutely opposed to the laws of Nature.

Knowing this human weakness for love of the pleasure of praise; thousands of persons do not have the courage to tell some friend or a near relation of theirs about any of his sins or evils, even when it is absolutely necessary and desirable, because they know that by their doing so, he would be hurt and would get estranged from them on account of this hurt and thereby their mutual relation would be embittered leading to positive harm of various kinds to them. It is, therefore, that millions of parents-even, do not intentionally point out to such of their grown up child who lives under their guardianship, such of his physical or spiritual defects or evils from which it is their parental responsibility to save him, and silently watch and allow the evil to go on. Several times these parents do not dare to tell their child his defects which they know to be defects, because they fear that the child will talk ill or disparagingly of them, which would be painful to them.

Though thousands of persons belonging to different religions, do not believe and accept some religious beliefs of their sect as true, yet, due to slavery to this love of the pleasure of praise, they continue to express and declare themselves to be the followers of that religion against their inner convictions out of the fear of incurring disapprobation of their co-religionists. They thus become hypocrites and thereby degrade their souls.

Thousands of slaves to this love of the pleasure of praise even when they know a prevalent ceremony, custom or usage to be false or harmful, yet follow it against their conviction out of the fear of incurring the 'disapprobation of their community. And through this hypocrisy, they degrade their own souls.

Being slaves, to this, love of the pleasure of praise, thousands of persons even when they know certain outer symbols of their religion to be unnecessary or harmful, not only continue to observe them themselves out of the fear of being condemned by some persons (and thereby become and remain hypocrites) but advise their children also to keep them on and, by making them habituated to their observance, side with falsehood and by their such hypocritical behaviour degrade their souls.

Q. Does this love of the pleasure of praise give rise to any low-hatred in man?

A. Yes, it does. Every pleasure-based low-love is related to some low-hate.

That is, whenever any event, opposed to the gratification of any of his pleasure-based low-loves occurs, than a feeling of hatred necessarily awakens in him in accordance with the immutable law of Nature.

Therefore, if you frankly tell a lover of praise even something which though true, offends against his praise, he would experience pain in his heart. And this pain will excite in him the feeling of hatred for you and he would get estranged from you. If very strong hatred were produced in him, he would withdraw his help if he formerly rendered any to you as a friend. But in case this feeling of hatred still more increases in him, he would take., you 'as' his enemy in place of a friend, and in this attitude of enmity or hostility towards you; he would seek the satisfaction, of this low feeling by harming you himself or getting you harmed by others in various ways.

In short, in accordance with the immutable law of Nature pertaining to soul-life, just as it is inevitable for every man who is lover of the pleasure of praise, to drift towards various falsehoods on various occasions, so also it is inevitable for him to do one or another kind of other evil deeds as well on different occasions.

2. Love of pleasure derived from honour

Q. What is love of pleasure derived from honour or respect?

A. Honour or respect means regard or deference. The strong craving to get respect or honour from others for oneself is called the love of pleasure of honour.

Being slaves to this pleasure derived from honour

(1) Thousands of persons spend hundreds, thousands and in some cases lakhs of rupees in order to secure this or that kind of prestigious government job or political position.

They try to get such a job or position by pleasing those persons from whom they hope to get that job through falsely praising them or doing some improper or evil acts for them or creating in them a good opinion about themselves by a false propaganda of their merits.

For the sake of securing this or that title or distinction from any government, thousands of persons besides lavishly spending money, try to please those whom they believe to be capable of securing their objective, by indulging in their false praises, by giving various kinds of presents to them or by executing some improper jobs for them when needed. By such worship of theirs, they please them and try to gain their objective through them.

(3) Thousands of persons in order to secure the honour of a seat in some political darbar of some government, adopt various such devices which in many cases are criminal and sinful.

(4) Thousands of persons in order to secure some position of honour in a religious sect or samaj or society or community or with the object of getting honour or respect from its people, resort to various improper actions whenever necessary.

Q. Do the lovers of pleasure derived from honour begin even to hate or harm a person who pains them by being an obstacle in the way of their getting such pleasure?

A. Yes, Sir. If someone exposes any true facts about any of their criminal, sinful, improper or unmannerly actions, they feel pained and hurt and cherish low-hate for him. Due to this feeling of hatred, they get estranged from him. If they previously gave any help to him, they in many instances, wish to stop it and do actually withdraw it. If this hatred assumes very strong form in them, they become vindictive and devise and adopt various ways and means of doing harm of different kinds to him, as well as to those connected with him. They satisfy their very low-feeling of hatred and thereby derive very base pleasure by thus doing harm to him or getting it done through others.

3. Love of pleasure derived from feeling of superiority

Q. What is meant by love of pleasure derived from feeling of superiority?

A. The strong craving for that kind of pleasure which a person derives from believing oneself to be superior to or better than others, or from telling others of one's superiority over them or from being accepted and acknowledged as superior to others or from showing oneself to be superior to others, is called the love of pleasure derived from the feeling of superiority.

Over-powered by this low-love:

(1) Millions of persons think, believe and declare themselves to be superior to one who is really abler, more learned or better or higher person than they, and think, believe and declare him to be inferior to them.

(2) Hundreds of announce express with special pride even some defect or evil deed of theirs on one or another occasion in the presence of others (especially those of their own outlook).

(3) Millions of persons even falsely boast of possessing a virtue which they do not have or highly exaggerate the virtue which they possess to some extent.

(4) Hundreds of persons suffer in various ways by courting uncalled for and undesirable conflicts with those who are their superiors.

(5) Millions of persons waste a lot of their money in order to show themselves big or superior before others.

(6) Thousands of persons even though, ignorant about some subject do not ask, enquire from or consult any other person who is very able or expert in that subject, sheerly out of false fear of being looked down upon. Thus they act blindly in their own way in that respect and thereby get harmed or harm others to a great extent.

(7) Hundreds of persons even when they are totally ignorant or possess very little ability in some respect, try to tell or teach, without occasion and in a most insulting manner, one or another thing to some other person who is far more informed or abler than they in that respect. For this impertinence they are on several occasions snubbed, disgraced and put to shame by him.

(8) Thousands of persons do not pay or like to pay any respect at all or even due respect to one who is definitely superior to them.

(9) Millions of persons behave disrespectfully in several ways towards the elders of their family or of their clan or other respectable persons.

(10) Millions of persons do not admit any of their true faults, crimes or sins or even any of their true weaknesses.

Q. - Is it true that many departed evil spirits led also by the love of pleasure afforded by the feeling of superiority, have falsely declared themselves as gods and have falsely claimed to possess different kinds of powers and thus created in people various false beliefs about themselves? Is it also true that dominated by this love of pleasure derived from the feeling of superiority, many persons living on this earth have also spread various kinds of falsehoods about themselves?

A. Yes, Sir.

(1) Many persons who on leaving their gross bodies became evil spirits, have made people their blind followers by creating in them false beliefs of this kind about themselves, that they were the creators and controllers of various kingdoms

of Nature; that they could perform various extraordinary feats or miracles; that they, on being pleased with them, could grant through their blessings, their own desires as well as those of their family and group members, and that they on being displeased could, through their curses, harm and torture them and their family and group members.

(2) Similarly, many living persons of this world have also made ignorant people their blind followers by creating in them such beliefs regarding themselves that they were gifted with powers of performing so-called extraordinary "miracles", and so-called supernatural "feats" and that they were capable of fulfilling their various kinds of wishes and longings.

(3) Different living persons of this earth have made millions of people their blind followers and disciples by creating in them such kind of false belief that they were incarnations (avtars) or accredited teachers or rulers &c of one or another mythical god.

(4) Different living persons on this earth have made thousands of people their blind followers and disciples by producing in their minds such kind of absolutely false beliefs about themselves that they had special relation with this or that so-called well-known god and threatening them on that score that if they acted in disobedience to the wishes of that God, they would be sent to some hell &c full of absolutely imaginary tortures and claiming to have the power of getting from that god not only a pardon of their sins if they believed in one or another faith of theirs, but further than that of getting them into a place called heaven, `swarg' or 'baikunth' full of some so-called luxuries or enjoyments of life.

Q. Does this love of pleasure derived from the feeling of superiority lead to the development of vanity in a man?

A. Yes, Sir.

Q. How does this happen?

A. When a man begins to love himself to such an extent that as a result thereof he regards his body, every organ of his body, his physical strength, his intelligence, his power of understanding, his power of speech or oration, his learning, his opinion and his beliefs etc., not only as excellent and without any blemish, but he even falsely, believes them to be far superior to others and falsely thinks and believes another to be inferior to him in respect of some virtue, then his such kind of false belief about himself is called the feeling of vanity.

It is not only that vain people regard false things as true and true things as false with regard to themselves alone, but they do not remain capable of seeing even the true beauty and real grandeur of those various kinds of better or higher qualities which have evolved in different departments of Nature. That is to say, due to this feeling of vanity, they gradually lose their capacity—if they possessed some such capacity previously—to see and to appreciate this kind of beautiful qualities and thus become spiritually blind. This spiritual blindness makes them not only incapable of seeing and, therefore, of truly appreciating and praising the glory of those higher souls in whom, in the course of evolution, various beautiful, praiseworthy and excellent higher virtues have evolved but also makes them incapable of evolving in their souls that feeling of true altruistic reverence which develops in a man on being able to see the beauty and grandeur of these higher virtues.

Besides this, persons dominated by vanity always believe themselves in the right even when in fact they have got perverted perception and hold false beliefs in various matters. And they always believe, consider and declare any such person to be mistaken, degraded and misguided who does not hold an opinion or belief on some subject similar to that of theirs.

Q. Is it true that various powerful persons from amongst such vain people, led by the feeling of low but intense hatred created in them against millions of people, because they did not share their beliefs and faiths about any so-called God or any of his mediums, have perpetrated on those people various kinds of most horrible atrocities and persecuted them in different ways and, in several cases, have even done them to death?

A. Yes, Sir. Such vanity-ridden powerful persons have under the pretext of religion, destroyed man's birth-right of true freedom of faith and thought, and besides persecuting people of different views in various ways, they have been guilty of the most heinous sin and basest crime of putting millions of persons to death.

Q. Do vain people feel hurt to hear some other person being talked of as better or superior to them in some respect?

A. Yes, Sir. When the vain persons do not believe anyone to be superior to them in any respect, it is but inevitable for them to feel hurt when somebody else is said to be superior to them in some respect.

Q. But do vain persons feel happy in falsely talking ill of others?

A. Yes, they do. They feel very happy. It is because of this that millions of persons on this globe feel very happy in slandering others. It is because of this that slander or calumny of this kind is rampant among the inhabitants of every country.

Q. Do the persons who love the pleasure derived from superiority or are possessed by vanity, develop low hatred also for one who tells them something which though true, yet offends against their vanity?

A. Certainly, yes. In accordance with the immutable law of the soul-life in Nature, it is but inevitable for vain persons to feel such hatred in a more or less degree. In the event of this low-hatred being aroused it is no less inevitable for such persons to feel estranged from the object of their low-hatred, to keep away from him or to avoid him, to decline even to see his face or to talk to him, to think evil of him and to manufacture and propagate various slanders against him, to refrain from doing any due service to him, even though he be their great benefactor; and in several cases when their hatred is intensified, they go to the length of inflicting some serious injury on him themselves or of getting it done by others.

When this low-hatred gets flared up and dominates the hearts of such vain souls against their elderly and respectable relatives or other respected persons, then the kind of feelings and thoughts which it gives rise to in them even in their relation are and can be approximately of this nature.

"He may be a big person in his own estimation but I do not accept him as such."

"You better not teach me; I can do this job much better than you."

"Once my mother pointed out an act of mine as bad. I grew wrathful with her and told such condemnatory things against her that she was at last reduced to silence."

"Whenever my father tells me something which goes against me, I silence him by telling him some condemnatory things against him."

"My elder brother never interferes in any of my matters out of the fear of being insulted by me."

"Once my father expressed his opinion about somebody else which was against my views. I was very much hurt. I felt so much hatred for him that I gave up talking with him. And ever since then I do not speak with him at all."

"Once my mother did not satisfy a desire of mine. I felt very much pained. In protest, I did not take my meals and in this way I too gave her much pain."

"I do not want to see even the face of such father of mine who points out and exposes any actions of mine as bad."

"When I steal some cash of my father ask elder brother, I do not admit to have stolen it even when they ask or inquire about it repeatedly, so much so that I refuse to confess this theft even when they begin to beat me and inflict very painful injuries upon me.',

"When I walk on a public road, I do not like to make way even for an old, weak or sick man or a woman or even any respected person who happens to come from the opposite direction."

"I broke all my connections with a certain society because when I was a member of its executive committee and representative assembly, then all other members of both of these bodies in those days, did not support my views but on several occasions they expressed their views against those of mine."

"On the way when I happen to meet any of my old teachers or even any other respectable person known to me, I do not on my own part, pay him any respects and show any regard for him."

"Even though I do several such acts that bring me great losses and even when I knew that had I consulted some person abler than about them I could have saved myself from such harm, then also, I did not consult some such able person thinking it to be derogatory to my dignity."

"I deem it below my dignity to accept Devatma as worshipful being for me, therefore I do not believe him to be Devatma."

The fact is that greater the vanity and hatred in the mutual relation of the people of a country, the greater is the amount of disharmony and of enemity between them. They break away from one another by producing absolutely false distinctions in their mutual relations. In such a strained condition, they do not and cannot develop into a prosperous 'nation' nor do or can they acquire or attain 'national' strength.

Vanity and hatred are the most degrading and most evil feelings in man.

4. Love of pleasure derived from selfishness

Q. What is meant by love of pleasure derived from selfishness?

A. Swaarth' or selfishness means "for one's own self." That is, when a person keeps his own pleasures alone as foremost in all his thoughts and actions and spends his money and energy at their altar he is disposed towards or loves the pleasures of selfishness. This form of disposition is called the love of pleasure derived from selfishness.

Q. Are those persons also lovers of the pleasure of selfishness who do some remunerative work and spend their money to secure pleasures for their wives and children?

A. Yes, Sir. If the husbands secure the satisfaction of their sex-instinct from their wives or besides that get various other pleasures from their services, if the fathers derive the pleasure of parental affection through attachment with their children; if the wives also obtain similar kinds of pleasures from their husbands, and if their children get several kinds of pleasures from both of their parents and all of them are attached to each other by the ties of such pleasures, then all of them have their relation with each other for their own pleasure and do different kinds of services for each other for their own selfish pleasures.

But when a lover of the pleasures of selfishness does not get nor expects to get some pleasure at any time by doing service to any other man or an animal or a tree etc., then he does not want to and does not bestir himself to do something merely for the sake of the pleasure of others.

Those persons who do not feel any pleasure in doing any physical labour, or in contributing their mental or educational energies or their wealth etc., for the good of any other person, do not do any such service for him. So such persons cannot and do not want to make any kind of sacrifice or surrender for the sake of any cause of public good.

Such persons are complete slaves to the pleasures of selfishness.

Q. What are the general characteristic features of persons given completely to the pleasures of selfishness?

A. Persons given completely to the pleasures of selfishness cannot and do not utilize any of their physical and mental energies, their knowledge, their wealth and property etc. for the good of other existences of Nature except for such few persons etc., from whom they get or expect to get at some time some kind of pleasure. Hence it is that:

Complete slaves to the pleasures of selfishness do not give in charity their wealth or their property for any cause of the good of others. They do not contribute any of their intellectual knowledge or industrial skill for any cause of the good of others. Even after receiving one or another kind of physical benefit from any one, they do not wish, even in return, to be of service to him. This is the reason why they do not do any service to him.

Even after receiving some spiritual benefit from a true soul-benefactor, they do not want to become serviceable to him and hence they do not become so.

They receive different kinds of physical benefits from various existences of the animal kingdom, yet they, on their own part, do not want to do anything for the good of that kingdom and; therefore, do not do it.

They receive different kinds of physical benefits from several existences of the vegetable kingdom, yet they do not want to be serviceable to that kingdom in any respect and, therefore, do not do any service to it.

They receive different kinds of benefits night and day from earth, water, air and other existences of the non-living kingdom, yet they do not, on their own, want to be serviceable to that kingdom and hence do not serve it.

The fundamental principle or 'mantra' which these utterly selfish persons repeat in their mind and practice day and night is of this kind -

"As far as it is possible, I should get one or other kind of pleasure for myself from others, but I should never do anything for promoting the pleasure or good of another—so much so that I should not do the work of another completely and properly even when I receive due remuneration for it."

A person entirely given to the pleasures of selfishness does not want to co-operate with or be a helping hand in the evolutionary work of any department of Nature. But on the contrary, motivated by the love of the pleasure of selfishness, he is ever ready to inflict, whenever necessary, various kinds of injuries on various existences of every department of Nature and feels pleasure in actually doing various kinds of harm occasion for it.

This disposition of such utter selfishness is most degrading and devilish.

The more the people of a country are dominated by this most degrading and devilish selfish nature, the greater is that country in a state of degradation.

Q. Does the love of pleasure derived from selfishness generate self-willedness too?

A. Yes, Sir. To desire the gratification of any of the pleasure-giving wishes or longings of one's own alone and to feel disinclined to comply even with any of the right and proper wishes or another on finding it opposed to some of one's own pleasures and to try to wriggle out of it, is called self-willedness.

A self-willed man is just like that unruly horse who does not wish to let even his own benefactor master to ride on its back or to be yoked in his carriage. And, if the master tries to ride it or to yoke it in his carriage, then out of anger he goes to the extent of biting, kicking or otherwise harming him.

This most evil-love is found in millions of persons. Dominated by this evil-love, even a very young human child manifests its characteristics.

He frets and fumes and feels pain even in obeying or acting upon any right and beneficial wish of his mother or his father, if it runs counter to any of his pleasure-affording evil-loves. And if he is not afraid of either of his parents to such an extent that in comparison to the pleasure to be derived from acting according to his own desires, he expects some greater pain to be inflicted by them which his heart is not prepared to suffer, then he point blank refuses to comply with such an order of theirs. If his parents do not have the strength or courage to check such a course of his, then by repeating his such actions he becomes more and more self-willed every day. He then becomes incapable or obeying any essential and beneficial laws of his family or society or any of the right orders of his officer, which offend against any of his pleasure-giving feelings.

Q. Cannot self-willed persons organize themselves into a big group even for some such legitimate gain of theirs which all of them accept to be right and necessary for them?

A. No. Neither an organized group can be formed by ignoring the principle of discipline, nor can any objective of it be properly achieved without it. No collective strength can grow in the absence of an organized and disciplined group. When the people of any land, on account of the feeling of mutual low hatred cannot unite among themselves, they cannot form themselves into a well-disciplined big group. They are therefore in a much weaker state than those who do not possess mutual hatred for one another to such an extent and who are able to follow the laws of discipline which are essential for the achievement of any common good and who in virtue of this ability can organize themselves into very big groups.

Q. Is obstinacy ('duragrah') also related to self-willedness?

A. Yes, Sir. When a person becomes so much of a slave to any of his pleasures that he does not wish to give it up under any circumstance and for its gratification becomes obstinate, insistent and improperly aggressive towards that person who can or is expected to satisfy it, then such action of his is called obstinacy or 'duragraha'.

Just as millions of human children from their very childhood become self-willed, so also when they unreasonably persist or insist on demanding the satisfaction of any of their pleasure-giving wish or desire from their parents or others, then every such act of theirs is called an act of obstinacy.

Q. Do some young and old persons also exhibit obstinacy or 'duragraha'?

A. Yes, Sir. Such persons also become duragrahi or obstinate when they unreasonably persist in demanding the satisfaction of some of their undesirable wishes or wills from some relative of theirs or others.

Q. Is there any 'sadagraha' or dogged persistence for a right cause also as opposed to duragrah or obstinacy?

A. Yes, Sir. When a man becomes truly conscious of a certain belief or faith to be false and a certain action to be degrading and harmful for his soul and soul-life and he never wishes to accept that false belief or faith or to do that wrong act out of any one's fear or pressure; and on becoming truly conscious of a certain action to be good and beneficial to his soul-life is determined to perform it and in doing it does not want to hear or accept anything against it from any of his relations such as, his parents, his brothers and sisters, his uncles, his paternal and maternal grand-fathers or his maternal uncles and aunts, his father's sisters, etc. or any of his friends or any other person or any social group and does not care for their threats or temptations and firmly stands on his such true consciousness and sticks to it with determination, then such action of his is called the true persistence or 'sadagrah'.

A country which has less of the 'duragrahis' or obstinate persons and more of 'sadagrahis' or men with grit to stand for the right, is much superior to those countries in which a state reverse to this exists.

Q. Are those persons in the right who on not getting any of their wishes or desires gratified at the hands of some person get hurt and pained and begin to hate that person and led by that feeling of hate, do not desire to pay nor actually pay, even due respect to him and consider and declare their such action to be right and necessary on the plea that to do so is opposed to their self-respect?

A. Not at all, Low hatred has absolutely no connection with true self-respect.

To do any kind of improper action which offends against the true dignity of the rank or position, occupied by any person in his family, his society, his religious community and in the governmental administration of his country, is certainly opposed to self-respect. But if on finding that a certain person, for one reason or another, does not accept some belief of yours or does not think you so capable in a certain respect as you think yourself to be in your own mind and thus differs from you in his views, then on this score of difference of opinion to refuse to pay due respect to him according to his dignity or still more to be determined to disrespect him, cannot certainly be an expression of self-respect. Some persons feel and cherish hatred for another on the score of difference of opinion and motivated by this hatred do not pay him due respect or still worse insult him. Such action of theirs has no connection at all with self-respect and it is in no way an expression of self-respect either. It is certainly opposed to good manners and justice. Therefore, it can never be right.

Q. Do self-willed persons feel hatred for anybody who causes any hindrance or obstruction against the gratification of the pleasure of their self-will?

A. Yes, Sir. They are fall of hatred even for one who rightly and justly interferes in the gratification of their self-will and develop perverted vision about him and see him and present him in a distorted way. If this feeling of hatred becomes intense in them, they are themselves ready to harm him in some other ways or get him harmed by others.

LOVE OF PLEASURE IN THE ORGANISM OF HUMAN SOUL DERIVED FROM THE AFFECTION OF CHILDREN

Man has descended in the course of evolution of mammals of the animal kingdom. He has consequently inherited love for children from them. But the parental affection found in millions of animals does not exhibit those degrading features which have gradually developed in the soul of man due to his love for children and which are specially harmful for his own soul-life and for the soul life of his children.

Due to his love of children, millions of parents, in order to please their children and also to please themselves thereby, serve them, on their asking or stubbornly insisting, with such foodstuffs or drinks which are positively detrimental to their physical health. It is not only their demand for harmful foods and drinks which they satisfy but they also minister to such of their wishes and wills which are harmful for both parties. The beings of the animal kingdom do not show such evil conduct while rearing their young ones.

Q. Do millions of human children also acquire various completely false and most harmful superstitions and beliefs and various kinds of most harmful habits from their parents?

A. Yes, they do. But the young ones of the animals are completely immune from such evils.

Q. Do millions of human parents who are slaves to the love of their children help them to grow and develop different kinds of most harmful pleasure-giving low-loves and low-hates?

A. Yes, they do. Millions of such human parents develop in their children the most harmful love of pleasure derived from the use of intoxicants such as tobacco, hemp, wine, opium, etc., taking of meat and eggs etc., and drinking of tea and coffee. They also stimulate and develop in their children false beliefs and feelings of hatred for others by falsely telling them that those people are inferior to them, because they belong to this or that religion or creed, this or that community, class, colour or group, or this or that profession. By such practices, they greatly harm their children and their own souls in various ways.

Q. Do not millions of persons possessing love or attachment for children also make their children hypocrites, thugs, cheats a perpetrators of other evils by their precepts and examples?

A. Yes, Sir. They certainly make them so.

Q. Do not millions of persons led by love or attachments of their children become partial to them and indulge in deliberate lies too on several occasions in order to cast a veil over some real sin or defect of their children?

A. Yes, they certainly do indulge in lies. Due to this attachment, it is inevitable for them to resort to such kind of falsehoods.

Q. Due to this love or attachment for children do not millions of parents, on becoming partial to their children, try to screen them as far as possible, on hearing some complaint about their bad, objectionable and criminal actions and establish their innocence by means of falsehoods etc.?

A. Yes, Sir. They certainly do so. Besides this, they feel hatred in their heart for the complainant and due to this low hatred they break away from him and harbour ill-feelings against him.

Q. Do not millions of persons led by the bias generated by this love or attachment for children become comparatively more attached to one child and less to the other one from amongst their children and thus on the occasion of any quarrel arising between them, perpetrate injustice or cruelty on the less-loved child by siding with the more-loved one?

A. Yes, they certainly do so. Being possessed by this low-bias, it is inevitable for them to be guilty of such a sin.

Besides the above horrible evils, those slaves to their children, are so much blinded that even when they know and see with their eyes that one or another of their sons has grown major and is able to maintain himself and has also become able to maintain his wife and children in the event of his getting married and that having grown out of the state of helplessness of childhood, he is able to live an independent life, even then they are not able to donate the whole or part of their wealth or property to some charitable institution or some cause of public good for their own welfare and for the welfare of their countrymen and thus cannot promote their own and others' soul-welfare. Thus by being slaves to this most degrading attachment or love they offend against the beneficial law of evolution and being callous to it they dedicate all their wealth at the feet of their children and thereby gratify their low-love.

Thus by siding with falsehoods and evils they degrade their own souls as well as the souls of their children. Their unfilial and completely selfish children, devoid as they are of self-respect, also feel no hesitation in accepting all the wealth and property of their parents.

Being avaricious, they want to have solely for themselves all such parental property which their parents could have subscribed as charity for their own as well as society's welfare.

Again, several parents, being slaves to this attachment, are so much blinded in relation to their children on account of this slavery that they want to leave all their wealth and all their property even to such a child of theirs who is squandering away money in various sinful acts in their very presence, and besides thus wasting their money he is also harming himself and others as well. The tragedy is that even when they see their property being thus wasted in evil ways and know it as a fact that after their death their property would be instrumental in making their child more and more degraded day by day and be spent in the dissemination of evil doing and that they in their turn would, by giving it away to him, prove an instrument and participant in those sinful acts and the most horrible consequences thereof, they would not however like, either during their life-time or by willing away their property after their death, to some charity or for some cause of public good and through such charity to do good to their souls as well as to prove serviceable to their own benefactor society or the people of their own country or of any other country. They want, however, to make an offering of the whole of their property at the feet of their sinful and evil-minded children. Alas! How most deplorable is the condition of millions of such slaves to their children.

84

Again, even when many parents know the truth that the wealth and property which they have acquired by their own effort if given to any of their children would never be donated by him to any cause of public good, and therefore, all the benefits which could be derived by various existences of different orders of Nature by such a charity, would certainly be lost, yet they do not want to cooperate in such a good or charitable cause due to low attachment to their children but, on the contrary, remain indifferent to it. And as the lover of a prostitute dedicates at the altar of his morbid love not only his own wealth, but in several cases even the money and ornaments of his wife by snatching them away from her and does not like to spend it in some truly charitable cause or for the promotion of the welfare of others and thus testifies by his such conduct utter aversion to the good of others, similarly these slaves to low-love of their children by becoming indifferent to their own good,-and to the good of others as well as to the great law of evolution, find satisfaction in making an offering of their wealth and property to their children. Alas! What a most regrettable and degrading state of human souls.

Besides this, these slaves to the low-love of children, due to their slavery, are ready even to submit to several such demands of their children when they insist for them and which the parent themselves know to be positively wrong. They dare not check or interfere in one or another evil or sinful activity of their children out of the fear that by such interference their children may break away from them. Thus they harm themselves as well as their children in various ways.

Again, lots of such parents know that their children whom they ardently love, do not reciprocate their affection and are void of all gratitude for them and who, ordinary occasions apart, even on any serious illness or difficulty of theirs do not render any service or help to them, but, on the contrary, inflict pains and sufferings on them by their various kinds of evil actions and some of them even pray for their early death, in order to get an early possession of their property, and thus on becoming their enemies behave inimically towards them. Even in such cases due to their low-love of children they allow all this evil to go on and are not able to cut off their mutually evil-producing and most harmful relation with such children. On the contrary, they want to give their wealth and property to such children of theirs in order to be helpful in their various evil acts in which these children seek their low satisfaction. In this way they become willing co-operators and helpers in evil life or adharma.

THE LOVE OF PLEASURE IN THE ORGANISM OF HUMAN SOUL DERIVED FROM POSSESSION OF MONEY & PROPERTY

Q. What is meant by the love of pleasure derived from the possession of money and property in a human soul?

A. When a man develops love for money or any other possession, such a disposition of his is called the love of pleasure derived from possession of money and property.

From an early age when a human child comes to know that those tasty things which he loves to take, can be had with money, he develops a frame of mind in which he begins to feel the necessity of and longing or greed for money. Generally, from then onwards, his longing for money continues to grow and gradually develops into love for it. Again, as he grows in years, he feels a greater necessity for money as a means to the gratification of his various other pleasures, and besides money, his longing for acquiring various other kinds of property also increases.

With the intensification of his such longing, he grows into a lover of money and various other kinds of property.

Q. What are the various evils caused by this low-love of money?

A. The greatest evil that results from the growth of this low-love of money and property is that for millions of person's acquisition of money and property becomes the summum bonum or supreme object of life. They spend their entire life in amassing wealth. Unless they die or fall prey to a disease which renders it impossible for them to earn money, they, as slaves to this low-love, employ their mental and physical powers in amassing wealth and property. Again, lacs of persons by gradually developing slavery to this most infernal love of money become spiritually so hard-hearted that they do not even remain capable of seeing and realizing this truth that money and property are only a means or an instrument to fulfil one or another physical and spiritual need of a man and not the ideal of his life. In this state of spiritual blindness, they become completely incapable of seeing the truth that there is a fundamental distinction between what is the end of life and what constitutes means to the realization of that end. But this is not all. They also develop perverted vision, i.e. they see the end as the means and the means as the end and thus spiritually perverted, and they participate and support falsehood.

Q. What are other evils that are caused by this low-love?

A. This low-love leads to various kinds of sinful acts or acts of misappropriation:

(1) Millions of men and women steal other people's money, ornaments, clothes, utensils, animals, fruits and various other things.

(2) Hundreds of persons forge one, or other kind of papers and various documents, and several persons make counterfeit coins and currency notes of one or another kind.

(3) Several medical practitioners and other men and women cause abortions of women for the sake of money.

(4) Thousands of persons indulge in various kinds of gambling by betting money &c.

(5) Thousands of persons open shops to sell intoxicants.

(6) Thousands of persons slaughter different kinds of beings of the animal world or get them slaughtered by others or purchase the corpses of slaughtered animals and sell parts of their bodies or even sell living beings to others for meat diet.

(7) Several persons suppress loans of money or any other article taken by them from others or adopt various sinful and evil means for not repaying it.

(8) Thousands of persons publish different kinds of false advertisements to promote the sale of their various commodities, and in order to attract customers to their goods, they also deliberately indulge in false praises of their articles and propagate various kinds of other falsehoods.

(9) Thousands of persons accept bribes from others for doing some work—even absolutely unjust work for them.

(10) Several persons commit highway robberies i.e., they forcibly rob a way-farer of his belongings.

(11) Thousands of persons give false evidence in different kinds of suits or cases.

(12) Several persons commit dacoities i.e., they attack the house, factory or shop of somebody and forcibly deprive him of his money and other possessions.

(13) Several people commit murders of others on receiving payment from someone.

(14) Several persons falsely pose as fortune-tellers or astrologers and cheat their believers of their money.

(15) Several persons make money by offering their daughters for prostitution or by selling them to others for the same purpose.

(16) Hundreds of persons exact dowry for their sons or daughters for giving them in marriage to somebody.

(17) Several persons make their wedded wives go to others for adultery. If their wives already commit adultery for the sake of money and that money comes to them or in case they expect to get some property by their wives committing adultery with someone, they allow them to do so.

(18) Several persons even sell their wives to someone for money.

(19) Lacs of women adopt the profession of prostitution either by openly running their shops in a bazaar or secretly indulging in adultery in their homes.

(20) Several persons, posing as patriots, collect funds from the public in the name of some public cause and embezzle it themselves. Or at the outbreak of some epidemic or famine etc., they issue an appeal for funds in the name of relieving the sufferers either on their own behalf or on behalf of a committee of a few men of their own choice and thus collect money. Afterwards, they spend some of this collected money for the declared purpose and misappropriate the rest for one or another work of their own society.

(21) Thousands of persons become untrustworthy by committing various kinds of frauds in connection with their own professions and thus embezzle the money of others.

(22) Thousands of persons suppress money or ornaments or any other thing which is kept by someone in their custody as deposit.

(23) Several persons take up the undesirable profession of gambling or speculation, etc.

(24) Hundreds of persons start big business concerns by borrowing money from others, which they cannot pay back on sustaining losses therein or on failure of their business.

(25) Hundreds of persons start some factory jointly with a few or many share-holders and themselves become its managing partners or directors. In that trusted position, they dishonestly put the run into such a loss that the other share-holders do not desire to continue the factory any longer. They then purchase the whole concern for a small amount and afterwards run it in their own name.

(26) Several persons on being private servants of somebody or on occupying some position in some mill, bank or shop, etc., betray their trust, and by adopting one or other evil means, they embezzle hundreds, thousands and even millions of rupees.

(27) Several persons when employed in the Government or state service, on getting a position of responsibility and control in some institution of public good, embezzle its funds by one or another illegitimate means.

(28) Several persons forcibly dispossess others of their houses or lands and thus become their owners.

(29) Several persons kidnap young children and sell them to others.

(30) Several persons try to bring some other state under their own control by one or another means; and by forcibly dispossessing another of the sovereignty of his state or country or some territory of it, they themselves become the lord, raja, nawab, king, and administrator thereof.

(31) Several persons declare themselves as alchemists and by making a false claim to possess the power of converting some base metal into gold or silver they loot many persons who blindly believe in them.

(32) Hundreds of persons wrongfully deprive others of their money by beguiling them into the false belief that they can fulfil their desires by the help of some 'mantras', charm, 'jap', prayer or blessing or that they are miracle-working sadhus, sannyasis, vairagis, fakirs, or sainies, etc: They also do so by falsely personating themselves as one or another government servant.

(33) Thousands of persons commit various kinds of unjust acts or cruelties in relation to their brothers or sisters or some other relatives in order to wrongfully possess their property.

(34) Thousands of persons sell one or another kind of their useful and serviceable animals to butchers and others for providing meat to meat-eaters. Several persons kill millions of silk-worms in order to obtain uncut silk threads from them. Several persons butcher thousands of various beautiful innocent and harmless animals and birds in order to earn money by the sale of their beautiful skins, feathers and extracted oils, etc.

(35) Thousands of persons become unjust to various kinds of their serviceable animals by exacting work much beyond their capacity.

(36) Thousands of persons sell intoxicants such as bhang, tobacco, ganja, opium and wines, etc., to those addicted to these intoxicants either in licensed shops or through smuggling them.

(37) Several persons purchase or seduce young and beautiful girls to open brothels or to sell them to others and thus make money. Several men and women conspire to entrap some person by deception into a compromising position and then blackmail him.

(38) Several persons tear out the eyes of children or maim their legs or break off their hands and thus cripple them and make them sit on the big thoroughfare to beg for alms. They spend a part of the money brought by these children through begging on their maintenance and use the rest for themselves.

(39) Several persons open liquor shops in which they make one or another customer to drink heavily. On his becoming unconscious, they pilfer all that he has on his person and then drive him out of the shop.

(40) Several persons defraud others of their money by creating a false belief in them that they possess the power to convert currency notes of small amount into

those of large one and ornaments of lower value to those of higher value. So on and so forth.

Q. Is there any other evil, which results from this low-love besides the above-mentioned different kinds of gross evils?

A. Yes, Sir. Slavery to this low-love also breeds miserliness. That is, millions of lovers of money and property, not only usurp the money and property of others by various ways but thousands of them become misers and in different ways harm their dependents and even their own body etc.

Q. How does this happen?

A. Enslaved by the love of money and on developing miserliness, they do not wish, as far as it is possible for them, to spend money even to satisfy the true needs of their own and those of their dependents. They feel it a torment and trial to spend money for the maintenance and development of their own physical health and that of their dependents, or for treatment in case of disease or for their own and their dependents' intellectual progress; and hence they do not spend it. In this way, they prove to be misappropriates or harmful in different ways in relation to themselves as well as their dependents.

Again, when such misers, even on possessing-sufficient money, lose the capacity to spend the requisite and sufficient amount in order to meet the ordinary needs of their own lives and the lives of their dependents and domestic animals etc., how could they be desirous to contribute any sum for the promotion of some cause of public good?

They could not be, hence they cannot contribute for any public good. If some of these misers are impelled at some time by the love of name or fame or popularity etc., to make a promise of contribution out of their money or property towards a charitable cause, then on several occasions they afterwards feel great repentance for having done so. It is because their beloved money makes an appeal to their heart in terms as these, "Thou art my lover. Why hast thou as such promised such a donation and thereby desired to part with me?" Listening to this appeal they feel ashamed and pained for their action, and to be loyal to their beloved money they refuse to pay their promised donation in charity on one or another false pretence. And if they have already given away some of their money in the name of charity, they even try to get back either the whole of the donated amount or as much out of it, as is possible, by some dishonest or sinful act of theirs.

Q. Does any evil consequence result even if a person amasses wealth by ways and means free from sinful acts such as falsehood, deceit, bribery, treachery, etc.?

A. Yes, Sir. If some person amasses wealth by means free from such kinds of sins, he can necessarily be safe from that soul-degradation which is the direct product of these evils. This is laudable so far as it goes. But he cannot save himself from the evil consequences of selfishness which is present in him. So long as he remains a slave to money and considers and makes the amassing of wealth as the ideal of life, and on being 'ignorant of what is good or evil for his soul-life, does not spend his money for the physical and spiritual well-being of other fellow human beings or for the good of other existences and thus remains indifferent and hostile to the most beneficial evolutionary process of Nature, he degrades his soul even though he does not amass wealth by various sinful means.

If the people of any land do not contribute or subscribe their money or their property for the sake of removing some evil or want or for the promotion of some kind of good of the people of their own country or those of any other, to the extent to which they can do on the basis of justice, then they prove by their such behaviour, based upon this low-love, that they do not wish by means of their earned money or their acquired property, to remove some evil or want or to promote some good of the people of their own country or those of any other and thereby be helpful in making them better than before. In other words, they wish to remain friendly to all those evils and inimical to all kind of good of them. Alas! How most deplorable is this nature of such persons! Thus, to the extent the people of a land possess this basest and most degrading low-love of money and property to a greater measure than those of another, to that extent the former people are in a worse, more degraded and weaker state than those of the latter country and they reap the horrible fruits of their degraded state.

THE LOVE OF PLEASURE IN THE ORGANISM OF HUMAN SOUL DERIVED FROM ACQUIRED IMPRESSIONS, ASSOCIATIONS & HABITS

Q. What is meant by the love of pleasure derived from acquired impressions, associations and habits?

A. Every human child by the help of his retentive power, acquires various kinds of impressions from his mother or father or both or from some other persons who bring him up. They are the first to assign him a name, to teach him some language and in the event of their being Hindus, it is they who teach him: "This is your mother"; "This is your father"; "You should call the first - as 'maan', 'mata,' 'amma' etc., and the other as 'pita,' 'bapu,' 'bhaya' or 'baba', etc." In accordance with the training given by them, he learns to call different persons by different designations such as sister, brother, 'taayaa or chaachaa' (uncle); maternal grandfather, matenal grandmother, maternal uncle, maternal aunt, grandfather, grandmother, 'phuppa' (husband of father's sister), 'bua' (father's sister), etc. From them, he learns that he belongs to a particular community, a particular caste, a particular class, a particular gotra or a, particular sub-caste, etc. From them he learns that he belongs to a particular religion or creed and its associated ideas of some god, or guru, or teacher, or religious book, or place of pilgrimage or ceremonies or symbols, etc. From his very childhood, he assimilates, after accepting as true, all such teaching which he gets from his parents or family relations or his community members, etc. He also learns from them various other kinds of habits in connection with how to eat and drink, dress and behave in relation to others.

Due to long association with all these kinds of beliefs—however false they may be—and with all these various modes of living—however undesirable or harmful they may be—he becomes gradually habituated to them. In the same way, he considers, accepts, and believes as his own all those persons with whom he lives and associates from his very infancy. He also learns to consider all those with whom he does not live or associate as not his own but as strangers or foreigners. This law is operative in all people of all lands. The attachment of heart or attraction or love which a child gradually develops in this way for such acquired impressions, associations and habits, yields him pleasure and slowly and slowly he gets enslaved to these kinds of pleasures. Such pleasures of his are called the love of pleasures derived from acquired impressions, associations and habits.

Q. Does a man suffer any harmful consequences due to his attachment to some pleasures of this kind of loves?

A. Yes, Sir. Every such person is certainly harmed to the extent to which he learns various kinds of false beliefs and becomes partisan to them due to these acquired impressions, associations and habits. These false beliefs generate and promote various kinds of harmful effects to his own bodily health as well as to other human and animal existences etc.

Q. How does all this happen?

A. It happens thus: Millions of persons, through the teaching and example of their family members and other relatives, develop habits of using intoxicating things such as tabacco, bhang, wine, opium and others. By the habitual use of these poisonous things they greatly harm their physical health.

Similarly, millions of persons form a habit of irregularity and do not take their meals or go to sleep or for natural calls etc., at fixed hours and by such irregular habits they harm their physical health.

In the same way, millions of persons form a habit of taking meat and eggs of the beings of the animal kingdom. And by this habit of theirs they directly or indirectly become party to the grave injustice perpetrated on the different kinds of beings of the animal kingdom and thereby they, besides greatly degarding their souls, impair their physical health in various ways by subsisting on this improper food.

Similarly, millions of persons get into the habit of keeping their bodies, clothes, homes and their other articles unclean. By such a habit, they impair their own physical health besides harming others.

In the same way, millions of persons become disrespectful to others in their talk and behaviour in different ways and thereby develop bad manners.

Again, millions of persons become transgressors and most harmful in various ways in relation to others by getting into evil habits such as theft, deceit, hypocrisy, and pretence etc. and thereby deteriorate their soul-life. Millions of persons get into the habit. of hating and falsely considering as inferior to themselves, all such persons who do not cherish a particular religious belief or faith or, who do not keep their bodies religious symbols like them or who pursue such vocations, though really desirable, but which they have been taught to consider as otherwise, or who do not belong to their class or caste etc. By manifesting in various ways their behaviour of hatred, ill-will and enemity against these persons, they not only deteriorate, their soul-life but also become most inimical to the cause of national and human unity and harmony. And so on.

Q. Does a man suffer from some other harms too from this kind of low-love of pleasure?

A. Yes, Sir. Due to the habitual residence in a certain house, village or town of theirs for a very long time, thousands of persons grow so deeply attached to them, that hundreds amongst them do not like to go away from there to some other distant place even for their absolutely necessary needs. This attachment deepens so much that if someone among such people is starving and is not able to earn his livelihood in his own place, even then he does not like to leave his place and go to any other distant station where he can get employment. Hence he does not go there and lets himself suffer.

Similarly, if someone among them is suffering from such disease which can be completely or substantially cured by his going and living in a different place, even then he feels a great wrench in going there. He, therefore, does not go there and does not adopt the right course for the cure of his disease and lets his body suffer. Hundreds of persons do not like to leave their homes for some beneficial tour or pilgrimage of different places even when- they can, afford money and spare time. Millions of persons who are attached to this pleasure keep such worthless things in their houses which are not and cannot be of any use to them, and which do not deserve to be stored. Due to slavery to this kind of pleasure, millions of persons physically harm themselves by improper bodily practices connected with their eating, drinking, sleeping, washing their faces, cleaning their teeth and taking bath etc. They feel themselves incapable of giving. Up any of these practices even when they know it to be harmful to them.

Considering themselves to be in such a state of utter helplessness, they continue that harmful practice.

Due-to slavery to this pleasure, millions of persons cannot cut themselves off even from such a harmful relation from whom they receive various kinds of evil, harmful and extremely painful treatment.

Q. Does affinity of temperament too, lead millions of persons to feel mutual attraction, attachment and friendliness?

A. Certainly it does. Due to this similarity of their natures also, they naturally feel attracted towards one another and become close friends or associates of one another. They like to seek each other's society and to live together.

Examples:-

A person has attraction for the pleasure of intoxication from drinking.

Two or three other persons also feel attraction for the pleasure of the same intoxicant. They are acquainted with one another and bear no mutual previous hatred. Under these, circumstances, they feel drawn to one another because of their similarity of nature. It is because of this mutual attraction that they like to sit in company to drink, as doing so enhances their pleasure still more. Thus they crave - to drink together rather than drink all alone in their own houses. Besides deriving pleasure from drink, they also want to wring added joy by carrying on talk in praise of intoxication and also the liquors which produce that intoxication. Such persons on such occasions want to eat one or another thing together. In, the same way, adulterous men and women addicted to illicit sexual intercourse; gamblers; persons following similar -pursuits and those interested in the same kind of sports, form friendships on the basis of their mutual, attraction. Several persons, being slaves to 'the-pleasure derived' from securing money or property by theft, feel mutually attracted and then form a gang to commit theft together. In the same way persons who are slaves to the pleasure derived from securing-money and other things by dacoity, commit this crime together. It has therefore been said about the mutual attraction of persons of similar nature:

"Prakriti miley man milat hai, un-milte na milaaye;

Doodh dahi se milat hai kaanji se phat jaye."

It means: similarities of natures or of temperament leads to kinship of minds of persons in the same way as milk mixes with curd and becomes curd. But the same milk having no inherent attraction for 'kaanji' (a sour drink) turns sour and curdles on mixing with it.

Again, it is said:

"Kunad ham-jinas baa ham-jinas parwaaz

Kabootar baa kabootar, baaz baa baaz."

It means: "In the animal kingdom, birds of the same kind fly together.

Pigeons fly with pigeons and eagles fly with eagles."

Again, in English it is said:

"Birds of a feather fly together."

Parrots feel attracted towards parrots but not towards crows or kites.

Therefore parrots fly together in dozens. But they do not fly or live with crows and kites. Similarly, the way in which scores of kites drawn together by natural attraction soar up and fly round and round in the sky and derive pleasure in it, they do not by in that way with crows due to the absence of the same kind of attraction for them.

It is due to this attraction based on similarity of nature that makes wolves to live in a pack of wolves, goats in a herd of goats, sheep in a herd of sheep and ants to live with ants.

Q. When several persons associate together on the basis of similarity of nature and take pleasure in indulging some sinful or evil action, is their evil association called bad society?

A. Yes, Sir. This kind of evil association, due to similarity of natures, is very much rampant in the human world.

Q. Can or does good association too come into existence on the basis of similarity of nature?

A. Yes, Sir. It can. If in some persons some such noble feelings have developed, that inspired by them they feel anxious to associate with one another and set up a 'sabha', society or club etc., for the cultivation of those feelings and make necessary sacrifices for it, they can certainly profit to some extent by their such association.

Q. Do not persons on becoming friends of one another by similarity of natures, form biases in favour of one another?

A. Certainly they do so. It is because of this that millions of person due to this mutual friendship render even such help to one another on different occasions which is absolutely based on falsehood, sin and injustice.

Q. Do millions of persons, due to this low-love of association, blindly believe as true the false recommendations or complaints of different acquaintances of theirs about some third person?

A. Yes, it is so. It is because a sort of attachment grows up in their hearts for those who frequently associate with them, and due to this attachment they feel bound with them. Therefore, when even a false recommendation or complaint about some third person reaches them through these associates, it gets a direct access to their hearts and they automatically accept it as true. Due to this false belief they form such an opinion about those, who do not associate with them, which is not true, or give a judgment or express an opinion against them which is positively unjust.

Again, millions of lovers of this kind of pleasure become so hopelessly enslaved to it that they not only lose the capacity of realizing their such harmful slavery as really harmful, but if some benefactor of theirs persuades them or in some other way makes an honest effort to get them out of some such harmful acquired impressions, associations or habits of theirs, then finding such persuasion or effort offending against their this low-love, they feel hurt and pained and feel hatred for that benefactor in their hearts and take him as their enemy in place of a friend and thus part company from him. By this most deplorable state of theirs, they become also unfit of securing various other kinds of benefits from him.

Q. Does some other evil also result from this low-love?

A. Yes, Sir. This low-love also produces various kinds of mental shocks and anguishes and various kinds of physical diseases and sufferings due to separation from the object of this low-love.

Q. How does it happen?

A. Every human being when he comes to love some person, animal or some other object, feels more or less hurt and pained in proportion to the intensity of his attachment to it when he gets separated from it by some, untoward phenomenon. Again, when some such hurt is great then not only does he writhe with agony from it and feels extreme restlessness and pain on account of loss of some beloved person or object of his, but his nervous system also gets shattered by it. This shattered nervous system also causes one or another kind of painful and harmful disease in his body.

Then besides mental sufferings he also experiences great pain due to one or another physical disease. However, if he has not sufficient strength to bear the pain or suffering arising out of such a great shock, then in this deplorable state he tries to free himself from his such unbearable pain by putting and to his dear body with his own hands.

By such an action, he not only dies a premature death but also an unnatural one. Others smother under such pain for some time and die a premature death. The proof of the various kinds of most horrible sufferings and shocks that millions of persons, due to the slavery to this most deplorable undue attachment; undergo in the event of some kind of separation by death or otherwise from their wives, husbands, children, friends or some other beloved persons or at the loss of their money, their property, their honour, their position etc., can be directly found in this very world from the lives of such persons of every country and community.

LOVE OF PLEASURE IN THE CONSTITUTION OF HUMAN SOUL DERIVED FROM VIOLENCE

Q. What is meant by love of pleasure derived from violence?

A. The strong desire to get pleasure by giving trouble or pain to some other man or animal or to do some kind of harm to him with the intention of inflicting pain on him, is called the love of pleasure derived from violence.

Millions of persons have inherited this low-love from their early ancestors who once used to seek and find their food by hunting like carnivorous animals. At first, those hunter ancestors of these people used to kill various creatures of the animal world exclusively for food; but on becoming thus habituated in this kind of practice for generations, they, besides killing for food, began to feel pleasure or joy even in killing some creatures for the fun of it. After this, they gradually began to seek and find pleasure or joy in inflicting pain on one or other of themselves by troubling, torturing and teasing one another. This very desire to get pleasure, by killing some creature or by troubling or torturing it in some way or by inflicting pain on it, is found in millions even to-day.

Such persons satisfy this love of pleasure in them by troubling some man or animal by one or other action of theirs, by making some child, boy or girl weep by some methods, by torturing some man or animal or by teasing someone, by breaking or damaging something of somebody. Lovers of this pleasure of violence on becoming hunters not only kill various kinds of animals for eating their flesh but they also kill, without reason, different animals whose meat they do not take.

Millions of lovers of this evil disposition for violence derive pleasure or joy by troubling or inflicting pain on another in the name of joking and jesting.

Then besides human beings this most degrading feeling is also found in some kinds of dogs and other animals who find pleasure in killing some creature not for eating its meat but for the sake of fun.

Q. Are there some such persons among the lovers of pleasure derived from violence, who obtain the pleasure of this low feeling by conveying to some person such absolutely concocted and false news that may give him pain?

A. Yes, Sir. Such persons satisfy this low-love of pleasure by giving news to someone about the illness or death etc. of some of his dear relations or by creating some false belief in him which makes him sad or pained.

VARIOUS LOVES FOR PLEASURE IN THE CONSTITUTION OF HUMAN SOUL DERIVED FROM FALSE BELIEFS

Q. What is meant by love of pleasure derived from false beliefs?

A. When strong attraction is formed in human beings for obtaining any of the various pleasures for themselves, they reach such a psychological condition that if someone, on knowing of their longing for that pleasure, were to give them even false temptation for satisfying it, they are prepared on several occasions even to accept this falsehood as true and, taking it to be true, believe it. And they experience pleasure in their hearts on the creation of such false belief.

In the same way, if someone were to tell them absolutely false and fearful stories about such pains or afflictions of which they are afraid, they even believe in them on different occasions and experience fear from them. If someone were to tell them some such absolutely false things about this fear of theirs, that they can save themselves from those troubles by such and such methods, they are prepared to believe in such things too and experience a kind of comfort or pleasure in their hearts through such false belief.

Longing for these two kinds of pleasures is called the love of pleasure derived from false beliefs.

Q. Is it not a fact that many subtle bodied evil spirits and many living human beings, knowing that man hungers or hankers after various kinds of pleasures and fears from various kinds of pains and wants to save himself from them, have, for the sake of obtaining one or another kind of pleasure for themselves, created in millions of persons, by giving them false temptations of pleasures and false fears of pains, various kinds of absolutely false beliefs which now go under the name of religion in different countries of this planet and in the most terrible web of which crores of people are caught and on account of which they are proving most harmful in various ways for themselves as well as for millions of other human beings?

A. Yes, Sir.

Q. How did the propagation of false beliefs in the name of religion begin in the first instance in the human world?

A. So far history is able to tell, the propagation of false beliefs in the name of religion began through the evil spirits. When some among these spirits came to know that by making one or another person in this world as medium, they could express their thoughts to others through them, they began to tell such false things to their relatives or others; e.g., if they offered such and such kind of eatables, drinks or scents etc., to them, they could make them very happy by satisfying various kinds of their heart's desires i.e., if they wanted children, they could give them children; if they wanted to be cured of an illness their own or of a member of their family - they could cure that illness of theirs; if they wanted to increase their stock of cattle, they could increase it; if they wanted abundance of produce in their fields, they could increase the crops in their fields; if they wanted victory in some war, they could make them win; if they wanted damage to be done to the property of any of their opponents or enemies, they could get that property damaged either by stealing it themselves or by getting it stolen by others or by harming it in some other way; if they wanted the abortion of some-one's wife, they could do so; if they were anxious to see some opponent or enemy of theirs to be ill and to suffer from that illness, they could give him lot of pain by making him sick; if they wanted the death of some son or some other member of the family of some enemy of theirs, they could bring about his death etc.

By believing in these falsehoods of theirs thousands of persons, in order to satisfy one or another of their heart desires, began to please them by making offerings of many kinds, and began to pray to them for the fulfilment of their desires, in the same way as lacs of persons, even to-day beg for the fulfilment of their wishes from the so-called one or another Devta (god) or one or another Devi (goddess) or some ancestor or 'Vad-vadera' of theirs or some so-called saint or wali or faqir or pir etc. And when in the course of the process of change in Nature some desire of theirs was satisfied, they attributed, the fulfilment of that desire to the kindness or mercy of someone of them and began to feel themselves grateful or indebted to him and to sing praise to him for his such kindness or mercy and accepting him as the giver of such pleasures to them, they began to adore or praise him in various ways.

Again when these evil spirits did not get the offering asked for themselves or for their mediums from some person, they denounced him as accused, criminal or sinner in their relation and in order to frighten him to subordination they said that they would inflict intense pain and torture on him by harming him in such and such way, e.g; they would bring about his premature death; they would give him great pain by making him ill; they would make his animals sick or kill them; they would ruin his crops by hailstorm or intensely heavy rain, or by drought or by getting them eaten by locust or by heavy storm of water; they would erase his house; they would give lot of pain to the members of his family by making them sick; they would make him pauper by robbing him of his wealth, etc. etc.

Gradually the satisfaction of such desires came to be called boon or blessing and its various contrary acts of giving pain, came to be known as 'shaap' or curse etc. It is in this way how in the beginning these evil-natured false gods and goddesses were created in the human world.

And then by declaring these false gods as omniscient, omnipresent and omnipotent etc., they further added to their false glory and propagated it and thus made people to falsely believe in their such qualities.

But in these early days, concocted ideas of hells and heavens were not yet prevalent. The false stories about these were manufactured and spread long afterwards. That is, when someone did not comply with their wishes to sufficient degree even by the above kinds of threats of harm, then they began to say that they would inflict even more painful punishment after their death than in this world on those persons who become sinners or criminals by betraying them and that those who would believe in them and make nice offerings of the things asked for by them and would sing praises to their glory and express gratitude in relation to them, would receive from them far greater pleasures after their death than those of this world. In accordance with these new concocted ideas the first type of place of torture was named 'narak', 'jahannam', 'dozakh' or hell, etc., and the second type of place of pleasures was named 'swarg', 'baikunth', 'golok', 'bahisht' or heaven etc. This is how the ideas of various kinds of absolutely false hells, and absolutely false heavens were created.

Even to this day the propagation of the temptations of the pleasures of this kind of absolutely imaginary heavens and the threats or fears of the pains of absolutely imaginary continues.

Q. Besides these false gods and goddesses, what were the other kinds of gods and goddesses whose worship was made prevalent?

A. When thousands of priests began to make good earnings through these false gods, then gradually many other clever persons also began to declare that, besides the evil spirits having real existences, different non-living things and living beings were residing places of one or another absolutely imaginary god who possessed the same qualities as the evil spirit and thus made their worship prevalent. For example, the worship of the Sun god; the Moon god; the Satan god; the Ganga goddess; the Yamuna goddess; the Banyan tree god; the Pipal (cassia religiosis) god; the Tulsi goddess; Sitla, the goddess causing small pox;

Mansa, the goddess fulfilling heart's desires; Saraswati, the goddess of learning; Lakshami, the goddess of wealth; Jwala, the goddess exhibiting flames; the cow goddess, the snake god and other similar kinds of absolutely imaginary gods and goddesses, also came to be prevalent.

Q. Besides all these what were the other false things which were propagated in the name religion?

A. The various false things, including these and others by the propagation of which millions of persons of this world have been made false believers, are broadly these:-

(1) As mentioned above, different kinds of false gods and goddesses, possessing absolutely new kind of imaginary and absolutely false qualities were propagated quite against the true and immutable laws of Nature.

(2) Similar kinds of false beliefs were also spread by declaring one or another person as the incarnation or devotee of or commissioned preacher or teacher etc., from someone of the false gods.

(3) The singing of various kinds of false adoratory songs, or false hymns etc., recitation of false sayings and incantation of false mantras in connection with qualities of such gods and goddesses were propagated.

(4) False beliefs were created in people by falsely declaring these various kinds of gods and goddesses and various other persons to be omniscient and by announcing one or another book as given as revelation of any of these gods, and its teaching to be absolutely free from error and absolutely trustworthy.

105

(5) By declaring as proper or good the different kinds of sinful or evil teachings and actions of these various kinds of so-called gods or of the so-called devotees of any one of them or of some so-called incarnation or relation of any of them or of some commissioned person of any one of them, false beliefs were propagated about them.

(6) By inventing false stories about the performance of extraordinary acts or wonderful deeds or miracles contrary to the immutable laws of Nature by these various kinds of so-called gods or some so-called incarnation of any one of them or some devotee of any one of them or some so-called commissioned person on behalf of any one of them or by some other so-called sidh, sadhu, pir, faqir, wali, guru, teacher, rishi, muni, sannyasi and yogi etc., false beliefs were spread among the people about them.

(7) False beliefs were spread as to how one gets the satisfaction of his heart-desires by pleasing, and thus getting the blessings of this or that so-called god or goddess or of some incarnation or devotee of this or that so-called god or of some so-called teacher, guru, wali, pir or saint contrary to true and immutable laws of Nature, and how one gets various kinds of sufferings by incurring his displeasure, or curse or ill-wishes.

(8) Contrary to the true and immutable laws of Nature, false beliefs were spread about the award of one or another kind of reward or punishment on men on their death, for their various kinds of actions by this or that so-called god.

(9) Contrary to the true and immutable laws of Nature, false beliefs were propagated about the re-birth of human beings in this world after their death, in the body of some animal or man as a punishment for one or another kind of their sins or to reap the reward for this or that so-called actions of theirs.

(10) By spreading various kinds of false stories about the blessings of various places and by declaring such places through such falsehoods as sacred religious places, various kinds of false beliefs were spread about them.

(11) Various false beliefs were spread about how human souls could be set free from the punishment or consequences of some really true and some absolutely false sins of theirs.

(12) In the name of getting "salvation" and "punnya" (blessing) but contrary to the true and eternal laws of Nature, various kinds of prayers, various kinds of 'mantras', various kinds of pledges, 'yogas', fasts, reading, incantations,

austerities and wearing of various kinds of symbols on the body were declared to be necessary and thus various false beliefs were spread about them in the people, and so on.

Now, if man had not been lover of various pleasures based on false beliefs and had he not been totally ignorant of them, there would never have been propagated such kinds of most harmful false religions on this earth and millions of persons would not have been entangled in the most horrible and most harmful meshes of these false beliefs and would not have brought about their spiritual degradation and ruin through this entanglement, nor would they have lost so much of their wealth and their property which it is not even possible to correctly estimate.

Besides these greatest harms, the teachings which have been given by the believers of these false religious faiths, in the name of religion, for the perpetration of various kinds of intense cruelties towards millions of persons, millions of animals and millions of various others having religious faith different from one's own, and the degree and extent of the cruelties which they have actually perpetrated on them, such and the same degree of cruelties have also not been perpetuated on the surface of the earth in any other way.

Again, leaving aside the past, even to-day, the amount of the harm which is being done in various ways to millions of persons of this earth by the false faiths, is also most horrible. The charity of millions of rupees which is being given every year to thousands of the so-called sadhus, faqirs, saints, mahants, pandas, worshippers, priests, Ganga putras, mullahs, phungies, and various other undeserving persons, thinking it to be an act of religion or 'punnya' due to such false beliefs, (which is doing no spiritual good either to the giver or to the recipient of the charity). If, instead of the charity being given to such persons, it is gifted away to some work of physical or mental welfare or better than both of these, to that of bringing about higher altruistic changes, then the various departments of Nature can be very much benefitted.

Q. Is it true that just as in the past knowing this most deplorable condition of men, thousands of persons had obtained their pleasure by getting the money and the property of people of different countries of this world by giving them some temptation of absolutely false pleasures and fear of absolutely false pains, in the same way, thousands of persons taking advantage of similar false beliefs, improperly get their money and property and thus live on their earnings and take various other kinds of services from them and hundreds of them satisfy their lust by violating the honour of hundreds of women and thousands of them obtain pleasure of various kinds of most harmful intoxicants bought with the money of others?

A. Yes, Sir.

Q. Do millions of parents of this world, being lovers of this pleasure derived from false beliefs, also implant various kinds of false beliefs in their children?

A. Yes, Sir. Millions of parents. Know that there is no such real existence as 'juju', 'haowa', maons etc., yet if their small children weep bitterly— especially in the night when their crying interferes with the pleasure of their sweet sleep—and when they do not stop crying soon, then in order to stop them from crying, they falsely tell them "Don't weep' stop crying very soon otherwise 'juju', 'haowa' or 'maon' will take you away". By implanting such kinds of false beliefs, they obtain their own pleasure. In the same way, thousands of parents for this same purpose say such things as "Bogey man will get you" i.e., that certain horrible man will take you away.

Besides this, thousands of persons being shop-keepers, just as they themselves earn money by cheating their customers and experience pleasure through obtaining as much money as possible by this method, in the same way, when they put their children in their trade, then, motived by this very feeling of pleasure, they teach them too, various kinds of ways of cheating for making money. They also implant in them such kind of false beliefs that "no shop works successfully without falsehood and cheating."

Thousands of other persons, by teaching that - one cannot win this or that case without falsehood, that certain political or social object cannot be realized without falsehood, implant various other kinds of false beliefs in mankind and make them hypocrite in respect of various matters.

Q. Is it not a most horrible act on the part of such persons, even when they are called parents, to seek and find, pleasure by implanting such kinds of false beliefs in the children of their own creation?

A. Undoubtedly it is. But just as the so-called gods and goddesses and other hundreds and thousands of well-known; persons being lovers of low pleasures have, by spreading in the name of religion various kinds of false beliefs in mankind, satisfied one or another pleasureful aim of their own, so in the same way, millions of parents, being lovers of the same pleasure, make their children believe not only in such different kinds of false beliefs which they receive from others in tradition and which they believe to be true, but they also implant in them such various kinds of false beliefs which they themselves know to be false.

It is due to the low-love of pleasures that mankind has reached this horrible degradation.

Q. Apart from these most horrible harms, what other harms are being done to mankind by these false beliefs propagated in the name of religion?

A. Crores of persons due to their becoming lovers and slaves to these false beliefs stick to them and by sticking to them, they greatly harm their most fundamental and essential thing i.e., soul, in various ways.

Millions of persons from among such blind believers reach such a state of deep degradation that they do not want to patiently hear or know anything from another against any of their false religious faiths or false beliefs and to think over it calmly, or to read some book or some other writing about it, and by continuing to be lovers of their false beliefs, they like to remain blind to true knowledge.

Again, many persons, who even though at heart know this or that religious faith of theirs to be false, yet being lovers of the pleasure of some political position or respect or praise or money etc.; or being slaves to some community connection etc., become hypocrites and falsely declare it to be true before the general public and in order to prove it to be true, they invent false arguments and deliver addresses and write and publish books and articles full of false arguments. And even knowing at heart some religious belief of their opponent to be true, they become absolutely hypocrite and, in order to demolish it, they invent false arguments and express them through speech or writings.

And these blind followers or hypocrites experience hatred even for the person who with good will exposes some of their false beliefs and their hypocrisy. And the persons in whom this feeling of hatred is strong, regard him as an enemy of their faith and of themselves and in order to trouble him by various means, to tease him, to torture him and to harm him in various other ways, they think out and adopt various schemes of evil and sinful character. By doing such most degrading actions and by becoming degraded through them, they satisfy their most evil feeling of hatred and enjoy its very low pleasure.

LOVE OF PLEASURE OR ALTRUISTIC PLEASURES IN HUMAN BEINGS

Q. What is meant by love of higher or altruistic pleasures ('saatvik sukhanuraag')?

A. In mankind there are lacs and crores of men and women who, apart from the members of their own family and some such persons with whom they are attached by the tie of some pleasure, do not perceive some pain, trouble or want of another person (with whom they are not attached by the tie of some pleasure) and do not possess any feeling, to remove it by some legitimate means, and therefore do not bestir on their own to do any such thing for any such person. However, if there be some person in this very mankind in whose soul there is some perception or, feeling to remove some physical pain or disease or some physical or mental want, or to help in the improvement of mental knowledge or to eradicate some really false belief or some evil custom or ritual of any such person or persons and if that feeling of his is also pure i.e., in doing some good to anyone through this feeling, he feels no longing for; getting praise or title, or position or reward etc., from somebody in this world or of obtaining the pleasures of some imaginary heaven etc., in the next world, and actuated by this pure feeling, he makes the sacrifice of some of his wealth or some of his property or some of his physical energy or some of his intellectual learning and knowledge etc., for the above-mentioned object, then such sacrifice of his, will be pure altruism. If this kind of feeling becomes so strong in a person that it overpowers his love of other pleasures and actuated by this feeling, he regularly or faithfully dedicates himself to the work and feels satisfied with the higher kind of pleasure or happiness which, in accordance with the laws of Nature, he experiences in doing such action, then his love of pleasure would be love of altruistic pleasure.

But until now there are comparatively very few in mankind in whom such pure, higher or altruistic feeling-has developed.

Q. What is meant by the presence in some person of the pure altruistic feeling to remove the pain or want etc., of some human being?

A. If some person sees with his own eyes, hears or comes to know from somebody else about the physical suffering, restlessness, distress or pain of someone and thereby feels pain in some degree in his own heart also and if he feels on his own, so strong an urge in his heart so as to render some assistance to remove the pain of that afflicted person that he is prepared on his part to render some help to remove his pain as far as it is possible for him, and actually does render some such help on his own and on doing this service he, except for the higher pleasure or satisfaction that he experiences in his heart, expects for himself no praise at all from the benefitted person or some other person or/and himself desires nothing whatsoever in return for that service from him or from anyone else, so much so that he feels no longing even to hear any expression of the feeling of gratitude from such benefitted person or persons and if some person instead of praising his altruistic service depreciates it or presents it in un-becoming or ugly colours, then, even on getting pained by it, he finds his altruistic feeling in no way lessened or feels in no way discouraged thereby; and even on realizing that this or that person has no appreciation at all for his good work and instead of praising him, he condemns him and declares him to be a bad man, he does not begin to hate his altruistic work by thinking: "what am I to gain by doing such altruistic action," but on the contrary, he feels some greater attraction in his heart for it, then and then alone his feeling can be purely altruistic in nature, otherwise not.

Q. Do you mean to say that when a man renders some kind of help to some distressed or afflicted or weak person and in return for this service he does not desire anything at all, such as praise etc., from the benefitted person or from any other person, then such action of his is motivated by pure altruistic feeling?

A: Yes, please.

Q. Is the experience of pain in relation to physical suffering of some other person called mercy?

A. Yes, please. This true altruistic feeling is also called mercy.

Q. If a person on his own opens some hospital for the cure of physical diseases of men or animals and establishes a requisite fund in order to keep it going on very well: or gives some capital fund or money for the purpose of research in and adoption of the means for the removal of some fatal disease or epidemic; or constructs some 'Dharmshala' or 'Sarai' (inn) etc., for the convenience of travellers and arranges for its proper maintenance by giving requisite money for it, or on coming to know about the paucity of water for men or animals of some place, constructs a tank or well or `bavli' or reservoir etc., or repairs or gets repaired some, bad road in order to remove the inconvenience caused to men and animals when passing on it, or plants a garden for the general public to stroll and enjoy beautiful and innocent scents of flowers, or opens an ashram for the maintenance and protection of incurably diseased persons and other various kinds of homeless and destitute women and men, so on and so forth; and in doing such good deeds, he does not desire for himself any praise or position 'or rank or some distinction or title etc., from somebody, and he in its return neither accepts from any person some reward or title etc., in this world, nor does he expect or hope after death to get some reward or prize from some so-called Devta, but remains completely satisfied only with the higher spiritual pleasure that accrues on doing such altruistic action, then would his such work be regarded as expression of pure altruistic feeling?

A. Certainly.

Q. It is said about some persons that they sacrificed their lives for a certain public or good cause and that such and such person from amongst them had devoted the whole of his life to it, then can his sacrifice of life in this manner be considered as based on pure altruistic feeling or altruistic love?

A. If there be perfectly true proof about a person that for his altruistic work, he did not accept from any society some fixed allowance or some regular monetary help and neither did he wish for himself some praise or some respectable position or some other kind of respect or distinction etc., nor did he hope for or expect the attainment of some pleasure in return for his such service from one or another Devta even after his death, then certainly his such service can be said and accepted to be an expression of pure altruistic love, otherwise not.

Q. What kind of service is that of those persons who engage themselves in some kind of noble work on acceptance of some regular monetary help or honorarium, from some individual or some society?

A. Such service of theirs is not, and cannot be, based on pure altruistic feeling, because a lover of pure altruism, apart from his altruistic pleasure, does not want and does not accept some regular monetary help or honorarium in return for his services.

Besides this when a person actuated by some altruistic feeling engages himself in some altruistic service, then, on the one hand, he does not shirk from work and, on the other hand, his love for that particular altruistic service in which he is engaged, gets intense or deep every day due to the daily pure exercise of it. Now if these two characteristics are also not found in him, then from the point of view of these two standards also his such service cannot be based on purely altruistic feeling.

Q. Then how some such service of someone may be considered or evaluated?

A. If some person takes up some altruistic work in hand and does notshirk it at all and does not consciously do the least harm to it in any way but can whole-heartedly devote himself to that work every day to the requisite duration of time or accomplishes the requisite amount of work in connection with it and in return feels no longing or expectation of some praise or respectable position or title or respect or appreciation, then though his such service cannot be based on purely altruistic love due to his acceptance of a maintenance allowance, yet it can certainly be beneficial or good for his soul to the degree to which he makes some sacrifice of his money for its sake.

Q. From amongst those persons who accept maintenance allowance, do those who devote what is regarded to be there, personal and private time to the work of some real good or service of another, get an additional spiritual gain for it?

A. They certainly get an additional spiritual gain for such extra service.

Q. Can some good action of such persons be regarded as noble or altruistic, who do it for the sake of getting praise, popularity, honour or fame from others and who fix or get fixed, some stone or tablet etc., on their own part as a mark to show this praise or make the fixing of such a stone as a prior condition to their doing such, good action?

A. Never. Not at all. Such action of theirs has the character of besiness,- and, therefore cannot be truly 'altruistic, but is only a, kind of commercial transaction.

Q. Will such noble action of a person be truly based on pure altruistic feeling, which is not done by him with the object of getting praise, name, popularity etc., in this world, but is done solely with the temptation of getting after death certain kind of physical or some other pleasures from one or another so-called Devta?

A. No. Never. So long in doing a good deed, there is an element of the impurity of expectation of getting some kind of pleasure from another or being saved from certain kinds of pains or troubles from another in this world or in the next world, till then such an action of any person is not and cannot be an expression of pure altruistic feeling.

Q. If a person helps or serves a truly destitute person on being moved by pure mercy alone, then will his such action be regarded as based on pure altruistic feeling?

A. Certainly it is so, if he does not desire anything from the helped person or somebody else in return for it.

Q. Can a person do an unjust act also on being moved only out of mercy?

A. Yes, please.

Q. How?

A. When some magistrate or judge, on seeing a truly accused person shedding even false tears in his presence, feels pain in his merciful heart and becomes partial to him and does not want to punish him even for his actual crime and being in such a state of mind releases him, then due to this feeling of mercy in him, he sides with injustice in the same way as a bribe-taking magistrate or judge sets free a truly accused person on the acceptance of a bribe. In the same way on several other occasions also a merciful person perpetuates several kinds of acts of injustice out of this feeling of mercy.

In short, just as man is led by mercy to do some good actions, so in the same way he is also led by it on many occasions to do many evil actions too.

Q. Are there other higher feelings also besides mercy which can be regarded as altruistic?

A. Yes, please. There are other higher feelings also which can be called altruistic feelings. For example, if a person, apart from his family relations with whom he is bound with ties pleasure has some pure feeling for the removal of some mental backwardness or for the advancement of intellectual powers of any other person or a group of them, then such feeling of his also is an altruistic feeling. We can call it the altruistic feeling of removing want.

Q. What kinds of actions a person does when he is motivated by this feeling?

A. If this feeling is present in sufficient strength in a person, he can open one or another kind of institution —i.e., open a school or college etc., for teaching some language, literature, mathematics or science etc., or for giving technical and industrial education of some kind; open some library for the public to benefit by reading different books on different subjects; start some paper or appoint some propagandist or teacher for some social or political, reform or for the propagation of some so-called religion etc. By doing so, he can also do some good to the public to some extent.

Q. But apart from doing some good, do those persons, not produce some kind of evil or harmful results for the human society, who sacrifice their wealth or their property for establishing such a school, college, library, paper or reading room or for the appointment of such a propagandist or teacher?

A. Yes, please. Certainly some evils are produced through them.

Q. How?

A. They become instruments of doing the worst kinds of harm to the human as well as to the animal world to the extent to which various kinds of falsehoods or different kinds of false faiths and beliefs in the name of religion are propagated through them as are opposed to real Nature and its true facts and laws; or teachings are given through them for doing some harm to the body or inflicting some kind of unjust act or acts on living beings.

Q. Do such schools, colleges, libraries, reading rooms, periodicals and teachers, and propagandists or preachers etc., also exist in this world which are the means of propagating the teachings of various kinds of false beliefs or false faiths and various other falsehoods and besides these of various kinds of unjust actions?

A. Yes, Sir, there are many. And due to the above kind of teachings given through them, worst kinds of harms are done to the beings of the human as well as the animal world.

Q. If a strong feeling to do research and find out various truths in some of the different departments of Nature awakens and developer in some person and in order to do research and find such truths, he devotes his physical and mental energies etc., then can his such feeling also be called altruistic?

A. Yes, please. If there is no element of the impurity of some temptation or hope of making money or getting praise, position title for himself from someone in his such feeling, then this feeling of his can also be altruistic.

Q. Are such men alone called "scientific men" or "scientists" who make investigations for finding out some truth in one or another department of Nature and who after finding one or other truth declare it to be so?

A. Yes, Sir.

Q. Is it always true what the scientists tell us about Nature, at any particular time?

A. No, Sir. In their declaring or giving out something as true there is sometimes some mistake or misunderstanding in their method of investigating truth; sometimes while drawing inferences from several kinds of true facts, they commit some mistakes of logical reasoning in their sequence of thought. And sometimes some of the these scientists do not accept some mistake of theirs as mistake, due to their being under the grip of the feeling of prestige and stick to it and declare it to be right, and several times they try to defend it even by different kinds of falsehood, etc.

But those of the scientists who, being anxious to remove such mistakes and to know, accept and propagate real truths, meet together to establish some scientific society and accept and propagate whatever appears to them to be completely true after co-operative analysis and criticism in such societies, they are certainly greater instruments in the propagation of truth.

Q. Are those who are called scientists also lovers of truth?

A. Such scientists, knowing that man cannot get any true knowledge about Nature without following some right method of Nature, certainly use the right method of Nature in order to discover truth. But they accept and follow this true method just in the same way, as a school boy does in learning arithmetic. Knowing full well that no correct answer to a question in arithmetic can be arrived at or known, without accepting and following the method of addition, substraction, multiplication and division, he accepts and follows the right method of learning arithmetic. But just as that boy inspite of accepting the right method of arithmetic commits various kinds of false and unjust acts, motivated by his various kinds of low-loves of pleasures and his low-hates, so also several scientists, on the one hand, being steeped in soul-ignorance are entangled in various kinds of false beliefs and, on the other hand, motivated by one or another kind of low-love of pleasure or low-hatred generated by such low-love, also commit unjust acts in relation to some existences in of Nature such as human or animal etc., and still more some of these scientists due to being intemperate in several matters with regard to their body even harm their bodily health.

Q. Do the souls of those persons reap some benefit from their altruistic work who do it with the desire to get praise, honour, position, title etc., in this world?

A. If the altruistic work of such persons is really of public good, then their souls will certainly benefit and thereby their soul-life certainly will be more or less prolonged or it will reap blessings to the degree to which their altruistic work produces real benefit for human beings or animals etc.

Q. From amongst all the various kinds of good which the pure altruistic feelings or loves produce in the human kingdom apart from the good they produce in other departments of Nature, what is the highest kind of good for human souls which is produced by some of these altruistic feelings or loves?

A. In the human kingdom there is, on the one hand, absolute ignorance about the nature and life of soul and on the other hand, there are rampant in it soul-degrading and soul-destroying activities consisting of various kinds of false religious faiths, various kinds of other falsehoods and various kinds of evil actions and various kinds of evil thoughts, due to various kinds of the loves of low pleasures in them and various low kinds of hates generated by these low-loves. There cannot be a work of greater good to mankind than that of giving salvation to man from such various false religious faiths and evil actions and to bring such fit souls under the refuge of the Devatma, (through whose higher influences of sublime powers alone a person can become fit to do such work of giving this kind of true salvation or freedom) and to open for them the path of soul- improvement according to their capacity. This and this alone is the highest—nay, hundreds of times highest—of all the altruistic work. No other altruistic work does nor can produce so much spiritual good to the soul of a lover of altruistic pleasure, than some such work. Therefore, a man cannot do that degree of true spiritual good to himself by some other altruistic work as he is able to do to himself to the extent to which he sacrifices his wealth and his property for this highest altruistic work, devotes the energies of his physical organs (i. hands, feet, etc.) for it, dedicates his mental powers of thinking an learning etc., to it and sacrifices for it whenever necessary e.g., his honour, his praise, his good name, his position, his physical health and his other bodily pleasures etc.

VARIOUS KINDS OF PLEASURE-GIVING LOW HATREDS IN THE ORGANISM OF HUMAN SOUL

Q. What is meant by low-pleasure-giving feeling of hatred a human soul?

A. The feeling of aversion which is produced in a man relation to the person who interferes with his love of some pleasure is called the feeling of low hatred.

Man wants to get that pleasure of which he becomes a lover. Therefore, whenever any person or animal or any other existence causes some kind of interference in his getting that pleasure, he develops this low hatred in relation to that existence. When this feeling is aroused in a man he becomes anxious to see that person or animate or in-animate existence come to some kind of harm or to hear about it or to think of or to do some harm to it or to get some kind of harm done to it by someone else, and gets pleasure or satisfaction or joy on hearing or knowing about some harm done to it or to some of its relations or on doing such harm to any of them himself or getting it done by someone else, then, the feeling which is the cause of manifesting various kinds of all such characteristics is the feeling of low-hatred in him. This feeling of hatred is of various kinds.

Q. What are the various ways in which these low hatreds are produced in the human soul?

A. There are four ways, viz.

(1) When one does not get from another the satisfaction of one's desired Pleasure:

When a person wants someone to be a party in the pursuance of some of his pleasure-giving desire (howsoever undesirable and harmful it may be for himself and/or for someone else) but the other person does not want to become his accomplice and does not support him, or cannot or does not want to satisfy, for some reason, even some proper desire of his, then being insane under the intoxication of his love of that pleasure and ignorant of his soul-welfare, he gets hurt and pain in his heart at this refusal by that person and develops in himself low hate in relation to such pain-giver.

(2) When one is attached to himself or some other person or society by some low-love:

When a person becomes attached by tie of some low-love, to himself or to some member of his family or to the people of his religion or his community or his country then naturally he becomes partial towards himself or to them. In such a state, if someone points out some true defect or wrong or some evil or shortcoming of his or of someone of them, then partly due to his self-love and partly due to the low-love by Which he is attached to them, he gets hurt and pain from him, and develops low-hate for him.

(3) When one's self-love develops extraordinarily:

When a person reaches such a state that in comparison with his own superiority, he does not like, nay feels pained to listen, to see or to accept the superiority of someone else in any respect whatever, though it may even be absolutely true, then he naturally feels low-hatred for the person eulogized.

(4) When a person becomes lover of one or another kind of his false traditions or false beliefs:

When a person becomes lover of his false traditions or false beliefs and therefore becomes partial to them, then:

(i) He hates a person or society on finding it holding a different religious creed or a different religious belief from his own;

(ii) He hates a person on finding him not akin to himself in his dress or manners or in his way of living or language etc;

(iii) He hates a person on finding him inferior to himself in some respect; and

(iv) He hates a person on account of difference in profession, colour or community etc.

Q. What are the chief characteristics by which we can recognize the presence of the feelings of hatred in a person?

A. When a person desires that:

(1) Every wish or will of mine—however evil and undesirable it may be in relation to someone else— should, be necessarily satisfied by everyone;

(2) No one should have a belief or opinion against any of my religious beliefs—however absolutely false they may be in the eyes of others—and against any of my opinions—howsoever wrong that may be in the eyes of others. And no one should ever express or propagate his opinion or view which is against my wishes and liking;

(3) No one should be considered or accepted, or declared to be superior to or better than I and no one should be praised more highly than I, in any respect and nor should he be given any respect etc. and

(4) I should not be considered or called, or accepted or believed to, be a person of demerit, lower or inferior by any one even when I have really got some such inferiority.

All such, characteristics are proofs of the presence of various kinds of low-hatred in a human soul.

DEGRADATION OF HUMAN SOUL

Q. What is meant by soul-degradation?

A. Degradation means to fall, to move downward, to disintegrate or to degenerate.

In Nature when some existence degenerates in some aspect from its previous condition, it is a case of its degradation. In the same way degeneration of the soul is called soul-degradation. Some of the examples of this soul- degradation are given below:

A person did not take hemp. Now due to some evil company he has started taking it. This is his degradation in this respect.

A person did not take wine before. Now he drinks. This is his degraded behaviour in this aspect.

A person did not take opium for the pleasure of intoxication. But now he has started taking it. This is his degrading behaviour.

A woman was not adulterous before. Now she has become so. In this respect, it is her degraded state.

A person used to admit some true fault of his when some benefactor of his pointed it out to him. Now he does not do so. Rather on feeling his ego offended by him, he is full of the feeling of hatred for him and starts harbouring one or another kind of evil thoughts about him and regards him as his evil-wisher instead of being his well-wisher. All these actions of his are degrading actions.

A shop-keeper did not cheat earlier while weighing something. Now he does so. This is his degradation in this respect in comparison to his previous condition.

A government officer did not take bribes earlier. Now he takes it. This is his degrading action in this respect.,

A girl did not steal before anything belonging to anyone else. Now, on finding occasion, she steals. This is her degraded condition in this respect.

A person did not hunt before. Now he has become hunter and kills different innocent creatures of the animal kingdom. This is his degrading behaviour in this respect.

A person used to give some money daily in charity for some public good. Now although he earns more than before, yet he gives no charity of this kind now. This is his degraded behaviour.

A person in order to get sublime light for his soul and his soul-life and to see and realize some truth in these respects in that sublime light (Dev Jyoti) used to study some book written by Devatma and meditated over its contents before. But now he has stopped doing so.

This is his degrading activity.

A person used to do some daily work earlier, in connection with freeing different persons from one or another kind of false beliefs or some sinful acts and giving them some knowledge about true religion.

But now he does not do any of these things or has lost the capacity todo any such work. This is his degraded condition.

A person in order to be helpful in some cause of public good used to devote twenty, thirty, forty or more days in a year for that work. Now he does not want to and does not actually devote himself even for a week or two for this work. This is his degraded condition.

A person did not accept as true the so-called gods and goddesses possessing different false virtues or characteristics. Now, he does accept them as true. This is a degraded state of his soul.

A person did not accept as his worshipful being any of the so-called false gods and goddesses devoid of sublime powers ('Dev Shakties').

But now he accepts one or another such being as worshipful. This is his soul-degradation. Formerly, a person did not worship any so-called god or goddess except the `Satya Deva' possessing true sublime powers 'Dev Shakties'. Now he does so. This is his degrading behaviour.

Formerly, a person did not accept as true the false teachings about salvation. But now he does so. This is his soul-degradation.

A person contrary to his inner true belief accepts one or another belief of a religion as true or keeps one or another symbol of some religion out of hypocrisy. This is a sign of his soul-degradation, A person contrary to his true inner belief, performs one or another domestic ceremony out of hypocrisy. This is his degrading behaviour, etc. etc.

In accordance with the immutable law of Nature it is inevitable for every human being on becoming and remaining lover of low-pleasures and their consequent low-hatreds to believe in different kinds of falsehoods in his various relations and to commit different kinds of evils and thus to disintegrate or degrade his soul organism.

Q. Are these low-loves of pleasure and their consequent low-hatreds responsible for all the different kinds of falsehoods in the human world and all the different kinds of evils perpetrated by man on men and animals and others?

A. Undoubtedly so. The real cause for all the different kinds of falsehoods found in the human world and all the injustice and evil perpetrated by man on lacs of creatures of the human and the sub-human kingdoms, are the low-loves of pleasure and low-hatreds.

THE VARIOUS KINDS OF FALSEHOODS IN THE HUMAN WORLD AND SOUL-DEGRADATION OF HUMAN BEINGS THROUGH THESE FALSEHOODS

Q. What are the various kinds of falsehoods found in the human world?

A. There are four kinds of falsehoods, such as:

(1) Various kinds of falsehoods connected with belief i.e., belief in a human being in various kinds of falsehoods about the fundamental reality of Nature, the immutable laws of Nature, and about one's own soul and various other existences in Nature.

(2) Various kinds of falsehoods connected with thinking i.e., when a human being thinks out and invents various kinds of falsehoods in his mind in order to hide some defect, fault, sin or shortcoming of his or to harm some opponent or enemy or foe etc., of his or to please somebody or to attract someone towards himself or to cheat someone for some other purpose.

(3) Various kinds of falsehoods connected with speech i.e., when a human being expresses through his speech or word or gesture various kinds of falsehoods invented or thought out in his mind for the fulfilment of some purpose of his.

(4) Falsehoods connected with various other actions i.e., when a human being contrary to his inner belief or knowledge keeps some religious symbol, or certain outward appearance, or performs some domestic or other ceremony or brings about some religious association or jatha or worships some so-called god or goddess or does some other action. And so on and so forth.

Q. Why does a human being become fond of falsehood due to some of his pleasureful low-love and its consequent low-hatred?

A. When a human being, on the one hand, finds and feels some kind of falsehood to be helpful in the satisfaction of some love of low-pleasure of his or its consequent low-hatred and, on the other hand, possesses no consciousness in his soul which could produce some hatred or pain for the varied harm done to his soul and body through that falsehood, then he becomes naturally prepared to side with one or another kind of falsehood and to use it and even deliberately forsakes truth to adopt the path of falsehood.

Again, when he, on achieving success in some purpose of his through falsehood, finds satisfaction, joy or pleasure, then on several occasions he preaches to the members of his family and others about the success of falsehood and the method of its use and expresses with enthusiasm and pride the necessity and grandeur of falsehood in proportion to the depth of his love for it.

Hence in accordance with the law of Nature, it is inevitable for every lover of low-pleasures and low-hatreds to become fond of falsehood.

Therefore, just as in the past, apart from others, the founders of various religious sects and their so-called various worshipful beings etc., had also made falsehood their support for one or another purpose of theirs, in the same way, several leaders of human society even to-day take the shelter of falsehood where-ever necessary for one or another purpose and do preach it to others.

Q. This is a very horrible state of affairs.

A. Undoubtedly. But it is inevitable for each and every lover of low-pleasure to side with falsehood—be he called a mahatma, muni, rishi, maharishi, guru, prophet, nabi, leader, buddh, siddbarath, jin, tirthankra etc., or some Ishwar, Parmeshwar or Parmatma etc.

Q. Then has falsehood been preached in different countries of the world even in the name of religion?

A. Yes, Sir. All those faiths prevalent in this world in the name of religion which are against the reality of Nature and its spiritual and other true laws and the true facts which can and do occur in accordance with these laws of Nature, are all of them fundamentally false.

Q. How were all these false faiths started?

A. Various evil and degraded spirits of different countries have called themselves gods and goddesses and different influential persons have given them out to be 'gods' or 'goddesses' and have deliberately given teachings in the name of religion about:

(1) False worshipful beings.

(2) False praises, false glorifying hymns, false adorations. False worships in relation to false worshipful beings.

(3) Different kinds of mortifications (Tapa).

(4) Different kinds of songs full of falsehoods.

(5) Different kinds of prayers based on falsehood.

(6) Different kinds of places of false pilgrimages.

(7) Different kinds of false fasts.

(8) Different kinds of false `Japs' or recitations.

(9) Different kinds of false readings and false concentrations.

(10) Different kinds of false beliefs about salvation.

(11) So-called religious books full of different kinds of falsehoods.

(12) Different kinds of false teachers or preceptors.

(13) Different kinds of ceremonies based on falsehood.

(14) Different kinds of false heavens.

(15) Different kinds of false hells.

(16) Getting of the pleasures of some so-called heavens by satisfying some false worshipful god or goddess, and undergoing various kinds of pains and other harms of various so-called hells by arousing their anger.

By propagation of all these kinds of falsehoods, they have made thousands and millions of persons believers in them.

Apart from this, in the name of religion but contrary to the true and fundamental laws of Nature:

(1) They have spread falsehood by declaring this or that god or goddess as creator of Nature.

(2) They have spread falsehood by declaring this or that god or goddess as omniscient, seer of the present, past and future, all-seeing, knower of the workings of our mind, and omnipotent.

(3) They have spread falsehood by declaring this or that god or goddess as incorporeal i.e., without an organized living body.

(4) They have spread falsehood by declaring this or that man or animal as incarnation of this or that god.

(5) Falsehood has been spread by declaring one's own self or someone else as performer of extraordinary feats or miracles.

(6) Falsehood has been spread by declaring one's own self or some other as the fulfiller of man's different kinds of worldly desires or as giver of blessings or boons ('var') about their fulfilment.

(7) Falsehood has been preached by spreading the false stories about the human soul being born again in this world in the form of man, animal or plant etc., in order to reap the consequences of good or bad actions.

(8) Various kinds of falsehoods have been preached through spreading various kinds of false stories in connection with salvation from sins or re-birth.

By hearing these various kinds of falsehoods (false stories) from their very childhood and accepting them as true, millions of persons come to believe in them.

Q. How do millions of persons from their very childhood come to believe in different kinds of falsehood?

A. When a human child is born into this world, he is completely ignorant and does not at all know even the words 'truth' and 'falsehood' and their meanings. Then when on learning some language, he begins to understand to some extent the talk of those around him, then he starts believing in various things—whether they are true or false—on their authority. All beliefs of this kind are called traditional beliefs or blind beliefs.

In such a mental state, soul is a distant cry about which he is in complete darkness. If he is told purely false things about his own gross body or some ordinary event of Nature even these he automatically believes as true.

Q. How does this happen?

A. This is how it happens: If some child is told in his childhood that small pox from which boys and girls and grown-up persons suffer, is due to the anger of some goddess, then he will believe this thing as true.

If he is told that all other kinds of diseases, which human body is heir to, are caused by one or another ancestor from among his dead ancestors, then he will also. Believe in this thing. If he is told that besides his dead ancestors there are other dead men and women who cause these diseases, then he will believe this thing also as true. If he is told, that various kinds of stars or heavenly bodies on getting angry cause various kinds of diseases in human body, then he will believe in some such thing also. If he is given this teaching that there is the statue of a certain woman of such and such name in such and such tomb or mandir and if she is given offering of some young one of a pig or a hen or some particular kind of sweet things to eat or she is presented with beautiful flowers for fragrance and some fragrant incense or some other thing is burnt before it, then on her being pleased, she cures the disease of some patient or gives a son to the woman who does not beget one, then he will believe these things also as true. If he is given the teaching that by bathing the statute of such and such god or goddess in such and such place, by offering flowers to it, by burning pleasant incense before it or by offering such and such eatables to it, such and such desire of a human being is satisfied, then he will believe it also to be true. If he is told that if the person who gets fever were to get tied round his throat or right arm some 'mantra' or charm written by such and such person, his fever disappears, he will believe in this thing also. If he is told that if such and such person were, after reading some 'mantra', to blow at some patient, then by his doing so, the disease of the patient disappears, he will believe in it also. If he is told that when a cow or a buffalo of someone does not give milk, then it is due to the anger of some dead ancestor and if that ancestor is offered such and such thing, then on his getting pleased, his anger is appeased and the cow or the buffaloes begins to give milk, he will believe in this thing also.

If he is told that there is a God, Ishwar by name, who makes the bodies of all men, animals and trees and it is he who has created the sun, the moon and the earth and it is he who is moving them, he will accept them as right and also believe them as true. If he is told that when a god named Ishwar, gets angry with human beings, then in order to take his revenge on them and to frighten them, he gives them various kinds of pains and troubles by spreading diseases like plague etc., and bringing calamities like famine etc., then he will also believe in this thing. If he is told that the God, Ishwar by name had come on this earth in such and such age by assuming the form of such and such man, tortoise or pig etc., he will also believe in this thing. If he is taught that the God, Ishwar by name, never assumed the form of some man or animal like pig etc., nor can he become so, he will believe in this thing also.

If he is taught that a God, Khuda by name, has taught in the scripture which he has given through his such and such messenger, that it is necessary and desirable for man to kill various kinds of animals and to eat their flesh, then he will believe in this thing also. If he is told that a God, Ishwar by name, has never permitted any man to take flesh of any animal and he has declared this act as evil and he is never pleased, rather he gets angry if someone does this act, then he will believe in this thing also. If he is told that God has permitted man to marry a second woman in the life-time of his first wife and to marry a third woman in the life-time of his two wives and to marry a fourth one in the living presence of his three wives, but he has not permitted woman to marry another man in the life-time of her first husband, then accepting these things as right he will believe in them also. If he is told that God has never permitted any man to marry a second woman in the life-time of his first wife and that he considers the men who go in for many marriages as evil and sinful, then accepting these thing also as right he will believe in them. If he is told that God is very much pleased if one utters some particular name or 'mantras' or sings his praises by some particular method so many times a day and besides showing various kinds of favours on this earth upon one who does so, he permits him on his death after certain specified period to enter and stay in some special place called 'Bahisht' or 'swarg' (heaven) where he gets tasty things to eat, intoxicating things to get intoxicated, many beautiful women to enjoy and glittering gold bangles ('kangans') to wear, then he will accept these things also as true. If he is told that God does not give intoxicants and other things and women etc., to any person whom he keeps in heaven, but makes him happy only by his proximity ('darshan') then he will believe in this thing also. If he is told that those who do not believe in God or Ishwara or do not accept some particular Book as written or sent or given by Him, He gets very angry with them and remains on the look out to take His revenge on them, and when they die, He keeps them in some such place which is called hell where snakes and scorpions always keep biting them and where they get pus to eat, then considering these things also as true he will believe in them. If he is told that when God gets displeased or angry with some person, then on the expiry of a certain period after the death of that person, he throws him in such a hollow place ('kund') in which there are no snakes and scorpions but a fire is ever-burning with the Dev help of sulphur and being put into it, his body is not burnt into ashes nor does it die and that this God satisfies his heart by torturing him in this way till eternity, then considering these things as true, he will become believer in them also. If he is taught that though a person may do any number of actions against the will of God and however angry or displeased that God may be with him for these actions of his, yet if before his death, he has 'darshan' (view) of certain statue in a particular place, or takes bath in a particular river or big pond, or a particular staired well ('bavli'), tank or lake etc., or even drinks some water of some particular river or accepts some particular person to be the special son or the special messenger of God, then the whole of his anger disappears and on the contrary he gets very much pleased with him and gives him a place in his heaven, 'swarg', 'bahisht' or `baikunth', to stay and enjoy various pleasures, then he will become a believer of these things also. So on and so forth.

On receiving teachings of hundreds of such kinds of absolutely false things, millions of persons gradually come to believe in them from their very childhood and on the minds of lacs of persons such false beliefs get such a strong domination that they become incapable for ever to free themselves from their most evil influences. How horrible and how pitiable is this condition of such human beings!

Q. What are the various kinds of falsehoods that have come into existence through human souls?

A. 1. When a human soul motivated by his low-love of 'ego' wants that for a crime or sin which he has committed in relation to someone, he should not get punishment of any kind or that he should not be lowered in estimation or put to shame before someone, then for his such evil defense he exercises his mental powers to think out all kinds of means based on falsehood. Through such thinking of his, just as he misuses his power of thinking and thus makes it as well as himself diseased and degenerated, so also he becomes the source of producing falsehood.

2. When a human being, moved by his feeling of hatred born of revenge, engages himself, for its satisfaction, in thinking out ways for spreading some kind of false accusations and slander or other falsehoods against some person in order to harm

him, then by his such thinking he, on the one hand, produces various falsehoods and on the other hand also makes his soul diseased and degenerated by misusing his thinking power through such actions of his.

3. When a human being due to being attached to someone by some low-love becomes partial to him and thinks out one or another kind of false pretexts or ways in order to hide some crime of his or to save him from the punishment for some real crime, then just as he becomes the cause of producing falsehood, so also he makes his soul diseased or degenerated by instilling the poison of falsehood in his soul organism.

4. When a human being on becoming slave to the low-love of money and property wants to get hold of the money or property another by deceiving or cheating him and for such a fraud thinks out one or another kind of means based on falsehood and harbours them, then by such thinking of his, whereas he produces various kinds of falsehoods, at the same time he makes his soul diseased or degenerated by perverse use of his thinking power through such action of his.

5. When a man motivated by the low-love of lust thinks out various kinds of means based on falsehood in order to seduce some woman, then by such thinking of his whereas he produces various kinds of falsehoods, at the same time he degrades his mind-and makes his soul diseased or degenerated.

6. When a human being, on the one hand, does not want to satisfy some desire of another and, on the other hand, due to some reason, he does not want to make him angry by giving him the true answer, then in this state whereas he produces falsehood by concocting one or another kind of, false pretext, at the same time he misuses his thinking power and makes his soul diseased or degenerated.

7. When a human being out of some fear of a person who has committed a crime or out of some other fear, thinks of telling something against the truth about his such criminal action, the true exposure of which is absolutely necessary for public good, or of giving some kind of evidence opposed to truth in a public court, then by his such thinking whereas he produces falsehood, at the same time by such evil action, he perverts his thinking power and- makes his soul diseased or degenerated.

8. When a human being praises himself against what is true in order to falsely show himself to be learned in some respect, then by such action of his whereas he produces falsehood, he at the same time makes his soul diseased or degenerated by misuses of his power of thinking. So on and so forth.

Q. Are all the various kinds of stories which have been spread under the name-of 'miracles' or 'karaamaats'-or impossible feats, false?

A. They are certainly absolutely false to the extent they are against the true facts of Nature and its true and immutable law.

For instance:

A particular messenger of God had turned his dead stick into a living snake. The founder of a particular religion was not conceived in the womb of some woman in accordance with natural law, but he had descended from heaven and assuming the form of a white elephant had entered her womb and then born out of her assuming the form of a human child. The founder of a certain religion, was born of such a virgin girl who had no sexual intercourse with any man. A certain person had turned water into wine. A certain person had, by his will, increased some loaves which were not sufficient even to fill the stomach of two persons, into hundred times more and had thereby fed thousands of persons. A certain person had resuscitated the absolutely dead body of some person. When a particular prophet used to walk in the sun, the shade of his body did not fall on the earth. At the time when there were no human beings on this earth, Ishwar, by his will, had brought into being many young men and women who were not born out of any woman's womb in the form of babies. And though they did not know any language because they had no parents etc., present beforehand to teach them a language, yet when God inspired the minds of some of them with some sayings composed in a special language or conveyed some thoughts to their minds in that language, they were at once able to understand them and to explain them. Some god had given such a vessel to a queen that whatever articles of food of different kinds and in different quantities she wanted, they would all come out of it, of the same kinds and in the same quantities. And all alone she used to feed through it thousands of persons at a time with different kinds of foods. A devotee of some god had once turned the dead corpse of a human being into the form of a sweet pudding ('halwa'). Once when thousands of persons came to a devotee of some God named Ishwar, for meeting him and no other arrangement could be made for their food, then that devotee called one of his disciples and told him to shake a particular tree by climbing over it and that he would thereby get all the things needed for feeding the guests. And when he climbed up that tree and started to shake it, so many of eatables of different kinds like sweets etc., fell from it, and that thousands of people had their fill. So on and so forth. Hundreds of such kinds of other false things have been spread under the name of miracles or such impossible feats.

Q. Is the soul of a human being degraded by siding with some kind of falsehood even at the mental level?

A. Certainly.

Q. In what way?

A. When a human being, due to his vanity or feeling of hatred etc., gets perverted vision in relation to some person and sees and believes the true state or some true virtue of that person in a distorted way and having reached this condition he harbours in his mind some kind of thoughts based on falsehood about that person;

When a human being, in order to save himself from some pain or to get some pleasure, harbours in his mind some thought based on falsehood with the object of breaking some right promise in relation to himself or someone else;

When a human being, in order to hide some crime or fault of his, thinks out in his mind one or another kind of false pretexts or methods; and When a human being thinks in his mind some means based on falsehood in order to show himself superior in some respect to those from whom he is not really superior in that respect etc. etc.

In all such cases even though he may not harm or be not able to harm anyone through such thinking based on falsehood even then he degrades his soul through every such thought based on falsehood.

Q. If a human being makes use of such different kinds of falsehoods whereby he cannot get any punishment according to any law of a government, does his soul become degraded even through them?

A. Undoubtedly:

If a human being, due to some false belief of his or due to his hatred, does not accept the true virtue of someone in the presence of someone i.e., does not acknowledge the presence of that virtue in him;

If a human being, due to his hatred in relation to someone, does not accept some truly good action of his as a good action; If a human being, even on coming to know at some time that some or all of his religious beliefs are false, deliberately declares them as true on account of his being believer and lover of these false religious beliefs from his very childhood, or still further when he gives false arguments in defense of them;.

If a human being, even on coming to know the truth of some true law of Nature or some true event of it to be against some previously ingrained false beliefs of his, does not accept it to be true, nor declares it to be so;

If a human being, deliberately adopts some means based on falsehood, for some social or political purpose in the name of religion or some other name, i.e., takes shelter of some hypocritical policy or behaviour;

If a human being, even knowing some domestic or other ceremony as false, performs it or attends it by becoming a party to it;

If a human being, keeps one or other kind of some false religious symbol on his body even knowing it to be false and thus becomes a hypocrite;

If a human being, with the object of getting the pleasure derived from honour and superiority, falsely praises some of his ancestors or his pedigree or his self, or some member of his family or some object of his, etc., then, even though he may not be considered guilty by any penal code of any government, yet he degrades his soul through every such action of his.

Q. What is the difference between a man in error and a man swayed by falsehood?

A. There is very great difference. A man in error, believing or knowing a certain false thing as true, sincerely tells and declares it as true or does some other act or behaviour in relation to it. But a man swayed by falsehood, even knowing various things or events as false, falsely tells and declares them as true before others through hypocrisy and tries to deceive them through his hypocrisy.

Q. If a person, having received some false belief since his childhood, sincerely propagates it by declaring it as true before someone else then is he not a man swayed by falsehood?

A. No. But if some person, due to some false belief of his, himself commits some unjust or sinful action in relation to some human being, animal or other existences or instigates some other person to commit some -sinful act in relation to someone else, then even though he may propagate the commission of that sin with sincerity, yet he degrades his soul by doing so.

For example, if a person gets from his childhood such beliefs through the teachings of his parents or someone else that to eat meat, to kill some living creature for meat-eating or hunting, to marry again in the life-time on this earth of a wife or a husband or to torture or kill a person holding religious beliefs different from one's own, is right, and motivated by such beliefs even if he sincerely performs some such action, he certainly becomes sinner and degraded through it.

Q. If some person holds, contrary to truth, some such beliefs, through which he neither commits any sinful or unjust action in relation to someone else, nor instigates someone else to commit sinful or unjust acts—such as that this earth rests on the fangs of a cobra or the horns of a bull, or that the sun rotates all around the earth or the river Ganges has descended from 'golok' (heaven) or the earth is not spherical but it is flat—and believes these views to be true, he sincerely declares them as true before others, then is he a man swayed by falsehood?

A. No. But in view of these false beliefs he is certainly in a state of ignorance or darkness and it is necessary and desirable for him on getting a chance, to get free from them.

Q. Are those persons not swayed by falsehood who bring in one or other kind of imaginary things in the writing of some novel, story, tale or some other article?

A. To the extent that a person does not deliberately use his power of imagination to produce some such writing, by the reading of which some person gets false knowledge about some existence or some aspect of Nature or by reading of which some person feels some urge to commit some unjust or cruel act in relation to some human being or animal etc. he does not become lover of falsehood through any fiction writing of his.

Q. Is it not falsehood to mask oneself in the form of another in order to obtain innocent pleasure through some dramatic performance or theatre, i.e., to imitate the form and speech or some other action of another and through that farce to give out and show oneself as different from what one is?

A. No. But if some person indulges in such a farce which is really insulting for another or is unnecessarily painful to the followers of a religion, then its performance cannot be proper.

Q. If some person puts such a question to another, to which the other person, on the one hand, is not bound by any true spiritual law to answer and on the other, giving of true answer to it brings harm to him or to someone else or there is risk of such a harm, what should the latter do?

A. He should in such a case refuse humbly to answer every such question

i.e., he should say, "I do not want to give any answer to this question of yours. He has every right to do so.

Q. Is it an act of falsehood or not when one says or tells something deliberately against truth in order to catch a thief or a dacoit?

A. It is certainly an act of falsehood. All such kinds of deliberate falsehoods are the cause of soul-degradation. Therefore, the ordinary moral law which is necessary for one to know in connection with all such situations is this: So long as a person motivated by his powers of imagination or imitation does not on his own part deliberately involve any person in some kind of misrepresentation or false belief or other falsehood by some talk or question or writing or article or sermon etc., of his and does not urge any person to commit unjust i.e., sinful, cruel or harmful action in relation to any living or non-living existence, till then he can use them in the way he likes for some proper and useful purpose and thus become helpful in the various kinds of progress of the human society. But as has been said before, he remains certainly responsible in every such action for the creation of any mistaken impression about truth and goodness.

THE DEGRADATION OF HUMAN SOULS THROUGH THEIR UNJUST OR USURPING THOUGHTS & ACTIONS.

Q. What are unjust or usurping ('apharankari') thoughts and actions?

A. The thoughts or actions indulged in by a human being, motivated solely by some love of pleasure or by a consequent feeling of hatred of his, by which he deprives himself or some other living or non-living existence, of some Nature-given just right, are called unjust or usurping thoughts and actions.

Q. What are the various kinds of these unjust or usurping thoughts and actions?

A. Fundamentally they are of four kinds, viz:

1. When a human being thinks out a thought in order to injure the just right of some existence of living or non-living world of Nature.

2. When a human being gives some such training to some other person or some being of the animal world which harms the just right of someone else.

3. When a human being, without any reasons of discharging some right duty or performing some right spiritual exercise and, solely motivated by his love of pleasures or feelings of hatred, indulges in activities in connection with his organized body which harm his health.

4. All such actions of a human being in connection with some existence of any living or non-living world of Nature which deprive it of some of its just rights.

But it is inevitable for every human being, motivated by one or another kind of low-love or one or another kind of low-hatred of his, to be unjust or usurper to some extent in relation to the living and non-living existences of Nature. Therefore, it is also inevitable for him to produce various diseases in his soul and to make it diseased, disfigured or degraded through his such various kinds of unjust or usurping inner thoughts and external actions.

Q. What are the various kinds of usurpations or deprivations of any of the just rights of the living beings of Nature i.e., some human being or animal or plant, or of some of its non-living existences?

A. The various kinds of usurpations in which he indulges are these:

1. Usurpation of the wealth of some human being.

2. Usurpation of some other property or thing of some human being.

3. Unjustly depriving some human being of his honour.

4. Unjustly depriving some human being of his fame.

5. Unjustly depriving one's self or another human being or animal of his health.

6. Unjustly disfiguring the form or qualities of one's own self or that of some other person or animal or plant or material object.

7. Unjustly depriving some person animal, plant or other object of some good quality.

8. Unjustly depriving some human being or animal of some right pleasure of his.

9. Unjustly depriving some human being or animal of some just peace of mind.

10. Unjustly depriving some human being or animal of some of his strength.

11. Unjustly depriving some human being or animal of his normal longevity.

12. Unjustly depriving some human being or animal of his life.

13. Unjustly depriving some human being of his just position.

14. Unjustly depriving some human being or animal of some physical organ of his.

15. Unjustly depriving some human being of some of his true beliefs.

Q. Are such various kinds of actions of usurpation or injustices also called sinful actions in ordinary language?

A. Yes, please.

Q. Do human beings alone, motivated by their low-loves of pleasures and their low-hatreds etc., indulge in such kinds of various sinful actions, or besides them did some so-called gods i.e. Ishwar, Parmatma, Lord, God, Jehova, Allah, Khuda, Vaheguru etc. or some so-called incarnation of any of them or other worshipful beings also indulged or even now indulged in them?

A. Though a person, be he an ordinary human being or be he called a mahatma, maharishi. rishi, saint, mahant, buddha, siddha, tirthankra, acharya, guru, nabi, pir, wali, etc. or be he called a god or goddess or Some of their special relative or devotee, or friend or incarnation, etc. yet if he has got one or another kind of low-love of pleasure and its consequent one or another kind of feeling of hatred, it is inevitable for him to indulge in one or another kind of sinful actions and to give teachings of various kinds of sinful actions to others.

Q. Have such so-called gods etc., besides propagating falsehoods and indulging in false behaviour, also done various sinful actions of usurpation themselves and given teachings to others also for committing various sinful actions?

A. Yes, Sir. The so-called worshipful beings and founders of the various religions etc., have done various kinds of sinful actions even themselves and besides this they have also given teachings to others to commit various kinds of sinful actions. For example:

1. Various so-called gods have asked from human beings the sacrifice for themselves even of human beings besides that of various kinds of animals and, on getting such sacrifice from them, they have got them killed and eaten them or sucked the fine particles of their blood.

2. On getting angry with some human being, they have out of revenge either themselves stolen his things or got them stolen by someone else.

3. On getting angry with some human being or animal, they have killed that human being or animal.

4. On getting angry with a human being, they have blinded him, or on getting angry with someone, they have made him sick or created some other trouble for him.

5. They have themselves committed adultery with someone.

6. They have given teachings of adultery to their believers.

7. They have permitted their believers to kill animals for eating their flesh.

8. They have deceived others:

9. They have permitted their believers to take such poisonous things as liquor, wine or hemp etc.

10. They have permitted their men believers to marry many other women during the life-time of their first wife and they have not permitted a widow to marry at all and under any condition whatsoever.

11. They have commanded their believers to kill those who do not believe as true the false teachings of their so-called Inspired or beloved ones.

12. They have required their believers to loot the belonging of those who do not believe as true in the gossips of their so-called inspired or beloved ones.

13. They have asked their believers to forcibly capture and make slaves of those who do not believe as true the myths of their so-called inspired or beloved ones. They have given them teachings to commit acts of incendiarism such as to demolish the places of their gods and memorable relics of some founders or gurus of theirs or to set fire to their houses etc.

14. They have commanded their believers to excommunicate or banish those who do not believe as true the myths of some of their so-called Rishi etc.

15. They have permitted their believers to snatch away the wives of those who do not believe as true the myths of some of their so-called inspired or beloved ones and to make them their own wives.

16. They have permitted their believers, besides having sexual intercourse with their wedded wives, to commit adultery with the women slaves or maid-servants of some one. So on and so forth.

Q. It is said about some of these so-called but most sinful and degraded worshipped gods that they will sit as judges or magistrates to take account of the sinful actions of human beings, immediately after their death or later on, on a special day, and to give them the punishment of hell or re-birth for such actions of theirs, or on being pleased at the recommendation by someone, or at some belief or action of theirs, to reward them with the pleasures of heaven etc. Are not such beliefs absolutely false?

A. Certainly they are absolutely false. Because if it be necessary, according to some so-called just procedure, for such hundreds of persons who are in comparison less sinners than these so-called magistrate Devatas, to undergo various kinds of painful punishments on being put in hell or on rebirth, then why is it not necessary according to the same so-called just procedure that these so-called magistrate Devatas who are in comparison to the ordinary people much greater sinners, to be sent to some greater hell than the ordinary ones or in some future birth to be born as insects in some sewage? Certainly it is. But the believers of false religions do not want to and do not accept some such true argument.

Q. If some human being indulges in such bad actions which are not regarded as crimes by the penal code of any government then is his soul degraded through such actions?

A. Yes, please, certainly it is degraded. To illustrate.

If some human being on becoming lover of the pleasures of some kind of play or show, adultery or gambling etc., squanders away his wealth or his other property;

If some human being, motivated by his vanity, squanders away his wealth or other property in order to get the pleasure of showing himself superior to others and being praised by others or out of fear of being condemned by others;

If some human being, on becoming lover of the pleasure of acquiring wealth or other property for himself, starts a business by taking loan so far beyond his capacity that he cannot pay it back, in order to become wealthy and man of property very quickly or tries to become rich very quickly through the bad habit of some kind of gambling such as speculation ('satta') or betting;

If some human being, on account of being lover of the pleasure derived from acts of violence, troubles or teases some human being or animal or kills some animals or deprives them of any of their just right in order to get the pleasure of that low feeling;

If some human being, on account of becoming lover and slave to his money and property on which he has absolute right, does not want to and does not contribute it to some altruistic work;

If some human being, instead of doing good to himself and others by giving away his money and other property, on which he has absolute right, in charity for some work of public good, wants to give it and does give it to some undeserving or unfit person or persons out of his tie of some low-love with them;

If some human being, on becoming lover of money and knowing that he will get nothing in return for whatever money he will have to spend on the upbringing and marriage etc., of his daughter, does not pay sufficient attention and does not put in sufficient effort in her upbringing and protection and by such behaviour of his the girl dies a premature death;

If some man marries another woman when an already married wife of his is alive on this earth or a woman renounces an already married husband of hers in his life-time and lives with some other man;

If some human being arranges the marriage of his children with someone before they attain the proper age of their majority and without obtaining their consent;

If some human being, in order to get the pleasure of intoxication, himself eats or drinks some intoxicating or poisonous thing or gives it to someone else for the same purpose or persuades him to take such a thing;

If some human being takes meat;

If a human being, on account of being a slave to the pleasures of money or any other possession of his or to his body etc., breaks, without some true, just and sufficient cause, any of his such right promises which he makes with someone in order to give him some money or some other thing or to see him or to do some work for him at a certain appointed time; etc. etc.; then though he may not be considered a criminal in accordance with the penal code of some government, and may not get any punishment for his such actions, yet he necessarily degrades his soul by his such actions.

THE CHIEF SYMPTOMS OF THE DEGRADATION OF HUMAN SOUL

Q. What are the symptoms of the degradation of a human soul?

The four chief symptoms of the degradation of human soul can be known, are these:

(1) Insensitiveness or hardness of soul and resultant soul-darkness and soul-blindness.

(2) Perversion of soul-vision.

(3) The creation of various unnecessary and most harmful pains for soul.

(4) The destruction of the constructive power of soul and its complete death.

Some explanation of every one of these is given below:—

1. Insensitiveness or Hardness of Soul and Resultant Soul-darkness and Soul-Blindness. ('Kathorta aur Andhita')

Q. What is meant by the insensitiveness or hardness of soul?

A. A human being who on becoming conscious of some of his low pleasures becomes a lover of and a slave to them and considers the getting of these pleasures as his ideal and engages himself in the task of getting them and spends his various energies in their pursuit, violates the Nature's law of evolution (which can be fulfilled in the life of a soul by following the path of truth and goodness) by causing various kinds of falsehoods and various kinds of evils through various kinds of his activities.

By the violation of this grand law of Nature, the organism of human soul gets into such a bad condition that he gradually loses the capacity—if he had inherited any such capacity from his birth to see the truth in connection with his soul-life, and when he loses it altogether he becomes completely blind. This state of blindness of human soul is called his state of insensitiveness or hardness.

Q. How is human soul harmed by the production and growth in it of this insensitiveness?

A. As the soul of some human being grows insensitive, the path of the entrance of the rays of that highest light called Dev Jyoti or sublime light goes on closing, by the illumination of which he could see various kinds of truths about the entity or being of his soul, its diseases or its degraded state, its salvation from that degraded state of it, the necessity of the evolution in it of the energy-giving higher feelings and the method of acquiring them etc., and by which he can get that rare knowledge about these truths which is called the knowledge of true religion.

As the rays of the Sun passing through a clean glass can enter a closed room but they cannot penetrate into it through its wooden doors or walls, in the same way, if the soul of a human being becomes so insensitive that the most intense rays of the sublime light (Dev Jyoti) cannot enter into it, then there is and can be no such illumination in his soul by which alone his own real condition can appear before his spiritual sight and he can see or realize through his mental sight, some of his degrading beliefs or some of his thoughts and actions motivated by some low-love or low-hate of his, in their harmful aspect and can obtain some true knowledge about the entity of his soul, its constitution and its condition. Therefore such a soul remains in a completely ignorant, unaware and blind state about its being, its degradation and diseases and their consequences.

Q. Are there persons who, on the one hand, due to their spiritual blindness are bereft of that sublime light which is necessary in order to see various truths about the organized entity of soul, its diseases and its evil thoughts and evil actions etc., and, on the other hand whose souls have become so insensitive that the sublime light cannot enter in them?

Are such persons completely blind from the point of true consciousness or knowledge about their soul and soul-life?

A. Yes, please. All such persons—whether they are connected with any so-called religion or whether they believe in no religion at all and whether they belong to this or that country—are steeped in spiritual blindness. And being in this state of absolute darkness or ignorance, they do the greatest harm to the fundamental and real thing of their being, i.e., soul.

Q. Isn't this state of spiritual darkness of a human being or his spiritual blindness the most horrible condition?

A. Certainly. Just as in the inception and complete development of cataract, man cannot see anything with his physical eyes even in the light of the sun, because the rays of the sun cannot enter into him due to his hardened lens and cannot bring the picture of the form of any of his surrounding objects before his mental vision, and therefore even on possessing the mental vision he cannot see the forms of these things; in the same way when the soul of some human being becomes so insensitive due to his soul diseases that even on getting a good spiritual occasion no rays of the soul-illuminating sublime light enters into him; then his soul remains in a state of absolute darkness and no picture of its being, i.e. of the bad or degraded state etc., of its inner self in any aspect, comes before its mental vision and therefore he remains completely blind or ignorant of the truths about them.

Now, if any of the truths were to be explained to such completely blind souls about the being of soul, its low-loves or its low-hates, or the various diseases produced in it thereby, or the necessity of salvation from them or its method, or the necessity for it of energy-producing higher feelings or forces, and the method of acquiring them, etc.; even then no truth about these subjects would come before their most insensitive and therefore completely darkened souls. That is, if they were given for study some book giving true knowledge about the various kinds of false beliefs in which they are entangled in the name of religion and if they could read it and even if they do read it, even then they do not see the falsity of any of those false beliefs of theirs and even after the study of that book they remain blind as before.

Q. Just as when an eye surgeon by operating upon a person suffering from cataract takes out the hardened lens from his eyes (and fits glasses), then the rays of the sun enter into his eyes and present before his mental vision the picture of the form of one or another surrounding object and he becomes capable of seeing them; in the same way is there no such method by which the insensitiveness of the soul which is produced by its various diseases, can be cured?

A. No, Sir. The cataract patient knows very clearly that he did not suffer from it before and that he has got it now, that due to this disease he is experiencing various kinds of handicaps and harms, and therefore he can also wish to be free from this disease of his. Therefore, hundreds of persons suffering from cataract wish to be cured from this disease.

But millions of souls, due to their slavery to pleasure-giving low-loves and the low-hate created by them, do not consider themselves to be diseased on account of them and not only that they do not feel any pain for any of their pleasant though degrading thoughts and actions and for any degradation caused by them; but, on the contrary, they experience pleasure. And in such a state, they become so blind that apart from their so-called religious teachers, though false, they become incapable of seeing some true worshipful being or true religious teacher in the true aspect of his excellence and remaining steeped in this state of their increasing soul-degradation and their daily growing darkness, they feel completely contented and happy.

Q. Amongst the darkness-ridden human souls, are there some such persons too, into whose souls, if they have not completely become insensitive, some rays of the sublime light of the Dev Jyoti-giver can enter on getting a chance and who on receiving those rays of the sublime light became able to see, according to their capacity, one or another truth about their own being and its soul-diseases and the causes and consequences of these diseases, etc.?

A. Yes, Sir. In those human souls who have not become completely insensitive, the rays of the soul-illuminating sublime light can, under favourable circumstances, certainly penetrate and they can to more or less extent illumine their souls too, and can also show them some false religious creed or belief or some bad action etc., of theirs in its false and evil colour. But the blindness of those human beings whose souls become completely insensitive, cannot ever and anywhere be removed, and it is inevitable for them so long as they live, to remain steeped in darkness and blind and in this state to become more and more degraded every day.

2. Perversion of Soul-Vision (Ulti-drishti')

Q. What is meant by perverted soul-vision?

A. It is the distorted vision in a human soul by which he sees the various things in Nature in a perverted aspect i.e. in various things of Nature whatever is true he sees and believes it to be false, whatever is false he sees and believes it to be, true And whatever is good he sees and believes it to be bad and, whatever is bad he sees and believes it to be good.

146

Q. This is really a terrible state!

A. Yes, Sir. But it is inevitable in accordance with the immutable laws of Nature for a human being to have such perverted vision about various things due to his pleasure-affording low-loves and consequent low-hates.

Q. How does this happen?

A. The being of man is made up of the force and material objects of Nature. This very Nature has created his being. He is alive or can continue to live only by the help of various other beings of this Nature.

By the violation of the life-promoting immutable laws of Nature, he is degraded and then on the continuance of this degradation, he becomes extinct as regards his individuality. By the knowledge and observance of the laws of Nature his being can obtain safety and welfare. He sees all these true characteristics of this very Nature in a perverted manner.

That is:

1. Several persons from amongst those with perverted vision, see and believe everything in Nature to be a force alone and believe only this force to be true and eternal. They do not see and acknowledge the real and eternal existence of any matter in Nature as real and eternal, but believe it to be like a dream and transitory.

2. Many from amongst such persons with perverted vision, see everything in Nature in the form of matter alone and believe matter alone to be real and eternal. All the forces in Nature are believed by them to be the expression of matter alone and they do not see and acknowledge the truth of the reality and eternity of any of them.

3. Millions, from amongst such persons with perverted vision, instead of seeing their own beings and the various things in their possession as parts of Nature which alone is real and complete and therefore their utility to lie in helping the good evolutionary work of this very Nature, they, on the contrary, see their utility in using them for the acquisition of various kinds of pleasures for themselves alone.

4. Lacs of persons from amongst such people with perverted vision, even though capable of doing one or another kind of work, yet, due to being lovers of pleasure

derived from idleness, see their good to consist in remaining idle and their harm in doing some necessary labour.

5. Lacs of persons from amongst such people with perverted vision, being lovers of money or other property, see the fulfilment of their life to consist in continually increasing it, and on their becoming misers they cannot use it to sufficient extent and do not use it even for their own bodily needs or that of their dependants. They see no harm in this but see their gain in it.

6. Lacs of persons from amongst such people with perverted vision, see more gain in giving to their own offsprings or other relations their money, property, some of their physical energies and mental powers, their learning and skills than in contributing these things wholly or to a large extent for the institution of real public good and thereby doing their own spiritual good and the good of others.

7. Millions of persons from amongst such people having perverted vision, in order to obtain various kinds of pleasures for themselves, do not see any spiritual harm of theirs, in indulging in different kinds of falsehoods, hypocrisy, fraud, breach of faith and doing various kinds of unjust and cruel actions, but in doing so they see their great cleverness and their very great gain.

8. Lacs of persons from amongst such people with perverted vision on coming to possess the money and property of their parents etc., on their death and, even on being capable of very well earning for the upbringing of themselves or of their dependents, see their greater good in utilizing the whole of that inherited money and property or a great portion thereof merely for the pleasure of their own selves or that of their kith and kin instead of contributing it for the spiritual good of their parents or some good of others.

9. Millions of such persons with perverted vision, being conscious of various pleasures and being lovers of them, see merely the acquisition of those pleasures and not their good as the aim of their life which is not the true ideal.

10. Lacs of persons from amongst such persons with perverted vision, being completely unaware and ignorant of the organized character of their soul, its degradation and the various truths about its life and therefore having no true knowledge about religion, see, due to their superstition-born practice, as completely mistaken and misguided even some such persons who have become capable of getting some Nature-based true knowledge about religion on getting a good chance of obtaining the soul-illuminating sublime light of Devatma.

11. Millions of persons from amongst such persons having perverted vision, when on hearing a sermon or some talk even from some of their true benefactor and well-wisher (leaving- aside others) against some of their false or sinful though pleasant act, get a shock on their love of pleasure, and become filled with hatred for him, then due to this feeling of hatred, they see him in, the form of a foe instead of a friend. And they see those persons with whom they are connected with one or another tie of low love and who are responsible for their soul-degradation as friends instead of foes.

12. Millions of persons from amongst such people with perverted vision, due to their vanity born of self-love, see those various persons who are really superior to them on account of their higher consciousness and knowledge in a certain aspect as inferior to themselves, though they themselves possess neither any higher consciousness nor any true knowledge in that respect.

So on and so forth.

13. The Production of Various Unnecessary and Most Harmful Pains for the Soul.

1. Various kinds of most harmful bodily troubles and pains which bring man's premature death—

Millions of human beings, on becoming lovers of the pleasures of taste, intoxication, sexual indulgence and idleness, so much exploit or misuse the various digestive and other organs of their bodies that these organs of theirs are damaged and they cannot discharge their functions properly. On account of the improper functioning of these organs, the toxins in their blood are not properly eliminated out of their bodies and on remaining therein, they produce various kinds of diseases in accordance with the immutable laws of Nature. By the production of these diseases, their health is lost and various kinds of troubles and pains develop in them. In the case of thousands of such diseased persons, these pains become so terrible that they writhe, very miserably weep and cry on account of them, and several of them, not having the strength to bear these pains and agonies and getting terribly worried by them, become ready even to kill with their own hands their very bodies (which they previously never liked to prick nor thrust even a needle in), and in such a state, hundreds of persons commit suicide.

Again, those persons who even on experiencing some kind of such most terrible troubles and pains at times, do not commit suicide, however produce various kinds of such incurable diseases by their various kinds of intemperate habits that they suffer pains from them for years and in some cases due to the atrocities of their such intemperate habits or excesses, they suffer for their whole life-time.

From amongst such persons those whose brains get greatly spoiled, become insane.

In the same way, the life of those persons who develop diseases like tuberculosis etc. by the infection of destructive germs in their bodies— and such diseases are developed in many cases even before youth or in youth—is shortened very much and in such condition lacs of persons die at an early or young age.

II Various kinds of most harmful pains for the soul, produced by bonds of undue attachments— Lacs of husbands are so attached to their wives and lacs of wives are so tied with their husbands and all of them are so tied with their sons, their daughters, their wealth, their ornaments, their one or other kind of animals and various other kinds of objects through their various low-loves that at one or another time, when any of their such ties is broken and by the breaking of the tie, they get separated, i.e. when due to death, running away, becoming averse or the occurrence of some other mishap in Nature, their relation is broken and they are cut off from each other, the tragic scene of the various shocks produced thereby and of the various kinds of pains which are produced by such shocks and the way in which such persons feel restless, weep, cry and writhe due to that pain, can be witnessed in every country of this earth. Had such persons, instead of thinking some human being or animal or any other object in Nature as their own and getting tied with it through one or another pleasure-affording low love, not considered it as their own and, instead of binding themselves with it through some low-pleasure, built their relation through some higher feeling, they would never have suffered these most intense pains.

Various kinds of most harmful pains produced by frustrated hopes—

Millions of persons on not being able to get a wife or a husband for themselves through marriage, millions of persons on not getting children even married, millions of person though having children yet on not getting a son married millions of persons on not getting the various kinds of political getting political or social positions and honours for which they possess strong desire, hundreds of persons on not getting through the examination concerning some intellectual knowledge in which they want to get through, hundreds of persons on not getting their ardent ambition of marrying a particular woman or a particular man fulfilled, thousands of persons on not getting the praise or receiving condemnation, for any reason from those front whom they have strong desire to get praise or not to get condemnation, hundreds of persons on not getting employment after continued search for it, thousands of persons on not getting cured of the disease from which they strongly wish to be cured, millions of persons on experiencing aversion or disloyalty from those family relations or others from whom they strongly desired true loyalty to them, millions of persons on not getting that pleasure from someone from whom they are anxious to get one or other kind of pleasure; hundreds of persons on being disappointed in love of some woman, man or boy for whom they feel love of some kind and whom they wish to return their love and millions of persons on not getting fulfilment of any of their other desires of such kind and on being unsuccessful and disappointed in them suffer, various kinds of mental pains, and in many cases, experience most intense and terrible pains, and thousands of them not being able to stand some of such pains go to the extent of committing suicide and die a premature death. The scenes of such pains can be witnessed in every country of this earth.

IV Various kinds of harmful pains produced by superstitions—

Millions of persons on acquiring from their very childhood, false-beliefs and teachings either in the name of religion or about various other matters from their parents or others become blind believers in different falsehoods due to their superstitions. Due to these superstitions also they suffer great pains at various times.

Being entangled in the meshes of such kind of most harmful false beliefs, thousands of women, in order to get children, take certain things in the name of medicine on being told by someone.

They get no children but on the contrary get one or another disease and continue to suffer from that disease.

Thousands of persons bring about several troubles for themselves by indulging in various kinds of acts in the name of magic or incantation on the suggestion of some one. Several persons fall in the trap of some alchemist and on losing even their own money or their existing property, suffer the pain of its loss. Hundreds of persons on becoming desirous of getting some pleasure of an imaginary heaven take to various kinds of mortifying exercises and through them suffer various unnecessary pains. Millions of persons on becoming greedy of getting the pleasures of some imaginary heaven through pleasing some imaginary god, take to pilgrimage to far off so called sacred places suffer various kinds of unnecessary pains. Several persons on being strongly desirous of getting some pleasure through 'yoga' form the habit of various such physical actions by the exercise of which their health is lost for all times and by becoming a prey to some disease they suffer its pains, and so on.

The true instances of such kinds of troubles can also be seen on this earth.

V Most harmful pains produced by jealousy—

Those human beings in whom the love of 'ego' or 'self' becomes so strong that apart from their own true or false praise, they cannot conveniently hear the praise of a true attribute of someone else and on hearing it, feel hurt in their heart and suffer pain, or they experience pain instead of pleasure by seeing or knowing any one superior to or happier than they in some respect. All such pains of such persons are called pains of jealousy. Thousands of men and women on this earth smart and smother under such kind of jealousy pains. And those in whom this most low feeling of jealousy is accompanied with a strong feeling of revenge, try to do one or another harm to persons of whom they are jealous.

VI Most harmful pains produced by revenge—

The most low feeling produced in some persons, on getting hurt or pained on their failure to get their object or desire fulfilled by someone, which stimulates them to settle scores with him by harming that person or his dear ones, either themselves or through others is called the feeling of revenge.

When this most low feeling in relation to someone even in relation to some well-wisher of their is aroused in them, thousands of persons burn in their hearts and experience pain in relation to him. Those persons in whom their feeling of revenge assumes a strong form, are goaded by its strong excitement to say even in presence of others, "Till I am able to perpetrate that particular harm to him—and in several cases to murder him—my burning heart will not be satisfied and my aching heart will not get peace."

VII Most harmful pains produced by vanity—

Due to their vanity produced by the love of ego, millions of persons falsely consider and believe themselves to be superior in - comparison to others even in those respects in which they are in fact very inferior to them or in which they have no true knowledge at all. They, due to the same evil feeling also falsely put much higher values on themselves than on those superior to them. In such a state, such persons receive great hurt and pain in their hearts when they hear some complaint or some beneficial talk from someone—even from some well-wisher of theirs--about some of their really undesirable action or conduct and smart under it for quite a long time. In this state of aggravated vanity, they get entangled and pick up quarrels etc., even with such persons from whom also they suffer various kinds of unnecessary pains. Several persons out of vanity about their physical power, in order to show their superiority, become careless in walking and running etc., or in attacking a human being or animal without any cause and thus suffer pain of various kinds by thus breaking some part of their body or causing some other harm to it.

Various kinds of harmful pains produced by crime—

Millions of persons being slaves to the arious pleasures of money and property etc., when in order to get them, indulge in theft, cheating, bribery, robbery, dacoity, forgery etc.

Again, thousands of persons being lovers of the pleasures of various other things commit various other criminal actions and due to their such actions are caught in the grip of the penal code of some country, then they suffer the pain of the fear of punishment and besides several other troubles also undergo the pains of the punishment of jail etc. The instances of this kind of troubles and pains can also be directly seen in different countries of this world.

4. The Loss of the Strength of Soul and its Complete Extinction.

On the production of various diseases the organized body of a human being, besides suffering various kinds of troubles and pains, also loses its strength, and on the continued persistence of some disease its strength continuously and gradually goes on decreasing, so much so that when its strength is lost to such an extent that the organs which keep it alive become incapable of doing their function, it becomes completely dead. In the same way, when various soul-diseases are produced in the organized soul of a human being due to his pleasure-affording various low-loves and their consequent low hates and such diseases go on aggravating; and they continue to cause its degradation; then as due to this degradation, his spiritual strength goes on decreasing on the one hand, and on the other hand when his such strength in completely destroyed, his soul also gets completely extinct.

It is an immutable law of Nature about body that though it may not be diseased, even then in order to make up its decreasing strength it is imperatively essential for it to gain its used up strength daily by the intake of the required amount of various kinds of food, by obtaining the light and heat of the sun to a certain extent, by breathing and living in the pure air, by sufficiently and properly exercising its organs through work or movement and by being temperate in habits etc., and if there occurs any deficiency in any of these items, the body will not only not get the required amount of strength but it will also lose its previously acquired strength to the extent of such deficiency. The proof of the decrease of strength of body on totally abstaining from food or not getting it and on doing excessive labour can be witnessed everywhere in this world. In the same way, the soul of every human being—even though for the sake of reasoning, it may be granted that it is not entangled in diseases of falsehood and aggression etc—requires every day, in order to preserve its existing soul-power and to produce new power in it in accordance with the inevitable law of Nature, to do disinterested service to a certain extent for the good or benefit of the various beings of different orders of Nature and to develop various altruistic feelings for rendering some such service. If a human soul does not possess these altruistic feelings the bodybuilding power which it has already got will continue to gradually decrease in the absence of any thought or action which could create such power and that soul will daily become weaker and weaker. Again, if it has some such feelings through which it is able to produce some strength in itself by doing altruistic activities even then if some hindrance occurs in their working on any account or there is any decrease or complete cessation in their functioning, not only will its power stop increasing but it will go on decreasing. And on its power being completely lost, it will one day die in the same way in which its or some other person's living body dies on the complete loss of its strength i.e., it does not then remain alive and dies completely.

Q. How can it be known that the inner strength of the soul of a human being is decreasing and it is becoming weaker every day?

A. The four symptoms by which the decrease of the strength of soul can be known are the following:

1. Loss of the Power of the Feeling of Higher Hatred

If a human being had higher feeling of hatred for some such thought or action connected with his body or his soul or both which was harmful to him and by the strength of this higher feeling of hatred, he did not indulge in that thought or action and remained safe from its harmful consequences; but after some time, he reached such a state that he became bereft or deprived of that higher feeling of hatred for that harmful thought or action i.e., he lost this feeling; and thereafter it was not only that he had no hatred for that kind of thought and that kind of action but he on the contrary developed attraction for the pleasure derived from it, and motivated by the attraction of this pleasure he began to seek and find it, then this symptom of his is a proof of the fact that the power of the higher feeling of hatred which was formerly present in him has been lost due to one or another reason. The proof of this truth can be found in the lives of different persons of this earth.

2. Loss of the Power of the Feeling of Higher Pain

If some person used to feel some pain or burning in his soul on indulging in some such thought or action which was harmful to him, and due to that pain he used to repeatedly desire in his mind to remain free from it in future or took some other measure for this purpose; but he gradually has reached such a stage that now he feels no pain at all in indulging in some such thought or action, but on the contrary, he experiences pleasure and endeavors to get the pleasure from such thought or action. Then this symptom in him is a proof that the power of the feeling producing higher pain which was formerly present in him, is lost.

In the same way, suppose some person on doing some undesirable, criminal, unjust or sinful action in relation to someone and on becoming or being made conscious of it, not only used to feel pain in his heart but used to feel so much pain that he became ready to express it to the wronged person in person or through a letter, to undergo some punishment for it or to do right reparation for the harm done to him in some other way, and only after doing some such expression of pain or its retribution, he felt peace or comfort in his soul. But afterwards he has reached such a state in which he now feels no pain at all on doing some such wrong action and does not want to express and does not express any only pain in the presence of some person wronged by him, and nor does he want to do, nor does any reparation for it. Such conduct of his is a complete proof of the fact that the feeling or force creating higher pain which he possessed previously and motivated by the power of which he used to perform various actions for the purification of his soul, has been lost. This true symptom can also be seen in the lives of various persons of this earth.

3. Loss of the Power of the Feeling of Higher Attraction or Higher Happiness

If formerly some person used to get the sublime light which is necessary to see some true altruistic virtue of some other soul and higher than this, the beauty of some spiritual excellence of the Devatma or his work and not only that he was thus capable of seeing that beauty but also used to feel higher attraction in his heart for that beauty and still more by the strong promotions of this attraction, he used to sing to others also the glory of that beauty through his own tongue; and motivated by this feeling he used to realize himself too, his (Devatama's) glory through his daily personal meditation and performed the spiritual exercises for realizing through it his own weaknesses and making by such realization his soul humble or meek by removing its hardness and creating and developing in himself by this whole process the higher or altruistic feeling of reverence. By such spiritual exercises he used also to obtain a kind of higher happiness or bliss. But afterwards he reached such a psychological state that no higher attraction was left in him to see and realize some such greatness and through it to awaken or develop the feeling of reverence in his soul and he ceased to get any higher happiness or bliss from such spiritual exercises and his heart became as hard and irresponsive as it was earlier. If formerly he used to bring before himself the beautiful picture of the benefits done to him by some benefactor and used to feel grateful in his heart for that benefactor and motivated by this feeling of gratitude used to render some disinterested service to him, but now there is no attraction left in him for that service. If formerly he used to feel attraction for some altruistic work and used to render some kind of help in such work but now there is no attraction left in him for that altruistic work and he gets no happiness or bliss at all from any such good activity. All such conduct of his is complete proof of the fact that the higher attraction in all these respects which was present in his soul and due to which he used to get higher happiness or bliss by doing some good work or spiritual exercise, has been lost and his soul-power based upon that higher attraction destroyed.

4. Loss of Body-building or Constructive Power of Soul In accordance with the immutable laws of Nature, like the millions of organized life-forces of the plant and the animal worlds, so long as the human soul also possesses the constructive power to build for itself, an organic body comprising of the necessary organs of various kinds and to keep it alive, till then by building through it some organized living body just as it can, on the one hand express itself, and on the other hand, it can keep itself alive as long as it is possible.

Again, in accordance with the immutable laws of Nature too, whereas it is necessary for a human soul, on the one hand, to get freedom from and protect his constructive (body-building) power from the degrading or destructive influences of its own and various other kinds of forces of Nature and, on the other hand, it is also necessary for it to grow and evolve various kinds of higher feelings for its growth and evolution. If it does not or cannot become capable of obtaining some such freedom and some such evolution or though capable, does not get some opportunity to obtain them, then whereas, on the one hand, the strength of its constructive power will not increase in comparison to its decrease, and on the other hand, its own previous strength will gradually go on decreasing by going against the law of evolution of Nature. And when the strength of its body building power is totally lost by gradual decrease, it will not be capable of constructing any other body whatsoever, here or anywhere else on leaving or being obliged to leave its earlier formed body and in such a state it is also inevitable for it to die and to be completely extinct as an individual entity with the death of the body.

Q. This is a very dreadful state. But is this the immutable law of Nature about the death of every living body-building life-force ('shareer nirmaankaari jeevani shakti')?

A. Yes, please. First try to realize this truth about the life-forces of the plant world. Now, if you take some such, grain of wheat, gram, lintel or peas, which possesses the power of creating or building a new living plant and if you sow it in proper season and suitable soil, and then help in the work of its constructive power by water etc., then there can grow a living new plant of wheat, gram, lintel or peas. But if you do not give it by some method an opportunity to construct or build a new living plant and allow it to remain completely idle, then in accordance with the immutable law of Nature, the result will be that the power of constructing a new plant and of increasing or developing the strength of its constructive force by every-day activity, which was previously present in it, will become weakened daily by remaining idle, and after a certain specific time it (constructive power) will be completely lost.

And when its constructive power is completely lost, then if you, in order to grow a plant out of that grain, sow it even in some suitable soil and help it also by providing all other favourable circumstances to sprout and grow, even then it will not be able to grow a new plant. Why? It is because the constructive power of making a new plant which was present in that grain before, has been gradually lost in the course of time on account of the grain lying useless.

It is such an immutable truth which you can verify in this very world by your own right experiment.

Q. This is absolutely true. But what proof is there to show that the power of making a new plant or the living constructive power which was present in that grain has on leaving that grain, not made a new plant for itself at some other place and is not living in it?

A. It is not possible for it to do so in accordance with the immutable law of Nature.

Q. How is it so?

A. Suppose that it is the life-force of a grain of wheat and there is so strong a constructive power present in it that it can construct a new plant from that grain on getting favourable circumstances. But in accordance with the immutable law of Nature until and unless its constructive power is not stimulated by sowing it in some suitable soil and favourable season on this earth and is not helped by water etc., or it does not get some favourable environments in some other place, till then it cannot do the work of constructing and evolving a new plant.

Again, even if it gets some favourable environment to do this kind of construction even then whatever suitable material it needs in the beginning for constructing a new plant, it can get that for some days, in accordance with the fundamental law of Nature, from the nucleus of that grain alone and never without it. Again, if that grain is sown in some soil and it shoots out its roots in the soil, then after that its life-force can be capable of drawing, in accordance with the immutable law of Nature, from that soft and wet earth by its root or roots all that material, by the nourishment of which it can evolve still further the form of that plant. Now so long as all these conditions are not fulfilled in accordance with the laws of Nature, till then it cannot construct a living and big plant. Now, if you do not let all these immutable laws of Nature be fulfilled in connection with the life-force of that grain of wheat, it will not be able to construct some plant in any way and by any other method.

Besides this, if you do not allow the grain to do the work of construction of a new plant and let it lie quite useless, then by thus lying useless and due to the working of the unfavourable influences of the various forces of Nature by which it is surrounded, it is inevitable for it to gradually lose the strength of its constructive power and to approach death and one day to get completely extinct.

Again, even when its constructive power is intact, it cannot do the work of making its plant in the first place anywhere else and with the help of any other material except the material of the, particular grain in which it exists. Therefore, either it does get such favourable conditions, before the exhaustion of the strength of its constructive power required by it to make a new plant, which may stimulate and arouse it to get that material from its grain and after making a tiny little plant from it, it takes further material for its development from the soil in which it has driven the roots of its tiny plant, or by the working of surrounding unfavourable influences it would gradually lose completely the strength of its constructive power and one day get itself wholly extinct. Without the fulfilment of this immutable law of Nature it cannot remain alive anywhere else or by any other method and its death is inevitable.

Again, in accordance with this immutable law of Nature, if some embryo of an animal or of a human being is born very prematurely due to miscarriage through some mishap, its life-force too will not be able, due to the absence of its earlier favourable condition, to do the work of making from that embryo, the living body of an insect or a bird or a calf or some human being etc., and on the cessation of its constructive work just as it is inevitable for the life-force of that embryo to get destroyed gradually, in the same way it is inevitable for that embryo to become dead or destroyed.

These are the truths which can be completely verified on this earth by reliable experiments.

Q. Is it then necessary for every human soul to protect or free its constructive power from the destructive influences of its own forces and those of different kinds of forces of Nature and to increase and evolve that power by developing in it the higher forces which may enable it to do the constructive work in connection with various departments of Nature?

A. Yes, please.

Q. And if some woman or man does not do so or cannot do so, is it also inevitable for his soul to go on being gradually degraded, to lose the strength of its constructive power and then, in course of time, to be completely extinct or die as regards its individual entity on the complete exhaustion of its strength?

A. Yes, please. It is also inevitable for every person, before it's complete annihilation, to get and suffer various kinds of unnecessary and undesirable pains born of his soul-diseases and various kinds of other spiritual pains born of undue attachments etc.

Therefore, it is inevitable for a person who, on being an organized living soul and on having made an organized living body through its constructive power, on the one hand, does not or cannot or would not become capable of protecting its soul-organism from its soul-diseases and of freeing it from the destructive influences of its inner degrading forces from which it requires to be freed, and, on the other hand, cannot or would not develop and evolve his constructive power by growing various kinds of higher feelings in its constitution and by becoming serviceable thereby to different departments of Nature and thus does not and cannot fulfil the law of evolution of Nature in his being, to completely destroy his spiritual organism one day and be completely extinct from the point of view of his individual existence by thus going against this immutable law of Nature. So long as his being is not completely destroyed and he remains alive to some extent, till then it is also inevitable for him to get and undergo one or another kind of physical and various kinds of mental pains as a result of his degradation.

Q. Then is it the only summum bonum of man to get freedom and protection from the slavery of all those low-pleasure-affording soul-forces which decrease or destroy that constructive power which has appeared in his soul and to grow all higher or altruistic feelings which increase and evolve its strength?

A. Yes, please. Only a fit human soul who gets consciousness or knowledge about this truth, can see and realize that this prime object alone is to be his ultimate ideal. But one in whom this consciousness is not awakened or cannot awaken, cannot know this fundamental ideal.

In such a condition it is inevitable for him to remain ignorant or in arkness about this fundamental thing, to walk the path of degradation and by being gradually degraded and suffering various kinds of pains to become completely extinct as regards his fundamental existence.

THE TRUE METHOD OF GETTING SALVATION FROM SOUL-DEGRADATION

I. The Salvation from Some Degrading Behaviour by Awakening of Higher Hatred

Q. How can a human being get salvation from some soul-degradation of his?

A. Man, by his very nature, longs for various kinds of low pleasures and then by feeding this longing of his, he becomes lover of all or most of them. These various loves for low pleasure of his and their consequent various feelings of low-hatred are the root cause of his degradation, because motivated by these, it becomes inevitable for him, in accordance with the immutable law of Nature, to indulge in various kinds of falsehoods and various kinds of evils in his own relation and in relation to others and to become lover of them also and due to this love for them to violate the beneficial laws of Nature about his constructive power or to go against it or to acts against and to become degraded every day through all such actions of his.

Now, so long any human being possesses attraction or love for any kind of evil action and aversion or hatred to the required extent does not awaken in him against it, by some Nature-based method, till then he cannot give up that falsehood, or that evil action of his nor does he want to give it up. Therefore, he cannot be freed from it nor can he be saved from the degradation that takes place in him, through it. This kind of feeling of aversion or hatred against an evil or false hood is called the feeling of higher aversion or higher hatred.

Q. How can this feeling of higher aversion or higher hatred be awakened in a soul?

A. First, if some sublime light could enter his soul which could show him in its true colours i.e., as degrading, bad, ugly or harmful, any of his degrading activity based on falsehood or evil, that was felt by him as pleasing and hence beautiful or attractive, and secondly, when the sublime power is imparted to him which may produce in him so much higher hatred for this degrading or harmful action of his that it may destroy the feeling of attraction or love for it, formerly existing in him and then his heart may not hanker after it and may experience aversion towards it.

Q. How and whence a person can get this unique and wonderful light and this unique and wonderful power?

A. Both of these can be obtained from some such soul alone in whom they may have evolved in the evolutionary process of Nature.

Q. Who is that soul?

A. That soul is the same Devatma whose mention has been made earlier.

Q. Can the rays of his sublime light and his sublime power be absorbed by every soul?

A. No, Sir. They can be absorbed only by some such soul who has not become completely insensitive in respect of some pleasure of his through its love and who possesses some capacity to absorb them in that respect. Such a soul alone is called a fit soul.

Q. Can all such fit ('adhikaari') souls get the rays of his sublime light and his sublime power?

A. No. Only those fit souls can get them in accordance with their individual capacity who get the good or golden opportunity of receiving them on the occurrence of some blessed event in the process of change in Nature. The reception of these two kinds of rays is also called reception of sublime influences. Except those fit souls, it is inevitable for all other human beings on this earth whether they are connected with some so-called religion, whether have faith in some religion and whether they do not believe in any religion at all, to remain in a state of complete darkness or ignorance about soul and soul-life and to be entangled in the meshes of one or another kind of false religions due to this blindness and therefore not to get salvation from them.

Besides this, if those persons who indulge in various evil-producing actions in relation to themselves and others due to their various soul-diseases, can acquire sufficient higher hatred in relation to their degrading actions only through the reception of the sublime light and power of Devatma and through no other method except this, then they cannot also get salvation from them without receiving the sublime influences.

Q. But cannot a number of persons be freed from various kinds of evils which cause them some real loss of wealth, honour and some pleasure of the physical health of their own or of any member of their family, by a sermon by some other fit person?

A. If someone who possesses sufficient hatred for the loss of wealth or honour or physical health, were to explain the evils thereof to those who possess some consciousness of some loss of such things or to try to make them understand it and to appeal repeatedly to their pre-existing consciousness about their loss, then some fit persons from amongst them, will certainly give up such evils. But it is also true along with this that several other such persons, in whom several kinds of evils are not present before, come to contract them by the sermon, persuasion or association of this or that person.

But the true salvation which a fit person can get from his soul-darkness and his various kinds of false beliefs and his various kinds of other falsehoods and his various evil-producing thoughts and actions in relation to himself and others to the extent he receives the sublime light and power of Devatma and he cannot get such salvation to that degree from anyone else.

Besides this, the extent and degree to which a fit person can evolve his higher feelings and higher life in his soul, by being able to establish the relation of his soul with the Devatma through altruistic feelings, to that extent or degree he can also never evolve his soul by contact with anyone else.

Q. How long any fit person can get these rarest sublime influences ('Dev Prabhavas') of the DaVita?

A. He can receive these 'Dev Prabhavas' of the Devatma only so long as on the one hand, he continues to possess eagerness or, desire in his soul to get these sublime influences and on the other hand motivated by this desire, he can get them (Dev Prabhavas) by true spiritual worship of the Devatma through his own daily spiritual communion with him (Devatma) or on being incapable of such spiritual communion himself, can get a good chance, to receive them through association with and sermon of some disciple of the Devatma—who is able to convey these sublime influences.

Q. If some person gets so many rays of sublime light of Devatma through his own personal spiritual exercise or through the sermon of some spiritually good person who can convey these influences, that he can see thereby some of- his low-love of pleasure or some of his degrading thought or action in relation to himself or to any other existence of Nature produced by that low-love of pleasure, as degrading for his soul but no higher hatred at all or in insufficient degree is produced in him for it, then can he in such a state get freedom from that degrading activity?

A. No, never. When the soul of a person reaches such a state that on seeing some of his degrading activity as degrading, lie cannot feel for it any higher hatred at all or in such sufficient degree by which alone he can give it up, then it must be understood that there is no capacity in him to get salvation from that degradation of his and therefore he can never have salvation from it.

Again, if some person has no desire at all present in him to get sublime light of the Devatma in requisite degree in which he can see the degrading aspect of the degrading beliefs, thoughts or other actions which spring up in him in relation to himself and others and higher hatred-producing sublime power in the required degree to give him salvation from them, nor does he actually develops them (sublime light and power) through his personal religious exercises, then also he can never get salvation from his degradation at any time and by any other means.

Q. Does a person get permanent salvation from his such degrading activity for which he develops higher hatred?

A. In some case he gets permanent salvation but in others it is not permanent but for some time only. If a person develops higher hatred in the degree in which it is necessary, in accordance with the laws of Nature, for permanent salvation from some degrading action then hegets permanent salvation from that degrading activity of his. But if higher hatred cannot be produced in him, in the required degree, then the duration of his salvation will be according to the degree of the higher hatred that he gets and not more than that. Afterwards, he can again fall into the same previous degrading activity.

2. Salvation from the Evil Effects of the Degrading Course by Higher Pain

Although a fit person gets salvation from one or another degrading activity of his, temporarily or permanently, through production of higher hatred, yet be does not get salvation from that spiritual impurity which he has produced in himself by doing, to himself or to others, some harm through that degrading activity.

Q. What is this degrading spiritual impurity?

A. By damaging or usurping some true right of any existence of the living or the non-living worlds of Nature, or by other action which is opposed to the good of his body or his soul, hardness and darkness etc. are produced in the soul of a human being. Such kind of diseased or bad condition of his is called spiritual impurity.

Q. Can such deformed or impure condition of a soul be reformed by some method?

A. Yes, Sir. If he can awaken in himself true consciousness in sufficient intensity about his such impurity, in accordance with the law of Nature, then it too can be removed completely or to some extent. That is to say that he should develop this consciousness that by harming himself or another person, animal, plant or thing in Nature, on being dominated by such and such low-love of pleasure or such and such hatred of his, he has thereby harmed his own soul.

Q. What happens by the awakening of this consciousness of spiritual harm?

A. If this kind of consciousness can awaken in sufficient degree in a person then pain for this spiritual harm of his is produced in him and moved by this feeling of pain, he wants to make reparation for the harmful action of his. This reparation is of two kinds:

(i) Reparation in relation to the harm done by him to someone else.

(ii) Reparation in relation to some harm done by him to himself.

From among these, on becoming conscious of some harmful action done by him in relation to another, when a person does any such action or actions by which the harm done by him or the undesirable trouble or pain caused by him to another is removed as far as possible; then such action or actions of his are called the action or actions of reparation.

Examples:

A person used to earn money by the sin or crime of taking bribes from others. He used to be very happy whenever and whatever money he got through this sin. By some good circumstances in Nature his soul got the opportunity of receiving the sublime influences of Devatma. On getting his sublime light he saw his action in its true or sinful aspect, and on getting His sublime power, he developed higher hatred for that sinful action to such an extent that afterwards he completely gave up that sinful action. Whatever money of others he had usurped remained with him and he felt no trouble or pain in keeping that money with himself. Then there came a time when he got more of the sublime power of Devatma so that he realized the truth in respect of that money that when the money that he had got through sinful actions, was not really his but belonged to others, he had no right to keep it with himself or suppress it. By the repeated concentration on this truth by him, on the one hand he begins to experience pain and burning sensation in his heart, and on the other hand he begins to feel repeated urges that he should purge this poison out of himself and should free his soul from this poison and this pain. He should not harm his valuable spiritual life by remaining engulfed in the temptation or love of that money. Motivated by this pain and this urge, he reaches such a psychological condition that he desires to return all the money got through that sinful action of his to all those from whom he had got it.

He returns that money to those persons or their heirs with a penitent heart—still more he returns it with interest and with an expression of sorrow—and still more he does not want to keep with himself or use for his own purposes or give to his children etc., even the money of the wronged persons, whose owners are untraceable but gives it in some good cause in order to be of help to it and by doing this he gets freedom from that impurity of his heart (an impurity that had been produced in it through that sinful actions) and obtains true spiritual purity. Now, if through the sublime influences of Devatma higher hatred to a sufficient degree necessary in accordance with true law of Nature for getting salvation and true soul-purity from theimpurity of this sinful action had not been produced in him, he could never have got true spiritual salvation from the impurity of this sin by putting faith in some so-called god or goddess like Ishwar etc., or by any other of the various false beliefs. In accordance with this true method of Nature every person requires this kind of higher pain in order to get salvation from any kind of his soul-impurities.

Q. Is it also necessary for those persons who, besides the sin of bribes-taking, usurp others money or property by other sinful actions such as cheating, forgery, theft, robbery, loot and dacoity etc., to develop higher hatred in order to get salvation from their such sinful actions and to develop higher pain to obtain salvation or true soul purification from the impurities thereof?

A. Indeed. So long as this law of Nature is not fulfilled in the case of any sinner, till then he can never get salvation from his sins and from the soul-impurity produced by such sins.

Q. If someone has not usurped the money or property of another but has unduly deprived him of his rightful peace or some of his rightful pleasure, then is it necessary for him in accordance with the laws of Nature, to develop higher pain so as to get salvation and purification from its impurity?

A. Certainly. Further, if some person has done even no harm to any other human being but has indulged only in some unjust or sinful thoughts in his mind in relation to someone, motivated by some low-love or low-hatred of his and though he does not commit any unjust or sinful action in accordance with his such thought, yet soul impurity is produced in him through his such thoughts. Hence it is necessary for him to develop higher hatred in order to get salvation from the course of this sinful thinking of his and to develop higher pain to obtain salvation or purification from the soul-impurity thereof.

Example:

Some person motivated by some low feeling of his, indulges in some unjust or sinful thoughts in relation to the money, property or lands of someone or the wife or daughter or sister etc., of another man, or some woman indulges in some unjust or sinful thought, of such kind in relation to someone's money, property, or in relation to some man. But beyond this, none of them does any other harm to another or he does not get an opportunity to do any such other harm, yet in accordance with the immutable law of the spiritual world of Nature, his soul inevitably gets harmed and degraded by the course of his these unjust and sinful thoughts. And in accordance with the immutable law of, Nature, there is no possibility of his freedom or salvation from this degrading activity of his or the impurity thereof till he develops higher hatred in respect of that activity of his and higher pain in relation to that soul-impurity.

Q. But how can those persons who experience only pleasure in doing some unjust or sinful overt action or some unjust or sinful inward thoughts in relation to someone else and in doing so they neither feel hatred for such activity of theirs, nor do they feel any pain for it, as is the case with thousands of persons connected with the various so-called religions of this world, get salvation from their those sinful actions or their such spiritual impurity?

A. In accordance with the immutable law of Nature, it is impossible for them to get salvation from both of these till the time that they, on possessing capacity for obtaining such salvation, get in sufficient degree, the higher-hatred producing and higher pain-producing sublime influences of some true deliverer.

167

Q. On being dominated by or becoming slave to some pleasure of taste or sex or idleness etc., one does not want to or cannot give up some edible or some other activity of his even when he knows it to be harmful to the health of his own body. Does such a person besides harming his physical health, suffer some spiritual harm also?

A. Certainly he does suffer spiritual harm also. When he deliberately decides in relation to his body that he does not want to give up or cannot give up such and such intemperate habit of his, because by giving it up he loses such and such pleasure of his and that he does not care if his body suffers some harm, thereby i.e., it becomes or can become victim of some disease or trouble, he deliberately sides with and loves that evil or harm and therefore by this degrading love of his, he, besides harming his body, certainly harms his soul also.

Q. If some person develops hatred and pain in relation to some of his pleasure-affording but degrading inner thoughts or overt actions, but he does not possess them in such a degree that he might get complete salvation there from, though in such a condition, he feels within himself a longing that he should get salvation there from; yet when at times he falls into such pleasure-affording but degrading thoughts or commits such pleasure-affording but degrading actions, then after indulging in such thoughts or such actions, he also feels in his heart some hatred and some pain or burning for his evil thoughts or action and troubled by that action of his he also condemns himself; self; then by what method can he get salvation from such condition?

A. In order to get salvation from this state, it is necessary for him to take upon himself some such punishments which may help to increase that hatred of his and that pain of his which he feels in relation to some degrading thoughts and still more for some other degrading actions of his.

That is to say:

If he sleeps on a cot then as a punishment he should sleep on the ground for some necessary period; if he takes his meals thrice a day, he should take only twice; from amongst the tasty eatables of which he is very fond, he should not take one or another such thing for a necessary duration; on being lover of money, he should fine himself a sufficient amount and give or donate it for the help of some desirable and good cause; he should take upon himself the spiritual exercise of thinking over the evils of his such degrading thoughts or actions and in doing so write a good number of letters or articles in order to increase his hatred in relation to them; in order to do reparation in relation to some person towards whom he has done such harmful action, he should try to give some comfort or peace to the heart of the wronged person by writing him letters confessing his fault and expressing his pain for it or by expressing to him in true words such true feelings of his heart, and if he has done some harm to some animal, then he should make due reparation for it by giving his money in sufficient amount in order to remove that harm being done by others also to that animal or its species or to other beings of the animal world or through some other way. So on and so forth. By accepting such kind of various reformative exercises and by becoming capable of carrying them out sincerely, one can also obtain much or complete help in getting salvation from some such degrading thoughts or some such other degrading actions.

Q. If some person has developed some higher hatred for some of his degrading thoughts or some of his other degrading actions, but it is not in sufficient intensity or degree so as to stop it completely, then what methods can be suitable for the further development in him of this higher hatred?

A. If he has the capacity, he can adopt for this purpose the various methods given below:

(1) To study with attention and concentration some such article or book which contains true description of the evils of that kind of degrading activity and thus to bring before himself and realize through such study those evils, and to continue this exercise as far as possible every day or even several times in a day.

(2) To sing with attention and deliberation such song which truly describes the evils of that degrading activity, and thus to realize through it that evil or those evils.

(3) To repeat with attention within himself some such saying of a few words as "That activity of mine is very bad or is very harmful."

(4) To remain in company of such a person who has got salvation from that degrading activity and who possesses very strong higher-hatred for it. To hear with attention if he gives some sermon or says something on this subject and to deliberate over the truth of it and to try to realize it more and more.

But if he is not able to adopt any of these methods or exercises and cannot also get any help from some capable person, then it is not only that no other thing can be helpful in increasing his higher hatred, but if no check is exercised from some other quarter against that degrading activity, then it is inevitable for his former higher hatred to decrease gradually and to disappear completely.

Q. Are not all the teachings about salvation false, which are given by the founders of the so-called religions of this world or their followers or by the preachers of those religions and which are against the true laws of Nature?

A. All of them are completely false.

THE TRUE METHOD OF DEVELOPMENT OF HIGHER OR NOBLE LIFE

So long as there is no awakening in the soul of a human being of those two kinds of higher or altruistic forces or feelings, the sprouting and growth of which does and can lead to the evolution of higher life in a human soul, till then there is and can be no beginning of higher life in him.

Q. What are those higher feelings?

A. Explanation of the higher feelings of altruism out of those two kinds of higher feelings, has already been given in the 19th chapter of this book.

Q. When and how some higher feeling of altruism is evolved in some human soul?

A. (i) If some person gets in his soul the potentiality of some such higher feeling in inheritance from his ancestors; and

(ii) If he gets the favourable conditions in Nature, to the extent and of the kind necessary for awakening and growth of it.

And if out of these two conditions none is satisfied, there is absolutely no awakening or growth of the higher power or that higher feeling in his soul,—and never and by no method can there be such awakening or growth.

Q. If a person inherits from his ancestors some higher feeling of altruism in a potential form, does that feeling necessarily awaken or grow in him?

A. Not in every one's soul. But there is or can certainly be such awakening or growth in the soul of some such person who gets, before the complete extinction of the potentiality of that higher feeling, some favourable conditions which protect it from the inimical forces of destruction of that potentiality, otherwise not.

Q. Does the potentiality of some higher feeling which a human being inherits in his soul from his ancestors get destroyed also?

A. Yes, please. If the potentiality does not get any favourable conditions at all in order to sprout or awaken, it gradually dies after the lapse of a specific period. When it totally dies then that higher feeling does never and by no method grow in that soul.

Example:

In some such grain of wheat, barley, gram or maize etc., which has got the life-force to construct the plant of wheat, barley, gram or maize etc., respectively, gets no chance or is not given such chance for several years to construct such plant; then its life-force goes on losing its strength gradually and completely dies after a certain period. After its complete death, just as no life-force of the same kind will ever grow in that grain again, in the same way no plant will grow out of that grain even if it is sown in the best of soils, watered properly, and whatever other means are adopted for this purpose, it will never and by no method whatsoever grow into a plant.

In the same way even if some person gets in his soul the potentiality of some higher feeling of altruism but does not get any favourable conditions for its awakening before its complete extinction, then that feeling also dies for all times.

Q. Does it also happen that some higher feeling of altruism may grow in some soul and it may continue for some time but it may afterwards die gradually?

A. Yes, please. It does happen that some higher feeling of altruism awakens sometimes in a person but then, due to unfavourable influences of several kinds of forces, it completely dies after some time.

Q. What are the favourable and unfavourable conditions?

A. When the life-force of a human being, an animal or a plant gets an opportunity to get help of all those external forces of Nature necessary to make its living body or its living form and then through that living body to gradually exhibit or express its various kinds of other inner latent forces, then it is called the acquisition of favourable environment or conditions; and the obtaining of the conditions opposite to those is called the getting of unfavourable conditions.

Q. Does not the life-force of every human being or animal or plant get some favourable or helpful conditions?

A. No. Millions of them do not get it.

Q. Then what is their end?

A. If they do not get all those favourable environments in Nature which are necessary for them to obtain in order to construct an organized living body or organized living form for themselves, then in such a state all of them gradually die out. And if some of them get such favourable environment only for some period and again cease to get them, the course of their construction will continue for that period but after that, it will cease.

Q. Does it also sometimes happen that the potentiality of some altruistic feeling which a person inherits from his ancestors, not only gets no chance to sprout but gradually dies out on account of his living and breathing in the unfavourable influences from the time of birth?

A. Yes, please. Under such unfavourable environment even the potentiality of some such higher feeling certainly gets extinct completely.

Therefore, it is extremely sad for a child who has got in him the potentiality of some such higher feeling, but has in his parents or family and environment such influences which are unfavourable or destructive of his potentiality.

Q. Then for the growth of higher life in the soul of a human being, just as it is necessary that he should possess the potentiality of some altruistic feeling in him; in the same way, is it also absolutely necessary that he should get all such kinds of favourable influences which in accordance with the immutable law of Nature are necessary for the sprouting and growth of that potentiality?

A. Certainly. The fulfilment of both of these conditions in necessary.

Q. Is it possible for any altruistic force of disinterested service to progress for ever if a human soul has received that force in heredity and gets suitable atmosphere for its growth?

A. Yes, provided that:

(i) The altruistic force of his is progressive in its nature; and

(ii) He, on the one hand, possesses in his soul those stable, bonds of relationship (or feelings) which are essential to permanently establish and maintain his union or communion with evolutionary or ever-progressive forces, and on the other hand he has in his nature no such antagonistic force which is likely to weaken or destroy those bonds of union.

Illustrations:

The living rounded bulb of an onion sprouts up under the influences of the required degree of heat and humidity of the surrounding atmosphere, even though it is not sown in any soil. On getting suitable environment, the life force within it builds out of the materials present in the bulb some stems and shoots out certain roots. But the stuff or material present in the rounded bulb is not sufficient for the life-force to build a full sized plant out of it, with the result that after sometime when the entire material present in the rounded bulb is spent up, the further work of building a plant out of it ceases. The life-force present in the rounded bulb not being able, to strike the roots of the bulb in some suitable soil i.e., on not being united or connected by means of its roots with a soil, is not able to get sufficient material to build out of them a complete plant. Consequently, the life –force of the rounded bulb is not able on its own to make any further progress in its constructive work. Again, this life-force surrounded as it is by unfavourable conditions begins to lose of the power of its constructive power. When the power of this constructive force is spent up, the life-force also comes to an end and ceases to exist for ever.

Similarly, when any human soul gets any seed of altruistic feeling in heredity, he is able to sprout it under suitable conditions. That is, he will not be able to develop to full stature his innate altruistic capacity, according to the immutable and eternal law of Nature so long as he does not establish his permanent relation with some such sublime soul who possesses the sublimest psychic forces in their complete form by means of which the sublime soul is able:

(i) To evolve the altruistic forces of a fit human soul to the fullest extent of his limit;

(ii) To support and develop all such various feelings as he has not been able to evolve because of lack of suitable conditions;

(iii) To impart to him the soul-illuminating sublime light in order to remove his soul-darkness and develop in him higher repulsion for all such low-loves and low-hates as produce that soul-darkness and thereby give him true liberation or salvation; and

174

(iv) To produce in him the realization of all truths which pertain as to the nature and organism of human soul and its degradation and thereby develop in him true soul-knowledge and besides this, he is able to grow in him higher attractions for all higher-life-promoting truths.

Q. Who is that sublime soul who is an embodiment of all sublime soul – forces (Dev Shakties), the permanent union or communion with whom is calculated to develop an individual to the fullest consummation or apogee of his innate capacities and thereby confer on him all-sided blessings? What is the method which Nature has placed for a fit soul to establish his stable or permanent relation with this sublime soul?

A. Such a sublime soul is none other than the Devatma in whose soul Nature has evolved the sublime forces after millions of years of its struggles and whose highest sublime influences according to the laws of Nature, produce higher changes in the hearts of fit souls.

The second group of altruistic forces which are important and necessary to establish stable soul-communion with the Devatma are dealt with in the next chapter.

THE TRUE METHOD OF COMMUNION WITH THE DEVATMA

The following four higher feelings are from amongst those various altruistic feelings by means of which a fit soul is able to establish his soul-communion with the Devatma:

1. The true and unshakable faith in his true Dev Rup or sublime beauty.

2. True and unshakable reverence for his true or sublime beauty;

3. Unshakable feeling of gratitude towards his true 'Dev Rup' or sublime beauty; for the highest spiritual blessings received from him; and

4. The feeling of attraction for his 'Dev Prabhavas' or highest sublime influences, So long these four higher altruistic feelings are not present to some extent in a fit soul, he neither establishes nor can ever establish any soul-communion with the sublime beauty of Devatma.

The description of every one of the four altruistic (satwik) feelings will be found in subsequent separate chapters.

II

THE TRUE AND UNSHAKABLE FAITH IN THE SUBLIME BEAUTY ('DEV RUP') OF DEVATMA

Q. What is meant by true-and unshakable faith in the Dev Rup or beauty of Devatma?

A. When a fit soul basking in the sunshine of sublime light (Dev Jyoti) of Devatma, comes to realize or get direct apprehension of this fact that by developing love or partisan spirit for falsehoods and evil thoughts and deeds, one degrades his soul and vitiates its constructive power; and by siding with truth and good thoughts and deeds, he increases the spiritual vitality of his soul and thereby promotes and blesses his soul-life; and further he also comes to realize that the highest sublime life which the Devatma has evolved in his soul by the unfoldment of the forces of complete love of truth and goodness is one great reality, which is above all forms of doubt and can never be questioned or doubted; then, by such a two-fold realization, he awakens in his heart an altruistic feeling of true faith which faith directly apprehends the truth and is itself a witness of that truth.

Q. Is it necessary for, a fit soul to grow true faith in some other truths before he can develop true faith in the Devatma?

A. Yes, please.

(1) It is necessary to see and realize in the sublime light of the Devatma, that Nature which through its evolutionary process has given birth to Devatma is a great reality; and that all true existences in Nature are directly the product of various forces and materials in Nature; that all existences in Nature degrade and vanish under the influence of unfavourable conditions in Nature; and that every

existence in Nature becomes better and evolves its capacity through assimilating favourable conditions existing in Nature etc.

(2) It is very essential to realize and put one's faith in the truth that every animate or inanimate object grows comparatively better according as it participates in the evolutionary process in Nature and grows worse or degrades according as it obstructs, opposes or grows hostile to it.

(3) It is essential to realize this truth in the sublime light of Devatma and strengthen one's faith in it that love for truth and love for untruth are two contradictory forces and it is therefore essential that votaries of the two must come into conflict and that in this conflict and war the ultimate victory inevitably lies with the lover of truth and its partisan or supporter.

(4) It is essential to realize the truth in the sublime light of Devatma and strengthen one's faith in it that in Nature love of goodness and love of evil are two contradictory forces, and the votaries of the two must inevitably, according to the law of Nature, come to close grips and in this great conflict or war it is inevitable in consonance with the evolutionary process in Nature, that the lover of goodness and his co-operators or, supporters must ultimately triumph.

Now, if a person is unfit to receive the sublime light of Devatma which is necessary to enable him to realize the above truths for establishing faith in their reality, he can never develop the requisite true faith in relation to Devatma.

THE TRUE AND UNSHAKABLE FEELING OF REVERENCE FOR THE SUBLIME BEAUTY ('DEV RUP') OF DEVATMA

Q. What is meant by the unshakable feeling of reverence for the sublime beauty of Devatma?

A. When any soul, illumined by the sublime light of Devatma, realizes to some extent the true sublime beauty of the Devatma and the sublime forces which have developed in it and by means of that light is, on the one hand, able to realize himself as completely devoid of those sublime forces and completely dominated by various low-loves and their resultant low-hates and thus a sufferer from various soul-maladies and on the other hand he finds and realizes, in the sublime beauty of Devatma, full cure of all the soul-diseases and full and suitable conditions for soul-growth, then and then only he is able, on the one hand, to directly comprehend the true glory of the sublime beauty of Devatma and his own utter insignificance and Devatma as his only refuge, and on the other hand, he becomes desirous of singing the glory of the Devatma or longingly hearing others indulging in the similar melody of song to the glory of the sublime beauty. By awakening such a desire or longing, he spontaneously bursts in to singing of his praises and listening to songs sung to the glory of the sublime beauty and by such an experience derives in his heart higher or altruistic ecstasy or joy. Such a soul-experience or realization is termed altruistic reverence.

By the development of this altruistic reverence, the devotee awakens in his heart true humility in Devatma's relation. By the development of this altruistic reverence the devotee awakens in his heart true respect for him and is anxious to make that feeing manifest in his relation. In fact, he makes an actual expression of that feeling. It is only when this altruistic feeling is fully developed in a soul that he is able by means of his inner vision, to see the true glory of the sublime beauty of the Devatina, and is able to fearlessly and fervently propagate that glory before others.

THE TRUE AND UNSHAKABLE FEELING OF GRATITUDE FOR THE SUBLIME BEAUTY ('DEV RUP') OF DEVATMA

Q. What is meant by the true and unshakable feeling of gratitude in relation to the sublime beauty ('Dev Rup') of Devatma?

A. When any soul charged with the sublime influences ('Dev Prabhavas') of Devatma realizes the various spiritual favours which he has received from him, i.e. the various false beliefs from which he has been liberated and the true knowledge about the true religion and soul that has been imparted to him, the freedom which he has got from various false and harmful rites and rituals, the physical and domestic blessings that he has received, as so many debts and obligations and when with a view to discharge the load of these obligations, he feels an urge to do some disinterested service to him and gets ready to know his holy wishes respecting those men, animals and plants dependent on him or houses and property belonging to him and endeavours his utmost to serve or protect them and even after his (the Devatma's) departure from this earth, he feels the similar strong feeling of proving serviceable to him and above all he is ready and fully desirous of sacrificing his mental and bodily energies, his wealth etc.; at the altar of his services, then and then only such a noble feeling 'of his, is called the feeling of gratitude.

THE FEELING OF ATTRACTION FOR THE SUBLIME INFLUENCES ('DEV PRABHAVAS') OF DEVATMA

Q. What is meant by attraction for the sublime influences ('Dev Prabhavas') of Devatma?

A. When any fit soul awakens, under the rays of Devatma's sublime light, to the truth that it is by means of the sublime influences alone that he is able to get true freedom from various soul maladies which he develops owing to the operation of various low-loves, which diseases degrade his soul and vitiate his constructive power and thus make him a wayfarer on the path of degeneration and he further realizes that it is by these sublime influences alone that he has been able to evolve to some extent such of the altruistic forces which help him to establish heart-communion with the Devatma and awaken and grow to some extent some other altruistic forces also and which altruistic forces can be sustained and become stable under the same sublime forces; then and then alone by such a realisation, he evolves in himself a desire and wish to imbibe these sublime influences more and more, Such a desire or wish for the sublime influences is known as the feeling of attraction for the sublime influences. If such an attraction or feeling for assimilating the sublime influences has not awakened in a man, he would never by himself perform any religious exercise to get them nor would he be able to acquire them by his personal spiritual exercises ('sadhana'). In such a state of his soul he would not be able to establish any soul-communion with the sublime beauty ('Dev Rup') of the Devatma. Hence by himself, he will not be able to have the privilege of direct worship of the Devatma.

Q. Can it be true that a soul may have developed in his heart to some extent true faith in Devatma, and true reverence and true gratitude for him and yet he may not have awakened in him any attraction for his sublime influences—such an attraction as may help him to do his personal religious exercise (`sadhana`) regularly and every day and by such a sadhana assimilate the sublime influences?

A. Yes. In such a state of his heart, he will not be able to truly worship Devatma, which worship is most essential for his soul-liberation and for the evolution of higher forces in him.

Q. What are the various spiritual losses a soul suffers if it does not and is not able to truly worship Devatma?

A. In the case of such a soul, no direct and systematic way would open for him to get freedom from soul-maladies and to grow higher loves in his heart.

Q. Does he suffer in any other way also?

A. Yes, he does. If by continuous degeneration in this direction, he loses even a desire for higher companionship ('sangat') which alone can help him to receive the sublime influences or loses his capacity to assimilate sublime influences even if he sits in such a higher society, then in that case he would be completely shut out of the possibility or chance of getting the sublime influences. In this woeful condition and in consonance with the inevitable law of Nature, he would grow more and more degenerated.

Q. But suppose a fit soul has developed a capacity to receive in his personal spiritual exercise the sublime influences of Devatma, can he continuously grow and develop his attraction for the sublime influences by his personal spiritual exercise?

A. If a soul is able by his personal spiritual exercise to acquire the Sublime Light of Devatma but is not able to conduct his life according to that light and develop higher repulsion or better than that higher pain for any of his low or harmful words, thoughts and deeds in relation to the Devatma, a human being, an animal, a plant or any other existence in Nature, and is not able to grow higher repulsion and higher pain for any low-love for wealth, fame, self-aggrandisement, children, husband, wife etc., even when he has seen them in their horrible form and in such a disability he continuously disregards the light and is found happy and at peace in that lamentable plight, then he will not be able to develop his attraction for the sublime influences. On the contrary, he will go on decreasing whatever attraction for sublime influences he possesses, till he loses it forever.

In short, any fit soul will be able to grow and develop this attraction only to the extent he is able to decrease the control over himself of one or other soul-degenerating love of pleasure and to the extent he is able to develop higher repulsion for such a degenerating love. But if a soul is not able to awaken in his heart any higher repulsion for a low-love or any higher repulsion for his degenerating belief, or for his degenerating thoughts, words and deeds, then in that case it is not possible for him, according to the immutable law of Nature, to awaken higher attraction for the sublime influences of Devatma.

THE METHOD OF SPIRITUAL EXERCISES FOR THE DEVELOPMENT OF THE FEELING OF FAITH TOWARDS THE SUBLIME BEAUTY ('DEV RUP') OF DEVATMA

Q. How can the feeling of faith develop towards the sublime beauty ('Dev Rup') of Devatma?

A. So long as there is no concern in the soul of a believer for the intensification of his faith towards the sublime beauty of Devatma, till then he cannot even be desirous of accepting any one of the spiritual exercises connected with the development of this faith. And, if on receiving the sublime influences of Devatma on some occasion and on finding a momentary wave in his heart to take to someone of the spiritual exercises, he begins it, then he cannot continue any such spiritual exercise.

Q. What is meant by the desire or the will to develop this feeling of faith?

A. If on receiving the sublime light of Devatma, a fit soul gets some realization of the sublime beauty, then in this state of realization, he will realize this most important truth also that the sublime beauty which is indispensable for removing his soul-darkness; for showing the degrading character of his various kinds of degrading beliefs, his various kinds of degrading thoughts, his various kinds of degrading utterances and his various other kinds of degrading actions; and also for understanding truths about soul and religion and for appreciation of the beautiful character of noble feelings for evolution of spiritual life, is not in him but is in Devatma. Again, he will realize that the sublime power (Dev Tej) which is indispensable for gaining salvation from such of his degrading activities from which true salvation is possible and for developing and growing true spiritual life for which evolution of higher or altruistic forces is necessary, is not in him but is in the Dev Rup of Devatma. On the growth of this true faith when he also knows that if by any cause this true and beneficent feeling of faith in him dies or is destroyed then there can be no greater loss to him than this and therefore he should deepen, strengthen and develop most useful this feeling of faith in him so that it never gets weakened or destroyed but becomes completely stable and unshakable, such a desire or will is called the desire or will for the development of this feeling of faith.

Q. When some person motivated by this desire takes to some spiritual exercises in connection with increasing this faith, does he experience some high or altruistic gratification or pleasure from it?

A. Yes, please, certainly he does. And if no low-love of pleasure, of his interferes in getting this higher pleasure, and does not destroy it and his attraction grows for getting this higher pleasure, then not only can he take to one or other spiritual exercises for increasing the faith but can also continue it; otherwise he can neither take to any such spiritual exercises nor continue it.

Q. If a desire in sufficient intensity grows in some fit soul for the development of his faith in the sublime beauty of the Devatma, then by what methods can he develop this most sublime faith?

A. If some such fit soul has become truly desirous of realizing the unique sublime beauty of Devatma and has become capable and truly anxious for getting his sublime light, then he can grow or evolve this true faith by sitting in some clean and beautiful place alone or in company with fit souls like him, and take to the spiritual exercises of realizing the following fundamental truths which illumine the sublime beauty of Devatma.

THE SPIRITUAL EXERCISES FOR THE REALIZATION OF THE FIRST FUNDAMENTAL TRUTH

"Study of and meditation over the Life-story of the Development of the Sublime Life ('Dev Jiwan') in Devatma"

To study how in accordance with the laws of Nature after millions of years of evolution of human species on this earth, love of goodness and truth first appeared in potential form in soul of Devatma and then in accordance with the evolutionary process of Nature when and to what extent and in what way they gradually developed. One should study this history of evolution from books and articles written by Devatma and deeply meditate in connection with this life history of Devatma over the following four fundamental truths about him.

1. How Sublime Love ('Dev Anurag') of goodness first appeared only in potential form in the tiny soul of Devatma; how this potential love of goodness in him sprouted in accordance with the evolutionary process of Nature; and when, where and in what way it grew and after growth how it established relation with all the orders of Nature; and how it developed various kinds of love for various kinds of goodness in relation to every department of Nature. There should be repeated realization of the evolution of this unique love of goodness and various forms of it.

2. Opposite to Devatma's consciousnesses of goodness there are various kinds of evil-producing thoughts and actions produced in various orders of Nature by mankind. In relation to these, he has developed various kinds of sensitivities against them.

There should be repeated realization of the development of these unique sensitivities against evil in the world.

3. On the evolution of the consciousnesses of good and evil in his soul in relation to every department of Nature, he realized the truth of most evil-producing disharmony in human kingdom in mutual relations of its members and between it and lower kingdoms and he developed a strong aspiration to remove this disharmony and to produce goodness-producing harmony in them.

Motivated by this strong aspiration he wrote for fit souls of the human kingdom prohibitions and injunctions and explained the methods of spiritual exercises for their realization, so that they may see their state of disharmony with all departments of Nature and get freedom from it and develop goodness-based harmony with them by evolving higher consciousnesses. There should be repeated realization of the unique excellence of this unique teaching of Devatma by study and meditation over these prohibitions and injunctions. To remove evil-producing disharmony and to produce goodness-based harmony in all departments of Nature, he sends out good wishes by singing the lines given below. There should be meditation over the excellence of his good wishes expressed in the song:

"Sakal vibhaagon mein Nature ke Uchchgati-prad parivartan ho; Neech-gati ho vinashat din-din, Sreshth meil un mein utpan ho."

i.e., whatever higher changes are possible in all the departments of Nature, through my sublime influences let those higher changes come, and whatever evil activities in their mutual relation can be destroyed, let them be destroyed and thus sublime harmony be born in them.

4. How sublime love (Dev Anurag) of truth first appeared in the potential form in his tiny soul; how this potential love of truth sprouted in accordance with the evolutionary process and when, where and in what way it grew and thus growing how it related itself to all the departments of Nature; and how he, due to evolution of this love of truth became lover of true knowledge and only true knowledge about every department of Nature.

There should be repeated realization of this evolution in Devatma.

Then with the evolution of this love of truth, in what ways he gradually became more and more capable of gaining true knowledge about Nature and in Nature about soul and how various kinds of false beliefs traditionally received under the name of religion disappeared and how he grew and developed various kinds of consciousness in relation to various kinds of false beliefs, erroneous thoughts, false utterances and wrong actions which are spread in human beings of this earth under the name of religion or between mutual behaviour of human beings or in relation to other kingdoms. In this path of evolution at a particular time, he realised Nature-based truths about soul and soul-life and after realizing them, he declared all the teachings that are current under the name of religion as false and he wrote and published books on true religion and prepared and made current the method of spiritual exercises of study and meditation for getting true knowledge. There should be repeated realization of the evolution of the unique love of truth in Devatma.

The study and meditation over the above four truths should give the realization that the life history of the emergence and development of the sublime forces in Devatma is absolutely unique. Due to the absence of potentiality of the sublime forces, there is no such life history of evolution of his own nor that of any member of his family or any other relation of his nor that of any countryman, nor that of any person of any country of this earth, nor that of a so-called god or goddess, nor that of a so-called Avtar, nor that of a maharishi, rishi, muni, siddh, buddh, tirthankra, jin, yogi, bhakta (devotee), guru, sadhu, mahant, sannyasi, vairagi, paigambar, pir, vali, and saint, nor that of a so-called special son of the so-called God or any acharya etc. For if he or anyone of them, having a real being, had been gifted with these true sublime forces in potential form and if they had developed in him, or in any one of them, then his own life-history, or of anyone of them, would have found resemblance with the life-history of Devatma. But there is no such life history either of him or of anyone of them. Therefore, this story of the evolution of sublime life in Devatma is a complete and irrefutable proof of his unique sublime beauty and sublime life. By repeated realization of this fundamental truth, a 'sadhak' (person who engages himself in spiritual exercises) gets or can develop in himself the true faith in the true sublime beauty of Devatma.

THE SPIRITUAL EXERCISES FOR THE REALIZATION OF THE SECOND FUNDAMENTAL TRUTH

Study of and Meditation on Various Writings concerned with the Supreme Ideal of Devatma

If in some soul there is development of the sublime forces of truth and goodness, then in the course of evolution there comes a time when they so strongly come to dominate him that they completely become his motive forces, and then in accordance with the law of the spiritual world of Nature, it becomes inevitable for him to sacrifice his various energies for their further evolution, to take stand in order to fight against all their hostile forces, and on entering this spiritual struggle for the triumph of them and on getting triumphant to do spiritual good to every fit soul as far as it is possible and on, entering this incomparable struggle to evolve more and more of his sublime life also, and to know and feel this and only this work as the one and only ideal or supreme ideal of his manifestation, and to live for it and devote life for it.

Therefore, in the development of this progressive sublime life of Devatma, there came a time, when he declared his supreme ideal before mankind, which supreme ideal due to the absence of true sublime forces had not been declared earlier by any so-called god or goddess or any so-called avtar of theirs or by any so-called founder of religion etc., because in the absence of these true sublime forces none of them could make such a declaration.

In accordance with Nature's own method, at the appropriate time, Devtma, on his thirty-second birthday, declared his supreme ideal, in a song as under:

"Satya, Shiva, Sundar hi, mera param laksha hovey; Jag ke upkar hi mein, jivan yeh jaavey."

i.e., May beautiful, truth and goodness, My foremost aim represent, And in the service of the world, May my life be fully spent.

Some of the sayings which reveal this very supreme ideal of his are:

188

"Satyasya premi aham, satya mayaa jayang labhet,
Shubhasyacha premi aham, subh mayaa jayang labhet.
Asatyasya shatru rahang, astayang mayaa nashtang bhavet,
Anritasya shatru rahang, anritang mayaa nashtang bhavet,
Ashubhasya shatru rahang, ashubh mayaa nashtang bhavet."

i.e., "I am lover of truth, let truth always triumph through me. I am lover of goodness, let goodness always triumph through Me. I am enemy of untruth and falsehood, let untruth and falsehood always be destroyed through me. I am enemy of evil, let evil be always destroyed through me." No one on this planet before Devatma had ever declared this supreme ideal—neither any so-called Vishnu, Shankar, Brahma, Ishwar, Parmeshwar, Parmatma, Vah Guru, Allah, Khuda, Lord, God etc., nor any of their so-called avtars or any special son nor any so-called rishi, maharishi, muni, yogi, bhakta, saint, mahant, siddh, buddha, tirathankra, nor any paigambar, pir, vali or guru etc., for none, in the absence of those true sublime forces which have manifested themselves in Devatma could possibly declare such supreme ideal. Therefore no one except Devatma has ever declared this supreme ideal.

For the realization of this supreme ideal of Devatma it is necessary to realize the four fundamental characteristics of it as given below:

1. The Progression in Devatma of Sublime Sacrifice of all kinds of pleasures for the realization of his Supreme Ideal.

For the realization of this unique supreme ideal just as it became inevitable for Devatma to wage sublime war against those who loved and sided with evil and untruth, and work for the triumph of goodness over evil and of truth over falsehood, it became inevitable for him to sacrifice all kinds of his pleasures whenever necessary. Sacrifices of these pleasures are called sublime sacrifices of pleasures.

2. The Progression in Devatma of Sublime Sacrifice of all kinds of his relations of caste, creed and society and family etc., whenever necessary, for the realization of his Supreme Ideal.

For the sake of the realization of his supreme ideal just as it became inevitable for Devatma to wage sublime war against those who loved and sided with evil and untruth, so also it became inevitable for him to part company with those persons of his caste, creed, family and other so-called friends etc., who became inimical to or were interfering, disturbing or hindering in the realization of the supreme ideal. This kind of sacrifice of all his such relations is called sublime sacrifice of persons.

3. The Progression in Devatma of Sublime Feeling for accepting pain in order to take and bear different kinds of intense and terrible shocks for the realization of his Supreme Ideal.

For the realization of his supreme ideal it became inescapable for Devatma to wage sublime war with all those lovers and partisans of evil and untruth outside his fold who on becoming enemies became source of torture to him. It became obligatory to bear great heart-breaking shocks and pains and intense suffering, physical diseases and other kinds of harms by their pain-producing various kinds of evil actions. It also became obligatory for him to receive and accept on various occasions besides ordinary hurts and pains, great special sufferings and intense pains and terrible tortures from various kinds of most low-activities based on ignorance, vanity, revenge, selfishness, lack of sense of duty, self-willedness, disrespect etc., of members of his own family and of his society. Again, it became unavoidable for him to receive and bear great shocks and terrible pains on his sublime heart by the most ungrateful actions of those from amongst his benefitted persons who on becoming ungrateful became ready for troubling him and torturing him in various ways and doing other harms to him. Still more, due to the wicked actions of various such persons, he on the breakdown of his nervous system of body, had several times reached the brink of physical death. And the feeling due to the most strong hold of which, he accepted and bore on himself all these kinds of great shocks, great troubles, great worries and extremely intense pains, is called sublime feeling of accepting pain.

4. The Progression in Devatma of the Sublime Feeling of complete utilization of all his energies, physical and mental, and of Education, Wealth and Property etc., for the Realization of his Supreme Ideal.

For the realization of his supreme ideal just as it became obligatory for Devatma to wage sublime war against those who loved and sided with evil and untruth so also it became unavoidable for him to utilize all his energies—physical, mental and of education, wealth and property etc. for it. This feeling of utilization of all these energies is called the sublime feeling of complete sacrifice.

This unique supreme ideal of Devatma is the second complete and irrefutable proof of his unique sublime beauty ('Dev Rup'). By the repeated realization of this second fundamental truth the faith in the true sublime beauty ('Dev Rup') of Devatma increases or can increase.

SPIRITUAL EXERCISES FOR THE REALIZATION OF THE THIRD FUNDAMENTAL TRUTH

The Manifestation and Progression of Sublime Light In Devatma by the Evolution of Sublime Life

With the gradual evolution of true sublime forces ('Dev Shakties') in Devatma, sublime light (Dev Jyoti) gradually developed in him which sublime light due to the absence of those sublime forces had not manifested itself before Devatma in any so-called god or goddess, or so-called avtar of theirs or any founder of a so-called religion or any other human being, so none of them had knowledge of these most important truths about the organic form of soul, its diseases, its degradation, evil consequences of its degradation, salvation from these consequences and its evolution of true life which are or can be known in the sublime light alone and without it they can be known by no other method and by no other means. With regard to these truths the whole of humankind on this earth was in a state of complete darkness.

Devatma alone on becoming capable of gradually developing his unique sublime light has seen and declared the hidden and most subtle important truths on these topics in course of time.

Leaving aside other books written by the Devatma, in this very third part of the Dev Shastra the light which is thrown on human soul constitutes absolutely new teachings.

Only through true understanding of this teaching, a fit soul can get true knowledge of religion and this truth does or can dawn on him as also that before Devatma none in mankind had any true knowledge about religion and before him no so-called god or goddess or founder of any religion had propagated true knowledge about religion. In fact, its propagation was not possible through any soul steeped in spiritual darkness.

The fundamentals of the most subtle truths which dawned on Devatma by the gradual development of this unique sublime light, are the following:

1. Whatever true knowledge there is about the organized form of soul and its diseases, its degradation and death, its freedom from its degradation and growth of higher life, that and that knowledge alone is the true knowledge about religion. Apart from this true knowledge whatever beliefs or faiths are held on this earth under the name of religion— beliefs about one or another Imaginary god, about

his false praise, about false prayer to him, about recitation of some mantra about him or its name or about getting pleasure or bliss by some kind of union or by some other method etc. — none of these beliefs or faiths constitute true knowledge of religion.

2. The basis of true knowledge of religion is one true Nature alone. For this reason for the sake of getting true knowledge of religion it is necessary to know the fundamental truths about true Nature. So whatever and to whatever extent teachings current under the name of religion, in the various religions on this earth, are against the fundamental laws of real Nature, all of them are completely false.

3. Devatma, who is endowed with complete sublime love of goodness and truth and complete sublime hatred of their opposites, evil and untruth, is the only true deity and no real existence wanting in these sublime forces is a true deity.

4. Due to being true deity, Devatma alone is the only true worshipful being for all fit human souls, and no one other than him is true worshipful being.

5. Only due to the presence and motivation of various kinds of low-loves of pleasure and their consequent various kinds of feelings of low hatreds in human souls, all kinds of falsehoods and all kinds of evils are produced. These very low-loves of pleasure and their consequent feelings of low-hatreds in them are the main causes of all kinds of falsehoods and all kinds of evils in the human kingdom. It is through both of them, that human soul suffers degradation or death or extinction. So no pleasure whatsoever can be the ideal of the life of any human being.

6. To get freedom as far as possible, from all kinds of low-loves of pleasures and from all low-hatreds which are produced by them and from all those kinds of falsehoods and all those kinds of evils which are produced by both of them (by low-loves and low-hatreds), alone is true salvation and apart from it there is no other true salvation.

7. Only by awakening and development in some human soul of higher or altruistic feelings of service of others and of feelings which establish spiritual relation with Devatma, is there development of higher or true religious life. By gaining of this higher life, his life force or his constructive power is increased. Without the development of these higher forces there is neither growth of higher or religious life nor is his constructive power increased.

8. To whatever extent and to whatever degree true salvation is or can be got by some fit soul in accordance with his capacity, through getting sublime influences

of Devatma, that he does not and cannot get by any other method. In the better-gifted fit souls the extent to which their higher altruistic feelings can establish high spiritual relation with the sublime beauty of Devatma and on attaining to these higher altruistic feelings and establishing relationship with Devatma, the extent of the development of higher life which can and does take place, to that extent the higher development cannot take place by any other method. And the extent to which the path of progress of their future true salvation and future higher life can be opened by the establishment of their spiritual relation with his sublime beauty, to that extent that path does not and cannot open by any other means.

These are the most fundamental truths which Devatma alone has seen and revealed through his unique sublime light and which no human being or so-called god or goddess devoid of this sublime light had ever seen and had therefore never revealed them either. Again, a fit soul also can see these fundamental truths only on receiving the sublime light of Devatma and never without this sublime light.

The work of higher changes in fit human beings through this Sublime Light

1. When some rays of this unique sublime light of Devatma reach the soul of a fit person, then through it his spiritual darkness is removed, and many kinds of false beliefs which he had received earlier under the name of religion, appear to him false, which without this sublime light had never appeared to him earlier as false.

2. A fit soul on receiving rays of this very sublime light of Devatma is able to see one or another degrading thought or degrading activity of his as degrading or harmful for himself, which before receiving the sublime light did not appear as of degrading or harmful character to him.

3. A fit soul on receiving rays of this very sublime light of Devatma, is able to appreciate the beauty or utility of one or other higher or altruistic feeling for himself, which before receiving the sublime light did not appear to him in its beauty and utility.

4. A fit soul on receiving rays of this very sublime light of Devatma, is able to see one or other shortcoming of his, which before receiving the sublime light did not so appear to him at all.

For bringing higher changes in fit souls by this very sublime light of his, Devatma sings the song of good wishes in his daily spiritual exercises, some of the stanzas of which are these:

"Atma-timar-har Devjyoti mam;
Aatma-prakashak Devjyoti mam,
Aatma-bodh-prad Devjyoti mam
Chaaron dig veh parkeeran ho!
Timar se niklen jan adhikaari,
Aatma-rup dekhen adhikaari,
Aatma-rog dekhen adhikaari,
Aatma-paat dekhen adhikaari,
Aatma-hit dekhen adhikaari,
Aatma-gyan un mein utpann ho,
Satya-Dharma ka gyan utpann ho."

Translation:

Soul-darkness-dispelling Sublime-light mine;
Soul-illuminating Sublime-light mine;
Soul-consciousness giver Sublime-light mine;
Be that spread in quarters four;
From darkness be out deserving beings,
Soul's real form be seen by the deserving ones,
Their soul-diseases be seen by the deserving ones
Their soul-degradation be seen by the deserving ones
Their soul-welfare be seen by the deserving ones.
Soul's knowledge be in them awakened,
True Religion's (Dharma's) knowledge be awakened,

In conclusion, just as all these manifestations and characteristics of the sublime light are unique so also this sublime light which has developed in Devatma is the third complete and irrefutable proof of the true sublime beauty in Devatma.

By repeated realization of this third fundamental truth also, feeling of faith in the sublime beauty of Devatma is or can be increased.

THE SPIRITUAL EXERCISES FOR THE REALIZATION OF THE FOURTH FUNDAMENTAL TRUTH

The Emergence and Development of the Unique Sublime Power in Devatma by the Growth of Sublime Life

With the gradual growth of the true sublime forces in Devatma, there gradually developed that sublime power (Dev Tej) comprising of the following four sublime feelings, which also had not developed before him in any of the so-called gods or goddesses or their so-called incarnation ('avtar') or in any founder of any so-called religious society or in any other person devoid of his sublime forces of truth and goodness.

1. The Growth of Sublime Hatred in Devatma connected with his Sublime Power

1. With the gradual development of sublime loves of goodness and truth in Devatma there gradually grew, in accordance with the fundamental laws of Nature, apposite to these, the forces of hatred or feelings of hatred towards evil and untruth. These very feelings of hatred are called sublime hatred ('Devghirna').

2. With the gradual development of this sublime hatred in Devatma there gradually grew the feelings of hatred against all kinds of falsehoods about human souls and their all kinds of inner and outer evil-based activities.

3. Due to the development of this sublime hatred in Devatma, no kind of love of pleasure could or did grow in him in accordance with the laws of Nature; for by a love of pleasure alone various kinds of falsehoods and various kinds of evils are produced. Therefore, unlike human souls, Devatma never became, nor could he become and nor did he become, lover of any kind of pleasure.

4. Due to growth of hatred in Devatma, as it was inevitable in accordance with the laws of Nature, no love could or did grow in him for any of the objects of pleasure i.e., for any human being, animal, plant, or tree, money, land, house or any other object; and unlike human beings he never became nor could he become and nor did he become lover of any object connected with pleasure.

5. There being no growth of love in Devatma for any object of pleasure i.e., for any human being, animal, plant or tree, money, land, house or any other object, there could not and did not grow any kind of partiality for any one of them and unlike human souls he never became and nor could he become and nor did become partial to anyone of them.

6. There being no growth of love in Devatma for any object of pleasure i.e., any human being, animal, plant or tree, money, land, house or any other thing, there could not and did not grow slavery in relation to anyone of them at all and therefore he was not tied to anyone of them with low attachments and neither did he become and nor could became slave to any one of them.

7. There being no growth of love in Devatma for any object of pleasure i.e., any human being, animal, plant or tree, money, house, or any other thing, there could never grow any feeling of hatred towards anyone of them and unlike human souls he never became and nor could become and nor did come to hate any one of them.

8. There being no feeling of hatred in Devatma for any human being, animal, plant or tree of Nature, nor for any of its inanimate things, there could not and did not grow feeling of revenge, or retaliation or jealousy in relation to anyone of them and unlike human souls he neither became, and nor could become, and nor did become revengeful or jealous.

2. The Growth in Devatma of the Sublime Pain connected with His Sublime Power
In the human beings through their low-loves of pleasures and their low-hates, various kinds of completely undesirable intense sufferings and intense pains are produced in human world whether in their various mutual relations or in relation to lacs of beings of the animal world and various kinds of harms are done to the various existences of the still lower worlds and thus relations of mankind have become unjust or irreligious. The pain which has gradually developed in Devatma towards these irreligious relations of man is called sublime pain.

3. The Development of Sublime Enmity in Devatma connected with His Sublime Power

An inimical feeling has gradually grown with the gradual development of the sublime pain in Devatma, towards man's low- loves of pleasure and their consequent low-hatreds and all kinds of falsehoods and evils which are produced by them. The feeling of enemity which has become more and more intense towards these low-loves and these low-hatreds and various kinds of evils produced by them, is called the feeling of sublime enemity.

4. The Growth of Sublime Faith in Devatma connected with His Sublime Power

With the gradual progress of the sublime struggle in Devatma connected with the sublime power, just as his feeling of destroying all kinds of evils and untruths and gaining triumph over them grew from day to day, so did his engagement in sublime struggle. By gaining triumph with the help of evolutionary forces in Nature over the lovers and partisans of untruth and falsehood through triumph of goodness over evil and of truth over untruth, his faith in the triumph of truth and goodness connected with the evolutionary process of Nature went on getting stronger in him. This faith is called sublime faith. The following is the saying of Devatma in connection with this sublime faith:

"Asatyasay seh sangramme, Satya meyav labhte jaiyam;

Ashubhasay seh sangramme, Subh meyav labhte jaiyam."

Meaning: On there being a conflict with untruth, truth alone triumphs; on there being a conflict with evil, goodness alone triumphs.

The Work of Producing Higher Changes in Fit Human Souls through Sublime Power of Devatma

1. When some rays of this unique sublime power of Devatma find a chance to enter a fit soul, then getting the rays of the sublime light whatever belief or faith in regard to his soul or religion appears to him to be false, towards that false belief or false-faith higher hatred is produced.

This higher hatred was not in him earlier; and if the rays of sublime power can enter his soul in such an amount, which amount alone can, in accordance with the laws of the spiritual world of Nature, completely destroy his false belief or faith, then on the production of the higher hatred of that amount it becomes inevitable for him to give up that belief and to get true salvation from that dear false belief or faith of his.

2. When some rays of this unique sublime power of Devatma enter a fit soul, then on getting the rays of the sublime light of His whatever degrading thought or/ and action appears in degrading or harmful form to him, towards that degrading thought and action, higher hatred is produced which higher hatred was not in him before. And if rays of this sublime power can enter his soul in such an amount, the entry of which amount alone can, in accordance with the laws of the spiritual world of Nature, completely destroy that degrading thought and degrading action of his, then on production of higher hatred in his soul to that extent, it becomes inevitable for him to get true salvation from that degrading thought or/and action of his.

3. When some rays of this unique sublime power of Devatma enter a fit person, then on getting rays of sublime light of His, whatever spiritual distortion has appeared to him in harmful or degrading form for his soul, towards that spiritual distortion higher pain is produced which higher pain was not in him earlier. And if rays of this sublime power can enter in his soul in such an amount, the entry of which amount alone can, in accordance with the laws of the spiritual world of Nature, remove that degrading spiritual distortion of his, then on the production in his soul of higher pain to that extent, it becomes inevitable for him to do

reparation in relation to that spiritual distortion of his and through it, get as far as it is possible, true purity or true salvation from it.

4. When some rays of this unique sublime power of Devatma enter a fit soul, then on getting rays of sublime light of His whatever higher or altruistic feeling appears beautiful and useful for him, towards that he feels attraction. This attraction was not in him earlier. And if he can get rays of this sublime power of Devatma continuously and if he can assimilate them, then, on getting them in necessary amount, that feeling of attraction of his can still more develop gradually, in accordance with the laws of the spiritual world, and he can also become lover of the higher pleasure of that higher or altruistic feeling and on his becoming lover he can develop higher life in his soul through it.

For producing higher changes in fit persons through this sublime power of His, the Devatma sings His 'hymn of good wishes' in His daily spiritual exercises, which it is as follows:

"Uchch-ghrina-prad Dev Tej mam,
Uchch-dukha-prad Dev Tej mam,
Neech-raag-har Dev Tej mam,
Neech-ghrina-har Dev Tej mam;
Chaaron-dig weh parkeeran ho !
Uchch-ghrina paaven adhikaari
Uchch-dukh paaven adhikaari,
Neech-raag tyagen adhikaari,
Neech-ghrina tyagen adhikaari,
Aatma-rog se nistaaran ho!
Aafma-paat se nistaaran ho!
Neech-gati se nistaaran ho!
Parama-lakshya mera pooran ho,
Jeevan-brat mera pooran ho !
Uchch-bhaava-prad Dev Tej mam,
Uchch-raag-prad Dev Tej mam,
Chaaron dig weh parkeeran ho!
Uchch-bhaava paaven adhikari
Uchch-raaga paaven adhikari
Uchch-ang paaven adhikari
Uchch-gati paaven adhikari
Uchch-roop un mein utpann ho!
Shreshth-roop un mein utpann ho!
Aatm-bal Un mein utpann ho!

Jeevan-bal un mein utpann ho!
Parama-lakshya mera pooran ho;
Jeeven-brat mera pooran ho !"

Translation:

High-hate-awakening power-sublime mine,
High-pain-awakening power-sublime mine,
Low-love-dispelling power-sublime mine,
Low-hate-dispelling power-sublime mine,
Be that spread in quarters four,
High-hate be gained by the fit,
High-pain be gained by the fit,
Low-love be renounced by the fit,
Low-hatred be renounced by the fit;
They be free from the illness of soul
They be free from the fall of soul
They be free from the low-activity
May my ultimate aim be fulfilled
May my Life-Vow be fulfilled
High-feeling-imparting power sublime mine
High-love-imparting power sublime mine
Be that spread in quarters four;
High-feelings be developed by the fit
High-love be developed by the fit
High-capacity be developed by the fit
High activity be developed by the fit
High-form in them be awakened
Beautitude in them be awakened
Vigour of soul in them be developed
Vigour of life in them be developed
May my ultimate aim be fulfilled
May my Life-Vow be fulfilled.

Just as all these unique characteristics connected with the sublime power of Devatma had also not appeared and did not appear in any of the so-called gods or goddesses devoid of the true sublime forces, so also they never appeared and nor could appear in their so-called `avtar' or in founder of any so-called religion or any other human being.

By the realization of these four fundamental truths through the study of and meditation on the various books and articles written by Devatma in connection with the true sublime beauty of his, every fit soul can grow his true feeling of faith towards him to the limit of capacity.

THE METHOD OF SPIRITUAL EXERCISES FOR THE DEVELOPMENT OF THE FEELING OF REVERENCE TOWARDS THE SUBLIME BEAUTY ('DEV RUP') OF DEVATMA

Q. How can a person reverent towards the sublime beauty ('Dev Rup') of Devatma develop his feeling of reverence?

A. So long a person, reverent towards the sublime beauty ('Dev Rup') of Devatma, feels no concern to develop his feeling of reverence, he cannot even be desirous to take to any of the spiritual exercises connected with the development of this feeling of reverence. And if on some occasion, on getting the sublime influences of Devatma there is a momentary impulse in his heart to take to the spiritual exercises and even if he begins it, he cannot continuously do any one of them.

Q. What is meant by the concern to develop this feeling of reverence?

A. The growth of this feeling of reverence produces higher altruistic gratification or higher pleasure. When a person develops so strong an attraction for such gratification or pleasure that he, of his own accord, wants to get it again and again and feels pain on not getting it, then this craving of his in this connection is called his altruistic desire or will.

Q. Is such a desire not present in every reverent person of Devatma?

A. No.

Q. Does it also happen that such a desire awakens and persists in some rare persons for some days and then dies out?

A. Yes, please.

Q. Why does it so happen?

A. Such persons have in their souls various kinds of low-loves of pleasure, which due to being inimical to this altruistic pleasure remove or destroy it in some days and then they are not at all desirous of this altruistic pleasure and they are content to get these low pleasures of theirs.

Q. But if in some comparatively better soul there is produced a desire or will, strong enough for the development of his feeling of reverence in relation to the sublime beauty of Devatma, then by what method can he develop it?

A. The various methods by which such a person can develop this feeling are as under:

(1) It has already been described how the feeling of faith can be awakened and developed by the realization of fundamental truths through the spiritual exercises of study and meditation on them. A reverent person can intensify his feeling of reverence too, by the realization of the fundamental truths with the spiritual exercises of study and meditation on the sublime beauty of Devatma as stated earlier (in the last chapter).

(2) On receiving the sublime light of Devatma, such a reverent person, irrespective of time and place, gets some realization of His sublime beauty, and on knowing himself to be desirous of it, feels himself insignificant in comparison with this sublime beauty of His. In this state of reduced vanity, if he exhibits his true feeling of respect by doing salutation, by bending his head as low as it is possible in all humility before his sublime beauty, and if he makes it a habit of remaining in that state of showing respect to the extent to which he can, then by this spiritual exercise he can develop his feeling of reverence for Him.

(3) On the growth of true reverence towards the sublime beauty of Devatma, it becomes necessary for such a reverent person to grow the feeling of respect towards one or other person or animal, garden, tree, plant or house or various other kinds of things (especially books and articles written by Him) connected with Him. The feeling of reverence for Devatma is developed by giving heart-felt respect in necessary and desirable degree towards them.

(4) On possessing reverence for Devatma, it is obligatory for a reverent person not to feel inclined to hear anything against the true sublime beauty of His from

anyone of his haters or from any person of perverted vision or to read articles of such a critic or to sit near him, mix with him, or have his company, and to reduce or remove if such an inclination was ever present. So also on hearing from the mouth of some such inimical person anything against His sublime beauty or reading about it in some article, or on getting true information about it from someone else, it becomes obligatory for him to feel shock in his heart for such perverted criticism. Therefore, if on some such occasion of false presentation of Devatma, a reverent person does not sit quiet but tries to expose that falsehood, then through such spiritual exercises, he can also intensify his true - feeling of reverence towards Him.

(5) The parents who gave birth to Devatma, the place where he was brought up for years by His parents who were the authors of His existence, protectors, nurses and educators and the part played by His revered parents, His grand-parents and other ancestors in His emergence, by their sublime life, are objects of reverence for a reverent soul. The desire to gain knowledge of his birth-place and of His benefactor parents and other ancestors and a feeling of proper respect towards them and enthusiastic description of their qualities and urge to have `darshan' of them and if possible have a pilgrimage of His birth-place and place of His childhood, is necessary for a reverent person. By such spiritual exercises also a reverent person can grow his feeling of reverence towards Him.

(6) Besides His birth-place, if Devatma has lived at some places for specific periods and on any such place memorials inspiring higher feelings like reverence etc., have been preserved, and still more if some shrine of.

His has been erected, then it is obligatory for a reverent person to have desire for `darshan' of such places and such memorials and such shrines. Therefore, if a reverent person motivated by this kind of true feeling visits such places in proper attitude, then through these spiritual exercises his feeling of reverence can get deepened.

(7) On awakening of the sense of true reverence in relation to the sublime beauty of Devatma, every reverent person will experience life-promoting higher bliss by singing or hearing them sung, one or another hymn ('stotar') or religious song ('bhajan') in His glorification or `aarti' expressing the beauty of His sublime 'Rup' by singing the praise of His sublime beauty as also by hearing it sung by other reverent people; by reading, or hearing them read, the life-stories of His sublime life and by performing such other spiritual exercises or by joining those performed by others. In this way too a truly reverent person can develop reverence for Devatma by every such spiritual exercise.

(8) On the growth of the true feeling of reverence towards the sublime beauty of Devatma, it is obligatory for Very such reverent person of His to show respect to all such reverent persons of His who have been true believers in His sublime beauty and who have been reverent towards His sublime beauty throughout their life. It is also obligatory for a reverent person to show still more respect for such persons among them who have, besides reverence towards Devatma, gratitude and who have grown and developed some feelings of service towards His supreme ideal and who have given good proof of the presence of these altruistic feelings in their souls. By the study and meditation over these topics from the life stories of such persons and by study of and meditation over their sermons on these topics, a reverent person can intensify his feeling of reverence for Devatma.

THE METHOD OF SPIRITUAL EXERCISES FOR THE DEVELOPMENT OF THE FEELING OF GRATITUDE TOWARDS DEVATMA

Q. How can a person grateful to Devatma develop the feeling of gratitude for him?

A. So long as a person is not motivated solely by his feeling of paying off his debt or does not himself want to do some disinterested service to Devatma or does not feel higher gratification or higher pleasure on doing service to Him and does not feel pain on not doing any such service, there is no proof that there is growth in him of some true feeling of gratitude in relation to Him. If some person expresses himself orally or in writing as benefited or grateful to Him, then even such an expression is not a proof that there is awakening or growth of the higher or altruistic feeling of gratitude to Him. Therefore, so long as there is no real growth of this feeling of gratitude in a person, he cannot have desire or craving to evolve this feeling.

Q. What is meant by the feeling of paying off the debt?

A. Debts are of two kinds. One kind of debt is that which a person on reaching his majority, borrows money or some other thing. And the second kind of debt is that which a person receives from someone else, without wanting or asking for it. However on getting help or service in his state of physical or spiritual helplessness, he becomes by the law of true religion, a debtor to him. The examples of these two kinds of debts are given below:

A certain young man went and requested another person, "A guest is coming to my house, I need a cot for him; please lend me a cot for three days, I will return it to you on the fourth day." Some other person went and said to a rich man, "I need a hundred rupees; please lend me this amount of money, and if you want interest on it, I am prepared to pay it and I will return this money with interest within six months."

The first person was given a cot on his making a request and the second also received the hundred rupees on making a request himself.

Both persons were lent these things on the condition that in accordance with their promises they would return the things lent in time. This is the first kind of debt.

Examples of the second kind of debts:

A person brought up her own or someone else's helpless child for some years. She provided with him food, she purchased clothes for his wear, she washed and got dried his napkins full of faeces and urine. She washed his face and hands, she bathed and wiped his whole body. She gave him toys to play. She kept him in open air as necessary for the preservation and growth of his health. She got his dirty clothes washed from the washer-man and paid him for that, or washed them herself and bought soap for washing. On his being sick she treated and, nursed him and in doing so she sacrificed her proper pleasure and her proper comfort whenever necessary. On the coming of the proper time she taught him the pronunciation of various words and how to speak. She sent him to school for his education and taught him various other things. During the days of his education and schooling she paid the fees, purchased books and met various other kinds of expenses etc. For many years and in various ways she supported and served him and for that, besides physical and mental exertion, spent on him.

A person, though old, was in a state of complete darkness and ignorance about his soul and soul-life. He was slave to various degrading loves of pleasure and their consequent degrading low hatreds; and was getting degraded day by day, and through this degradation was nearing his spiritual death day by day. There was no spiritual force producing altruistic feeling or love in him motivated by which he could strengthen his soul-life. With regard to soul and soul-life, he was in most pitiable and helpless state and though he was in such a state he was not conscious of it. He himself had no desire or anxiety to protect his soul-life from degradation and destruction or to gain spiritual force for himself. Now, through getting of sublime influences of Devatma, there awakens in him the consciousness of his most pitiable state, and he gets, in accordance with his capacity, freedom from various kinds of most harmful and false beliefs, traditionally received under the name of religion, and he gains most rare and true knowledge, and on getting true knowledge about soul and soul-life gains freedom from one or other kind of unjust or evil-based conduct in relation to the members of his family and

THE DEV SHASTRA III

various other persons and animals and other existences of Nature and through this freedom as far as it is possible, there is protection from spiritual degradation. On becoming aware of someone of his evil actions, there awakens in him the feeling of doing necessary reparations, and by doing this kind of true reparation he gets purification from its defilement. On getting one or other kind of true or higher consciousness he becomes a man of morals and through it saves himself from his soul-degradation to some extent. On possessing potentiality to grow one or another true altruistic feeling, he develops some higher-life-promotings altruistic feelings. After realization of all this kind of rare good, he become conscious that the extent of spiritual good which has come to him in this way, and the extent of physical and mental benefits which have been gained by him through this spiritual good, and the money or property or respect or position etc., which have been gained through this spiritual change, has been gained by him through the getting of the most sublime influences of Devatma only; and if he had not got the rare occasion of getting His sublime influences he would never have gained all these kinds of blessings. If by bringing before himself those great benefits received from his greatest benefactor, he feels himself to be his greatest debtor and there awakens in him some true and sufficient desire to pay off this spiritual debt and he is prepared to pay off this spiritual debt and for that he takes to necessary spiritual exercises and finds higher gratification or higher pleasure in these spiritual exercises of his and feels pain or discomfort on not doing it, then such activity of his proves that there has awakened that true altruistic feeling of gratitude towards the bestower of soul-consciousness, spiritual knowledge, spiritual salvation, and spiritual life i.e., Devatma. By the development of this feeling of gratitude for Devatma through spiritual exercises he can on the one hand establish his spiritual relation with Him by this feeling, and on the other hand can evolve higher life and power in his soul also.

Q. If a fit soul reaches this sublime state of the feeling of gratitude, then by what kind of spiritual exercises can he deepen this feeling in him?

A. After the growth, in sufficient degree, this feeling of gratitude in his soul, a fit person can perform his spiritual exercises of paying off the spiritual debt to Devatma in the following ways and thus develop his spiritual life:

(1) By donating money as an offering;

(2) By donating as an offering, some land, house, shop, well etc.,

(3) By utilizing his mental powers i.e., his education, his skill, his thinking faculty, his writing capacity and his power of speech for Him; and ;

(4) By utilizing his body i.e., energies of his hands and feet etc., for Him.

To the extent a person motivated solely by the disinterested feeling of gratitude becomes capable of serving Him through any of these ways, to that extent by such service he does spiritual good of his soul.

Q. Does it also happen that even on awakening of the disinterested feeling of gratitude, a person due to low-love of money and property, does not have the strength to offer them in proper portion and therefore does not do so?

A. Certainly, it does. First, human beings are so dominated by their-self love that through degradation due to it their souls become so hard that generally there is no growth of the true feeling of gratitude at all in them; and not to speak of their feeling for the greatest benefactor of their soul, they do not experience this feeling of gratitude even towards the benefits of their ordinary benefactors like parents etc. Secondly, the very small number of persons in whom this feeling is awakened to some degree are so tightly bound to the love of pleasure of one or other kind that they cannot desire to offer at all some of their energies; and those energies which they do want to offer, they have not the strength to offer them in sufficient and necessary degree and therefore do not offer them to that extent.

Millions of most low and most degraded selfish persons want to have, as far as possible, all the money and all other property of their parents for themselves. Due to the absence of their feeling of gratitude towards their parents' services, they do not want to give their parents even their self-earned money for their spiritual good. Given their ungrateful character it is not possible for them that they should offer some good portion of money they received from the parents for their good and for the good of others.

On the contrary, millions of persons not only do not feel themselves as debtors towards any kind of benefactors and do not have any feeling of gratitude towards them, but thousands of them due to one or other reason on becoming ungrateful are prepared on the contrary, to trouble, or to give pain or torture or still worse even to murder some benefactor of theirs; and by such devilish activities they satisfy their devilish nature and give proof of the presence of this devilish nature in their souls.

Q. But if some persons have such inborn capacity that the true feeling of paying off the debt of gratitude towards Devatma can be awakened in a sufficient degree in them and if it is awakened in them, then by what spiritual exercises can they, by growing their feeling of gratitude, develop their spiritual life or spiritual force?

A. Such persons motivated by their feeling of gratitude will know in accordance with their less or more depth of feeling and understanding that for the growth of this feeling which of the spiritual exercises of service described above they can take to and to what degree and extent they have the anxiety to perform them. And again, if they take to and perform such spiritual exercises in accordance with their capacity, then, by doing so just as on the one hand, they can grow their feeling of gratitude, so also on the other hand, with the increase of this feeling there will be increase in their service.

Q. Even after the bodily death of Devatma, can a grateful person grow this feeling for Him?

A. He can certainly do it. Even if he has not offered Him in His life-time some money or some other property and if afterwards here awakens in his heart true and sufficient desire to offer any one of them, they, he can offer it for the fund which is called 'Bhaint Fund' and which He Himself has established. Besides this, if apart from cash money Devatma has left various kinds of property, house, land, garden, trees, memorial symbols etc., and such dependents who have been loyal or true to Him till His death; or animals, then he can truly protect anyone of them in accordance with the consent of the Trustee or Trustees. And motivated by his true and disinterested feeling of gratitude and by thoroughly doing every such service, he can through this spiritual exercise also develop this feeling in him and increase his spiritual strength.

THE METHOD OF SPIRITUAL EXERCISES FOR THE DEVELOPMENT OF THE FEELING OF ATTRACTION FOR THE SUBLIME INFLUENCES ('DEV PRABHAVAS') OF DEVATMA

Q. How can the feeling of attraction for the sublime influences ('Dev Prabhavas') of Devatma grow in a fit person?

A. So long a person does not awaken consciousness about the degrading character of some of his low pleasures and does not realize the most fundamental truth, that it is only by getting the sublime influences ('Dev Prabhavas') of Devatma, that he can get salvation from the degradation born of his love of low pleasures; and besides it, can also awaken and grow in him some such higher or altruistic feeling through which constructive power of his soul can increase, and on getting these true consciousnesses does not consider the getting of the 'Dev Prabhavas' as the supreme gain over all other gains of the world and does not feel happy and gratified on getting them; till then just as on the one hand, he cannot feel any attraction for the sublime influences of Devatma, so on the other hand, he cannot be desirous of taking some true and necessary spiritual exercises of sacrifice or dedication.

Therefore, on sufficient awakening of these consciousnesses, just as a person can become truly desirous of getting salvation from the slavery of the love of some low-pleasure in him, so also he can become desirous of those sublime influences through getting of which this true desire in him can be fulfilled. And when there awakens a true desire in a person in this way for getting the sublime influences of Devatma, then this desire in him is called the feeling of attraction for the sublime influences of Devatma.

Q. If true consciousness is awakened in a fit person about any of his degrading loves of pleasure or degrading feelings of hatred, which motivated him to indulge in some thoughts or actions of misappropriation or harm in relation to a living or non-living existence of Nature; and true consciousness is awakened about those evil thoughts or actions; and he becomes truly desirous of salvation from it; and if he also knows that only by getting the sublime influences of Devatma, he can get salvation from that low-love of pleasure or from some degrading thought or action produced by it and he has the true desire or craving for getting the sublime influences of His, then what various spiritual exercises may be undertaken by him for getting these invaluable sublime influences of Devatma?

A. He should sit in a solitary, lonely, clean and beautiful place and should first do obeisance to Devatma through His photo and then should pray to Him with sincere heart for getting of His sublime influences in this way:

"Oh true Lord! Let the rays of your sublime light ('Dev Jyoti') enter my soul, and through them let my soul be illumined and I may see that degrading thought or action of mine in its true form which I have done or am doing or can do in relation to you or some human being, animal, plant or inanimate object and let me be able to realize at this time its real evil nature in its true ugliness and be able to write fully about its ugliness in my spiritual exercise book. Besides this, oh Lord! Let those rays of higher hatred and higher pain producing sublime power enter my soul through whose getting the feeling of hatred or still more the feeling of pain is produced for this degrading thought or action of mine, by the production of which alone, on the one hand, I can get true salvation from it, and on the other hand; I can become capable of taking true spiritual exercises of reparation in sufficient degree in connection with it and by taking to such spiritual exercises, I can gain true purity of my soul from that defilement."

If some verse or song or music can also be helpful in this kind of true prayer, he should sing it with sincere feeling and union of heart. After this, if he has some article depicting that degrading thought or action in him in its degrading aspect by some believer of Devatma who has got salvation or purification from defilement of that very degrading thought or action through getting of the sublime influences of Devatma, then he should study it with attention and deliberation. He should as well study some such article by Devatma which is on this very topic and by whose study also his sublime influences can reach him. Again, on getting His 'Dev Prabhavas,' he should write in his spiritual exercise book (which is kept for this very purpose) that degrading thought or action in him in relation to himself or some other injured person just as it appears in its evil or harmful aspect; and if he feels in himself a true urge to do reparation in relation to him, then he should copy down whatever he has written in his spiritual exercise book about the harm done to him or write a letter of this kind of description. After this, he should bring before himself the gift of the most rare and most invaluable sublime influences from Devtma that he has received and, in order to feel thankful or grateful towards Him, he should recall His sublime beauty and feel his insignificance in relation to Him by bowing his head again and again and by reaching a state of true obeisance should awaken his true faith and humility towards His sublime beauty.

After this spiritual exercise, he should himself hand over the copy of that letter to the injured person or send it to him by some other way. And, if there awakens in him an urge to go to the injured person in that connection and express his heart-felt sorrow or pain for that bad, wrong, faulty or sinful thought or action of his, then he should do so.

Or if there awakens in him an urge to do both of these things, then he should do both of them.

Q. If there is a 'sadhak' (one who engages in spiritual exercises) who wants to get still more of the sublime influences of Devatma in his spiritual exercises so that he should see in its true character i.e., in its degrading aspect that hidden thought or action of his in relation to Devatma or some person or animal or any other thing which is harmful for his soul about which he is in complete darkness and in relation to which he also wants to get those rays of sublime power (Dev Tej) by getting which there awakens higher hatred or higher pain in his soul towards the degrading aspect of it; then what else he should do for getting them?

A. In the spirit of the same spiritual humility he should pray again and again for the sublime influences ('Dev Prabhavas'). When on getting His sublime light ('Dev Jyoti') by such repeated prayers some inner thought or outer action of his in relation to Him or some person, or animal or plant, appears before him in its degrading aspect, or still more on getting rays of His sublime power there awakens in him higher hatred or, still more, a feeling of higher pain for that thought or action in him, then in accordance with the method described in the first spiritual exercise, he should again write down this situation and his feelings in his spiritual exercise book; and then send its copy, or some letter full of description of this kind, to the injured person and on his being alive on this earth and on his being capable of going conveniently to him in person, he should go to him and orally express before him his sorrow and pain; and in order to do reparations he should do whatever else he considers right to do through his bodily activities or his money.

Q. If some such 'sadhak' gets such sublime influences ('Dev Prabhavas') but the person, in relation to whom he has done some bad or degrading thinking or bad or degrading action, is not alive on this earth, then in such a condition how can he perform his spiritual exercise of reparation?

A. In such situation, if his spiritual exercise is really right or true, then so far pain is produced in his soul in relation to that injury, the waves of it, will spread through ether and on reaching that injured being i.e., the Devatma or some person or animal, produce effect of serenity on him and will also become source of purity of the soul of the 'sadhak'.

Q. Can such a 'sadhak' also take to some other spiritual exercises or means for this purpose?

A. Yes, he can do so if he has in him a true and sufficient urge to take to some such spiritual exercises.

Q. What can be the various such true spiritual exercises?

A. For the harm done by him to Devatma, he should accept punishment in the form of fine which he can give in the 'Bhaint Fund' (Fund of Offerings) or he can take to proper and disinterested service through his physical work for some such member of his family, animal, garden, or house etc., whose burden of bringing up or protection or looking after, Devatma had taken upon him-self till the time of His death; and if there awakens in his soul an urge to do this kind of reparation in relation to some harmed human being, then in this very way he can also be serviceable through money or physical work or both, to any such relation etc., burden of whose bringing up or protection, the harmed person had taken upon himself. And if there awakens in him a desire to do reparation in relation to some harmed animal or plant and that animal or plant is no more on this earth, then he can do true good to his soul by accepting some such kind of spiritual exercises in relation to its community or generation.

Q. If in a fit and capable person there has awakened a desire to get true knowledge about his soul and Devatma and he knows that there is necessity of getting sublime influences ('Dev Prabhavas') of Devatma for getting this true knowlege and that without getting His sublime light ('Dev Jyoti'), he cannot see in its true character, any truth in relation to those topics and so long he does not see or realize any such truth in its true character with his inner eye, till then he cannot have any direct true knowledge about it, then what kind of spiritual exercises should he perform to get the sublime influences of Devatma in order to get such direct true knowledge?

A. If such true desire has awakened in a person then he should sit in a clean, beautiful and lonely place and first remember Devatma through 'darshans' of His photo and by concentration on Him alone, he should get into spiritual union with Him; and then whatever kind of direct true knowledge whether of his soul or of Devatma, he is desirous or anxious to get, for that he should, with sincere feeling repeatedly and continuously pray to Him for His sublime light ('Dev Jyoti'). After such a repeated prayer when his soul is illumined by His sublime light ('Dev Jyoti') then he should study with full attention some article of His on that topic. Now, if he has got the amount of sublime light ('Dev Jyoti') which is necessary for realization of some truth about any such topic, he will certainly have direct perception ('darshan') of some such truth and through its 'darshan' he will gain direct true knowledge about that topic. But if he has not achieved such state of his soul or if the surrounding environments are not sufficiently favourable to him, then even by prayer to Devatma, he will not be able to get His sublime light ('Dev Jyoti') at all or in such amount by which he could see or realize that truth in that clearness, with which it is necessary for him to see.

In conclusion, so long the immutable laws of the spiritual world of Nature about getting the sublime light ('Dev Jyoti') of Devatma are not properly-fulfilled, till then no such 'sadhak' will get His sublime light in sufficient amount and the true realization of that truth which he could have on getting it would not occur, and therefore, he will not get the direct true knowledge which he desired to get.

Q. What is the favourable spiritual condition for a sadhak?

A. That condition of the soul of a sadhak is favourable in which some rays of the sublime light ('Dev Jyoti) of Devatma can reach through some true spiritual exercises. It is a condition in which his soul has not become so hard that no rays of the sublime light ('Dev Jyoti') could enter in him and even on sitting for the spiritual exercises he remains in the same state of darkness of his soul in which he was before sitting down to contemplation.

Q. Why so much hardness is produced in a soul due to which no ray of the sublime light ('Dev Jyoti') of Devatma can enter his soul?

A. The chief causes for the production of such hardness of heart are:

(1) Continuous growth of the various low-loves of pleasures.

(2) Continuous growth of low-hatred—especially growth or production of low-hatred, due to any reason, towards Devatma by whose sublime light alone, the

214

soul of a person on becoming illumined directly, sees some spiritual truth and thus can gain direct true knowledge about it.

(3) Continuous indulgence in some evil actions in relation to any existence of any department of Nature.

(4) Disregard of some truth even when there is direct perception ('darshan') of it in the sublime light ('Dev Jyoti') of Devatma, i.e., even on getting knowledge of some truth, not to give up one's false thinking, false faith, false sayings, and any false or hypocritical action giving up of which is necessary for his spiritual good; and not to accept or side with that truth, whose acceptance and support involves giving up of some pleasure-giving but degrading thought or action but in contrast to it to give superior place in his soul to falsehood and hypocrisy.

In accordance with the immutable laws of the spiritual world of Nature, a human soul can become hardened through any one of these four causes, and on gradually hardening of it when it becomes so hardened that no way is left for the entry of the sublime light ('Dev Jyoti') of Devatma in him, then no rays of the sublime light of Devatma can enter such a hardened soul and therefore do not enter it.

In this state he does not remain capable of seeing any, truth about what is good or evil in relation to his organised soul and his soul-life and he becomes completely blind.

Q. This is an extremely terrible state indeed! It is an extremely sad sight that a human being is incapable or becomes incapable of seeing any truth about his essential and fundamental part of him i.e., soul and soul-life!

A. Certainly.

Q. What are the external unfavourable environmental conditions for spiritual exercises?

A. The following are the main unfavourable conditions:

(1) Not to keep the body clean to the extant it is necessary to keep it pure or clean with water, but to keep it unclean or dirty.

(1) Not to put on clothes which are clean or beautiful.

(2) Not to keep the body clean to the extent it is necessary

(3) Not to have a clean or beautiful place for spiritual, exercises specially if it is very impure by its assimilating of his own or someone else's impure influences.

(4) The presence of some disturbing thing which disturbs the concentration of mind.

Q. If the inner condition of a 'sadhak' is also good and he has also got favourable external conditions and he has also some capacity for getting the sublime light of Devatma by sitting in his place of spiritual exercises and he is also anxious to get direct true knowledge about soul and Devatma and he also gets that amount of sublime light of Devatma by repeated prayers by which he directly sees some truth about soul and Devatma, then after getting 'darshan' of that truth, what else should he do?

A. After this, he should try to repeatedly meditate or think over that truth.

Q. What will he gain by this?

A. By this spiritual exercise whereas on the one hand that truth will appear before him in greater and greater clearness and on the other hand, it will get more and more deeply imprinted on his retentive faculty and he will be able to recall it quickly when necessary.

Q. Besides this, what other spiritual exercises he should undertake?

A. If he has sufficient power of thinking over such a topic and he also wants to view these events or facts in Nature that support the realized truth, then for this he should, on the one hand, pray with one mind to Devatma for getting more and more of his sublime light and, on the other hand, he should by union with Nature try through repeated thinking to bring before himself, in accordance with his capacity, those various events connected with the support of that truth which can come before him, and if they do not appear before him clearly then he should continue his spiritual exercise of thinking in the same way in connection with them the next day and in this way ever after, till he gets direct true knowledge about them.

Q. Besides this what else should he do for the growth of some such knowledge?

A. He should also study whatever articles on this topic by other thinkers he can get for the same purpose. By this study also he will get help in understanding these truths. Again, he should try repeatedly to fix them in his consciousness i.e., he should try to write them down in some note book or spiritual exercise book. By such spiritual exercises those truths will be very well impressed on him and at the time of necessity he will be able to explain them well in a speech or a writing or both when necessary.

Q. Can a 'sadhak' continuously increase this most valuable and rare knowledge of his through these spiritual exercises?

A. If the feeling of altruism is so highly developed in the soul of some such 'sadhak' that whatever truths about soul or Devatma he has himself become capable of seeing in the sublime light of Devatma, he will undoubtedly propagate them among such people who are ignorant of these truths and who on the contrary, believe various falsehoods as true and due to these false beliefs harm their soul or besides it their body or in addition to it do various other harms to themselves; and further if he accepts gladly the sacrifices and self-surrender which are necessary for their propagation, he will certainly become, through such kinds of his spiritual exercises, more and more capable of getting His sublime light ('Dev Jyoti') for seeing and realizing the truths more and more.

Otherwise, if on becoming selfish he becomes anxious to get more and more of this kind of rare knowledge for himself alone or he wants to show himself superior to others by explaining them to people and in this way shows himself superior and thus satisfies his feeling of vanity, then he will not be able to get any more this sublime light ('Dev Jyoti') and his path of progress for gaining this kind of invaluable true knowledge will be closed. Still more, if at the time of propagation of them he tries to produce this false belief among people that the knowledge which he is propagating before them, he has not got it from Devatma and by His sublime light but he has found it himself, then due to this false step there will be still quicker degradation and he will gradually lose also his earlier knowledge of the truths i.e., he will not even remain capable of seeing those truths which he could see before and therefore, he will return to the earlier state of darkness with regard to them.

Q. Then is it necessary in accordance within the laws of the spiritual world of Nature that whenever and whatever truth about soul and Devatma is seen or realized by a person through the sublime light of Devatma,

(i) That he should not express before any human being any of his beliefs or faith, nor write an article, nor keep a religious symbol, nor perform a ceremony against that truth; and

(ii) That he should propagate the truth with open heart and with complete courage and disinterestedness to people who are blind to this truth?

A. Certainly, otherwise he will not remain fit for getting the sublime light ('Dev Jyoti') of Devatma on these topics and for getting realization of more truths. And, still worse by siding with falsehood he will gradually become blind even to those truths which he was fit to see earlier.

Q. If some such desire has grown in a person that the constructive power of his soul be increased and that some higher altruistic feelings be developed in him in relation to some existence of Nature—whether for Devatma or a person or animal or plant etc.,—then what spiritual exercises he should undertake for fulfilling this desire?

A. Man, by his very nature, is pleasure-loving i.e., he is lover of pleasure.

Now, if no such higher feeling has awakened in his soul by whose motivation whenever he does any thinking or action, he experiences pleasure, then he can never himself become desirous or anxious for the awakening or growth of that higher feeling in his soul for increasing the strength of his constructive power. And, when there is not present in him any true desire or anxiety of this kind, then he cannot with sincerity take to any kind of spiritual exercise for its increase nor can he perform it.

But on getting 'Dev Prabhavas' of His if some higher or altruistic feelings like faith and reverence etc., for Devatma have already awakened in the soul of a person and by the satisfaction of this feeling, he gets so much pleasure that there awakens a desire in him for repeatedly getting it and on becoming enamoured of this pleasure, wishes the growth of that higher or altruistic feeling, then he can take to and perform those spiritual exercises which have been described earlier.

In the same way, if in some soul a higher or altruistic feeling of doing good in relation to man or any other kingdom of Nature is awakened and he has become so strongly desirous of pleasure of it that he does not want to destroy that feeling but wants to strengthen it, then he can, also for this purpose, take to and fulfil the same method of spiritual exercises for getting sublime influences ('Dev Prabhavas') of Devatma which have been described earlier. But if this feeling of his is not completely disinterested i.e., if on doing some service of someone he seeks in return, apart from the altruistic pleasure of doing good, some other pleasure of his own or somebody else's then, in accordance with the immutable laws of the spiritual world of Nature, not only will his altruistic feelings cease to grow by taking to such spiritual exercises, but to the degree that adulteration of pleasure of some low feeling is found, to that extent that higher feeling of his will go on decreasing day by day; and if its decay continues in this way, then one day that feeling of his will be completely destroyed.

In Conclusion: It does not lie within the nature of any human being that:

(i) even on knowing some false belief of his, some false thinking of his, some false saying or some falsehood- based action of his, he feels no hatred towards it and feels no pain towards it, but in such condition on the contrary he gets pleasure;

(ii) even on indulging in some harmful thinking or some action towards some human being, animal, plant or material object and he feels no hatred towards it even on knowing it to be harmful and experiences no pain towards it but on the contrary experiences pleasure;

(iii) even on awareness of his being ignorant of or in the dark about his being and in it of fundamental thing i.e., soul, he feels no hatred towards this ignorance or darkness and feels no pain for this state; but on the contrary feels pleasure; and

(iv) on having no consciousness of his spiritual degradation and of those low-loves and low-hatreds of his through which there is soul-degradation; and there being neither hatred towards that state of degradation and nor any consciousness about a spiritual strength, nor any attraction for this strength-promoting higher feeling, even on knowing or hearing about it and on experiencing no trouble or pain on the daily destruction of his spiritual strength; he should ever and to any extent desire to get salvation from it or to awaken or evolve any higher feeling. In accordance with the immutable laws of the spiritual world of Nature there can be no such anxiety or desire of this kind in him. Devatma embodying in Himself true sublime forces, has emerged in the human kingdom on the one hand to give salvation to whatever person in the human kingdom has such capacity that in him there can be produced some degree of that hatred and that pain for some degrading belief of his or for some degrading action of his etc., by whose production in sufficient degree it is possible for him in accordance with the laws of Nature to get true salvation from such falsehood or evil-based thought or action of some kind; and on the other hand to evolve or grow any higher feeling in whatever soul it is possible, because without the emergence of Devatma no such good changes could come in the human kingdom.

WHAT ARE-THE CAUSES WHICH KEEP A HUMAN SOUL INCAPABLE OF GETTING SUBLIME INFLUENCES ('DEV PRABHAVAS') OF DEVATMA EVEN AFTER COMING UNDER HIS REFUGE

Q. Due to what degrading feelings of his, a human soul does not remain capable of getting Devatma's sublime influences ('Dev Prabhavas'), even after he has come under His refuge through receiving His spiritual influences ('Dev Prabhavas') and on getting a spiritual change in necessary degree?

A. Besides his various other low-loves of pleasure by slavery to which he becomes indifferent to Him and does not want to and does not establish his spiritual union with Him, his various kinds of feelings specially connected with the love of self, make him and keep him indifferent to Him; and they reduce him to such a state of degradation that if he had ever before the capacity of getting sublime influences ('Dev Prabhavas') of His, then, on being reduced to this state of degradation, he does not remain capable of getting His sublime influences ('Dev Prabhavas') and, therefore becomes bereft of getting them.

Q. What are the degrading feelings produced by the love of self?

A. These most degrading feelings are as under:

(1) Strong hold of the love of the pleasure of selfishness.

(2) Strong hold of the love of the pleasure of vanity.

(3) Strong hold of the love of the pleasure of self-willedness.

220

(4) Strong hold of the love of the pleasure of low-hatred.

1. Strong Hold of the Love of the Pleasure of Selfishness: This low love sets a person:

(i) Not to feel any kind of relation with Devatma even on receiving various kinds of spiritual and various other benefits from Him and not to keep relation of any kind with Him but only with his partner in life or his child or any other such person or persons with whom he is tied by one or other kind of low-love of pleasure of his;

(ii) not to wish to become helpful, in any way, as far as possible, in connection with His supreme ideal even on getting most rare spiritual good from Him;

(iii) not to have desire in himself for seeing or realizing the greatness of His (a) Dev Rup; (b) Dev Prabhavas; (c) True teaching about religion; (d) supreme ideal; and (e) unique work and for remembering His benefits to him or members of his family and for thinking over his selfish or some other undesirable or harmful action of his in relation to Him; and

(iv) for the work being done in his village or city or in any part of the country of removing from people false beliefs about religion and some kind of social evil of theirs or some kind of sins or some other kind of good work through the sublime influences ('Dev Prabhavas') of Devatma for their such unique and most useful work, he does not have any feelings for giving any donation of his money and property, and excepting his sons, not to wish and not to do good of his own soul or his country by giving his money and his property for such good work; and as far as it is possible, not to utilize and nor to wish to utilize any of his physical or mental energies for the progress of some such work.

2. Strong Hold of the Love of the Pleasure of Vanity

(i) Motivated by the feeling that, 'I should not appear inferior in the eyes of any one or be taken as inferior even on being so', he does not accept any of one's wrongs, sins, bad actions, or faults in relation to any one, nor actions based on ignorance, injustice or fault in relation to any one. And not to admit any of one's disobedient actions, one's mistakes, any of one's wrongs or any of one's sins in relations to any one, or still more to coin falsehood of various kinds for hiding any one of them or still more to falsely accuse or blame another for the wrongs and thus by siding with falsehood day by day, he steeps one's soul in darkness.

(ii) Being incapable of seeing various truths about soul and soul life due to one's being only a human soul devoid of the psychic forces of Devatma and embodying various kinds of low-loves and low-hatreds and even on having no consciousness in one's soul about one or another kind of real evil and goodness, to think or believe oneself as having more knowledge and consciousness on these topics than Him.

Ignoring some truth or true facts of the spiritual kingdom of Nature due to bias for some old false belief of one's or some low-love of pleasure, to consider or believe oneself to be always right in accordance with the promptings of one's own feeling of vanity and if some teaching or action of Devatma is against it, then to think or believe Devatma to be mistaken and by getting habituated day by day to this great falsehood to increase darkness in one's soul.

(iii) On having a difference of opinion with Devatma to think of oneself as superior to Him and in order to show Him as inferior to boast of one's such false superiority from place to place, to talk ill of Him and to propagate amongst other people falsehood and irreverence in relation to Him.

(iv) Due to the feeling of vanity to see and think and believe as inferior to oneself even such a person who has come under the influence of Devatma and who on getting changed by the sublime influences ('Dev Prabhavas') of Devatma has made much greater sacrifice in comparison to oneself for getting a higher spiritual life and who is to a much greater extent serviceable to the supreme ideal of Devatma in comparison to oneself.

3. Strong Hold of the love of the Pleasure of Self-willedness

(i) Not to accept any instruction of Devatma which goes against any of one's loves of pleasure, howsoever degrading or harmful it may be to oneself or beside oneself to some other and on the contrary to feel pain, and therefore to act in terms of one's own wish on this topic and not to side with His good wish and not to follow it.

(ii) Not to listen to such a thing from any elder or even from one's head or not to like any check against any of one's love of pleasure, howsoever degrading its getting may be for one's soul, and still more howsoever harmful it may be for another; nay, on the contrary to feel hurt and therefore to try to act in accordance with one's own wish in that connection and thus by such activity of one's own, to keep on harming oneself or besides oneself some others also.

(iii) Due to one's love of pleasure of self-willedness even on being in some institution of Devatma, not to feel oneself bound to work in accordance with one or other of its good rules or one or other of its proper and right method in connection with that institution and not to do one's duty well in relation to it and to prove oneself harmful in its relation by remaining in such a low state.

(iv) On accepting responsibility of service of some kind to the supreme ideal of Devatma, not to work, in accordance with one or other method established or the one accepted by Him which is found working against any of one's pleasures and by working in accordance with one's own will or wish alone in this connection and to prove oneself as devoid of the feeling of discipline and harmful in relation to that work and still more not to work to that extent and not to attend to that extent to which extent it is necessary to do, but to attend for oneself, in that connection and to remain satisfied and happy even on doing harm to it due to indiscipline and in this way to prove oneself as incapable of remaining under an organized group or society or to work in accordance with its regulations or to follow them.

4. Strong Hold of the love of the Pleasure of Low Hatred Love and hatred are contrary to each other. A feeling of hatred is produced in a man in more or less degree towards a human being or animal or any other being, when he receives any kind of pain against any love or various pleasures from that human being or animal.

This hatred is called low hatred. This low feeling of human soul is most degrading one. Just as lacs and crores of people in the human kingdom motivated by the strong promptings of their low-loves of pleasure, indulge in various kinds of falsehoods and do other bad or unjust actions in relation to others so also they, by the promptings of various kinds of low feeling of hatred in them, do various kinds of actions based on falsehood and injustice.

(i) The human soul who hates any human being or animal etc., wishes for his harm, i.e., he wishes him evil.

Therefore he gets pleasure or feels gratified to see or hear about any kind of evil happening to such a human being or such an animal etc., whom he hates.

(ii) Due to this most degrading feeling of hatred, human soul comes to have perverted vision i.e., whomsoever he hates, he sees and presents his various things in perverted form. He sees and believes a well-wisher or benefactor as his evil-wisher or enemy and some real evil-wisher or enemy and real evil-doer of his as well-wisher or friend.

(iii) Due to this most degrading feeling of hatred, a human soul becomes revengeful in relation to another human being or human beings i.e., he feels comfort or is gratified to do one or other kind of harm himself in accordance with the occasion and his capacity, to the person or persons whom he hates.

(iv) Due to this most degrading feeling of hatred, a human soul becomes ungrateful to his benefactors i.e., instead of feeling indebted to his benefactors for the favours and of becoming serviceable to them in order to pay off this debt, he gets ready to trouble and torture them in various ways. It goes so far that some persons on becoming ungrateful, ease or satisfy their soul by going to the extent of murdering their parents or some other benefactor.

These persons, who have no capacity for any degree of salvation from the domination of these four kinds of most degrading but pleasurable feelings produced by self, even on getting the highest privilege of coming under the influence of Devatma, do not remain capable of getting His 'Dev Prabhavas' and on remaining devoid of getting them, gradually continue to become more and more degraded.

THE FALLACY OF THE FREEDOM OF HUMAN SOUL

Q. There are people who say or believe that man is created or made by their "god" named Ishwar, Parmeshwar, Parmatma, Brahm, Vah-guru, Allah, God, etc., and He has given man such power or freedom by whose virtue, if he so desires, he can completely free himself and keep himself free from any one of his such thoughts or actions which has been denounced as bad or sinful by that God of his. How far is this saying or belief of theirs true?

A. This saying or belief of theirs is absolutely false:

(i). This saying or belief of theirs is itself absolutely false that man is created or made by this or that God of theirs.

Therefore, when no such so-called God is producer or creator or maker of man, then their saying or belief that the God by giving this much or that much power to him, has given him the freedom that if he so desires he may do or not do some bad or harmful action in relation to himself or anyone else, is nothing but false in accordance with true laws of logic.

(ii). Every human being by his daily true introspection sees or can see the truth that in relation to the feeling of low-love and low-hatred of his, by coming under whose domination he has become its absolute slave, even on knowing that by satisfying it certain harms do come to himself or to someone else, he has no strength or power in him to give up that pleasure and he cannot free himself from the domination or slavery to it, and that he, has no freedom in relation to the pleasurable love-force to which he has become subordinate.

Whenever a human being wishes something and whatever he wishes, he wishes it due to the presence of some feeling and its promptings in him, but he can satisfy this feeling or wish of his only when no other feeling of his stronger than it or no other power of Nature outside him becomes a hindrance to it i.e., in comparison to the strength of that feeling of his, the other power should not be stronger, otherwise even on wishing something he cannot be capable of fulfilling it.

Examples:

If some child or youth who, due to some physical disease, has become so weak that he cannot even sit on his bed without the help of someone, he wishes in this state, that he should himself get up from the cot and run for a mile or a half, then such wishing of his will prove a failure and he will never be able to do it. If an old man of eighty or ninety desires that just as in boyhood and youth his physical strength had gradually increased in comparison and his physical organs had comparatively grown stronger, so also now his physical strength should go on increasing day by day and his physical organs should go on getting stronger; then such a wish or desire of his will never be fulfilled and his physical strength will not increase day by day and his physical organs will not get stronger day by day, because this wish or desire of his is against the immutable laws of Nature about physical body.

In the same way, if somebody is being carried away by a strong current of such stream the strength of whose flow is greater than his physical force, then even on wishing that he should, not be carried away by the flow, he will not be successful in this wish of his and if in this state of his he does not get necessary help by some favourable circumstances, then it is inevitable for him, by gradually losing his strength, to die by drowning in the water of the stream. And is it not true that several persons, even having no desire to die, do die by helplessly drowning in the water of some stream or sea? Certainly, it is true.

But, if a person on feeling some annoyance wants to drive away a fly from his face and for fulfilling this wish or desire of his, there is also sufficient strength in any of his hands and there is no other hindrance in it from anyone else, then in accordance with his wish, he can certainly use that hand for driving away or removing that fly. On the fulfilment of this very law, he can also do any other work connected with his walking, sleeping, awakening, eating, drinking etc.

In the same way, if a person wants to eat some sweets and if he can get the sweets from some sweetmeat-seller only, and he has also that amount of money which is necessary for buying it, and at that time the power of temptation or love of money is not so strong in him that it should become a hindrance to that wish or desire of his, and he has also strength in his body for going to the shop of the sweetmeat-seller, and the feeling of idleness is not so strong in him at that time which may be a hindrance or check to his going or moving, and there is also no other hindrance in this wish of his at that time, then on the fulfilment of all these conditions, he will certainly fulfil this wish of his; otherwise not.

Therefore, even if a person (1) knows some evil or sin as evil or sin; and (2) he even does not wish the harm which is done to him or someone else by it, but if he has become completely subordinate to the power of the pleasurable temptation of it, then, even on wishing, he cannot free himself from its subordination or its clutches or from that harm which is done through it to him or someone else. He clearly realizes this truth through his own self-examination that by wishing alone he cannot free himself from the domination of any such low or degrading power in him and he himself cannot get salvation or freedom from any such pleasure-giving power of which he has become subordinate or slave. And in this condition even if there is a possibility of his salvation from this degrading state, then he can realize it only through someone else; and he by himself and by his wishes alone, cannot get salvation from it.

Are there not such lacs and crores of people in the human kingdom who do not like to save themselves and never want to get freedom from any such evil or low actions of theirs or any such sin of theirs by which they get pleasure or gratification? Is it not true that lacs of people, take poisonous and health-destroying things for the sake of the pleasure of intoxication; eat and drink various health-destroying things for getting the pleasure of taste or palate; indulge in adultery for the sake of getting sex-pleasure; cheat for getting the pleasure of wealth; take bribes, suppress deposits, steal, gamble, tell lies and give false evidence and do various kinds of other unjust or misappropriating actions; observe some convention or custom or ceremony etc., of their faith or community or "bhaichaaraa", samaj, society or religion even knowing it to be false and keep one or other religious symbol even knowing them to be false and do various kinds of other hypocritical actions out of slavery to the feeling of superiority; and they do not themselves want to save or free themselves from these pleasures of theirs? Yes, still more if some other person, even their own parents or someone of the other benefactors, tries to save them from such pleasure-giving action and says or exhorts them against this pleasure-giving action of theirs, then they, on the contrary, experience hurt and pain in their heart and in several conditions, do not even want to listen to such things of his and still more look upon him with hatred. Then is it not absolutely fallacious to call or believe these persons, who are in such a state, as free? Certainly it is!

In conclusion, when a human being due to being in complete subordination to any degrading but pleasure-giving force of his does not remain its master or lord but becomes its slave, then he is not free but is a salve. And he who is a slave, how is he free? Therefore, those who are slaves are not free. Being by nature lovers of pleasure, human beings, of whatever pleasures they become slaves, in relation to them, they are not free but slaves.

Having reached this state of slavery or subordination produced by love of pleasure whatever spiritual degradation crores of persons do to themselves through evil conduct of theirs, from that degradation they cannot themselves get freedom or deliverance or salvation; nor can any of their so-called God or Avtar or 'bhagat' of that God or so-called yogi, rishi, muni, sant, mahant, siddha, buddh, jin, tirthankra etc., devoid of true sublime forces, give them true salvation from that slavery to the extent that it is possible.

A fit soul can get this kind of true salvation only by getting, on some good occasion, the sublime influences ('Dev Prabhavas') of Devatma, and by no other way.

Q. Then is not man free in relation to any of his thoughts or actions?

A. Whatever kind of thoughts come to a man and whatever kind of false and injustice-based actions he does and whatever actions of eating, drinking, sleeping, awakening, passing stools, walking, moving his body, speaking, sitting, lying etc., connected with his body he does; he indulges in them motivated by his various kinds of feelings only.

Therefore:

(i) He cannot and does not indulge in any thought or action in relation to a subject, for which there is no feeling present in him to think or act;

(ii) For that kind of thought or action for which there is some feeling in him to indulge, for checking or completely destroying that thought or action connected with that feeling, so long there is no other feeling in him, till then on being motivated through that feeling it is inevitable for him to indulge in some corresponding thought or action. Therefore when a person in connection with his body is feeling hungry or thirsty, is feeling an urge to pass stools, or is sleepy, or some other feeling of this kind is getting into motion some organ of his or some mental thought, then through this feeling of his that urge or action or thought is necessarily produced and if he tries to check or keep in check its satisfaction for some time, then it will be caused by either some other feeling in him or there will be some other force of Nature outside of him; and if none of these powers become checks, then motivated or prompted by that feeling of his, he will necessarily do some action for its satisfaction.

Q. If every human being indulges in some bad or good thought or any other action solely motivated by some feeling then why is he given punishment by a government for doing some crime in relation to someone?

A. The punishment is given for the reason that some other or others be saved from that harm which is done to them by that action of his, because the other person or persons do not want any such harm to be done to them through him and they have in them the feeling to save or protect or keep themselves safe from that harm. Therefore, whereas some (innocent) persons cannot protect themselves from any kind of harmful action or actions of one or many such (criminal) persons, there are other persons who due to one or other feeling of theirs get ready for doing this kind of work and through them such work gets done. Such people determine or accept in accordance with their feelings some method of punishment in relation to various kinds of crimes which is called penal code. This penal code is of various kinds from the point of view of its inferiority or comparative superiority. And through this penal code, as far as it is possible, various persons are protected from various kinds of harms of the criminal persons. Just as some tiger or lion, although motivated by some feeling of his, wants to kill and eat some cow, lamb or goat of someone, yet the person to whom that cow or lamb or goat belongs does not want, in accordance with his own feeling, to get that killed by the tiger and, therefore, on there being necessity, wants to harm or kill that tiger himself or get it killed by someone else and wants to protect its and his own right; or some other persons by accepting money or even without accepting it, protect that proper right of his; so also those persons who protect in this way the proper rights of the citizens of their own country or others and as far as it is possible, keep peace among them or still more try to do one or other good to them, their method of work of this kind is called government, and just as it is right, in order to protect one from the undesirable attacks of the lion, to give the latter necessary pain or do harm or kill him; so also for the protection of the proper right of any person of mankind, it is a proper and necessary action to give one or other kind of punishment to any person or persons improperly aggressive.

In conclusion, every human being only on being motivated through one or other kind of feeling, indulges or can indulge in any kind of thought or action, and never without it. Therefore, in true meaning of the term there is no freedom of his.

HIGHER CHANGES CAN TAKE PLACE IN A SOUL, ONLY ON THE BASIS OF PLEASURE OR PAIN

Man by his very nature is pleasure-loving i.e., he has deep love towards various kinds of pleasures. He accepts to undergo pain against the pleasures he has love for, only to the extent to which it is not possible to get that or some other pleasure, without undergoing it.

Therefore, whenever he wants to accept pain of any kind or to sacrifice pleasure of any kind, he makes such acceptance or sacrifice only for getting some pleasure. He has love for pleasure and pleasure only. He has in his soul a craving for pleasure only and lives or wants to live for pleasure only. In conclusion, all his thoughts, and all his other actions are for getting pleasure or avoidance of its contrary pain.

Therefore, when a person becomes lover of some such pleasure which he gets through some physical organs of his, then for getting it he becomes intemperate because it is inevitable for him. In this state, he eats and drinks various kinds of things which feel tasteful to him. Then on becoming a slave to pleasure of such taste, he does not refrain from doing injury even to his physical health.

In the same way, on becoming lover of the pleasure of intoxication or sex-pleasure or pleasure of idleness etc., he in various ways harms or wrongs his physical health or his physical organism. On becoming lover and slave of the pleasure connected with offsprings he, in bringing them up, produces various kinds of evils or harms whether for their body or for their soul and for his own soul. On becoming lover of money, property, superiority etc., he takes shelter in various kinds of falsehoods and various kinds of unjust actions for getting these pleasures; and besides the harm to his soul, he several times also harms his body greatly. Sometimes on getting mad in the love of some pleasure, he kills his own living body with his own hands. In conclusion, to whatever extent and of whatever kind, evil is done through man whether in human kingdom or in the lower kingdoms, whether to himself or to others, all that is caused by the pleasure-loving nature of his.

On being lover of pleasure and on having pleasure-loving nature, no human being can go against this fundamental nature of his because, in accordance with the immutable laws of Nature, it is impossible for him to do so.

Then, if some sublime or higher changes are possible in accordance with the laws of Nature in this pleasure-loving nature of man, then that is possible in him only by this one method—and that also not in every human being but only in some fit souls—and also among those in whomsoever and to whatsoever extent, spiritual hatred can be produced for any kind of false belief, for any false thought of theirs or for any kind of falsehood-based action of theirs or any unjust or cruel action of theirs or in special circumstances some spiritual pain can be produced towards any one of them. Only when that hatred and that pain is produced, then and then only, they can be free from it, otherwise not at all. Again, it is also necessary that on getting free from it, they should experience no pain but feel comfort or pleasure.

In this way there are persons who are lovers of the pleasure of self. If against that pleasure some such higher feeling can be awakened on whose production they get or can get some kind of pleasure and that feeling grows in them, then by the attraction of that pleasure of theirs, they do some good or excellent action for themselves or others, otherwise not. Devatma has emerged for fulfilling this true and immutable law of higher changes of Nature in pleasure-loving mankind.

THE EMERGENCE OF DEVATMA
FOR BRINGING IN A NEW ERA

After the coming into being of man there has been an extremely slow progress whether of his brain and of his mind and other powers. For a very long time, man was so much of a savage that even with regard to the relation between man and woman, he had not established the relation of a married couple. Then, when the attraction of the various kinds of pleasures of the relation of man and woman increased in him and he gradually took to family life and besides other things when his mental powers of thinking etc., were put to greater exercise for bringing up children, there was some more progress of his. In the same way, one or other kind of pain also set his various kinds of powers into motion to some extent and gradually helped in their progress to a certain degree.

In the beginning the number of human beings on this earth was extremely small, but with the passage of time it increased gradually.

For thousands of years man knew neither how to make fire, nor how to make cloth, nor wore any clothes, nor knew how to dig metal out of the earth and to make something out of it, nor had he any village or town, nor any shop, business and nor did he know how to read and write, but he lived a life like most of the ordinary animals of the jungle.

Then, when on the one hand comparatively greater path opened of the evolution of his mental powers of thinking etc., and, on the other hand, his loves of pleasures gradually increased, then by the motivation of these loves of pleasures just as there opened a greater path of progress of various kinds, so also, by the increase of such various feelings of pleasure etc., he gradually became more and more low—so much so that with regard to various actions of his, he became very low even in comparison with animals.

Leaving aside various kinds of cruelties done towards the animal kingdom, man in relation to his own kingdom has done murders, has committed misappropriations, has done injustice to the weaker sex; strong men have made by force weaker men, women and children their slaves, sold them to others like animals and have made money by doing business in this slavery; man has propagated various kinds of false and most harmful religious faiths, and on becoming believers of false religious faiths, people of various countries have tortured in various ways those not sharing their religion, have burnt them alive by putting them in fire, have troubled and tortured them in various other ways and have, murdered them. On the alleged wishing of one or other kind of the so-called gods, but in reality low spirits, they have made sacrifices of the blood of human beings, by cutting their throats, besides that of animals; by accepting instruction of one or other so-called god they have made unjust wars on the followers of other religious faiths. In such wars one side of people, on triumphing over the other, have looted their villages, have burnt them by setting fire to them, and besides making their women and children slaves they have spoiled the honour of their women. For misappropriating the property of widows on the death of their husbands, men by producing the false belief in them that the widow who dies by sitting on the pyre with her dead husband not only goes to heaven but also takes her husband to heaven, have also burnt them (the widows) in fire with the dead bodies of their husbands. By condemning women and other thousands of persons as inferior, they have kept them deprived of the progress of their intellect. Men have checked and denied widows the right of remarriage, and for getting the pleasure of sex etc., they started the practice of polygamy; motived by vanity and feeling of hatred, they have without reason, by calling lacs and crores of people as inferior in comparison with themselves, have condemned them as untouchables and have done various kinds of cruelties to them; they have propagated various kinds of absolutely false distinctions. On becoming slaves to the temptation of money, property and position they have taken to the path of various kinds of cruelties for getting them. On becoming rulers, they have set up most terrible methods of punishments in accordance with their degraded nature. For getting food and other things they have declared proper or legal the killing of various kinds of animals; and they have propagated various kinds of most cruel actions. For all these there is well-grounded proof in history of mankind.

This is a dark picture of mankind, which is certainly so terrible and so bad that it cannot be worse. And this state of affairs has been produced through its own various kinds of low-loves of pleasures and his low-hatreds.

But side by side with this most sad and most devilish stage of affairs there has been a gradual change of mankind in another direction which is certainly very beautiful and therefore very pleasing. This beautiful state of affair has also gradually evolved by the increase of the love of pleasure. After thousands of years, when several persons on knowing that Nature alone is the fountain head of their various kinds of pleasures and in its various things and powers, there is a source of their pleasures, there was awakened a desire in them to get knowledge about them, and this desire gradually increased. Then such persons of various countries on finding that the method used earlier for gaining knowledge of Nature which was merely imaginative, was not giving proper results, gave it up, and for getting the right knowledge of Nature, they discovered the right method which was necessary and adopted it. Since then, in accordance with this new method, they have achieved great success in getting true knowledge of Nature. It is this method which is called the scientific method.

On the one hand, by working in accordance with this right method and, on the other hand, by the help of mathematics which had progressed very much long before, amongst the people of different countries, the path of the progress of this new kind of knowledge opened more and more. By the opening of this new path, a new era of getting various kinds of new pleasures was ushered in on this earth for the people of several countries which can be called the age of technology.

By the coming in of this new age, man, by bringing under his control, various physical forces of Nature and by harnessing them for various kinds of purposes of his own, has been able to get various kinds of new pleasures which pleasures were not obtainable earlier by people of the human kingdom. With this there has been very great progress of his arts and industries.

Again, after experiencing cruelties and various conflicts and various kinds of quarrels, and pains and troubles in mutual relations, there gradually came a further change in his nature and in this state of helplessness he accepted those rights of others which he did not accept earlier. On the acceptance of these rights there gradually came great changes for the better in their mutual conflicts and methods of punishments for crimes and various kinds of unjust methods which were prevalent earlier, disappeared. There came into being various kinds of peaceful conditions in the relation between his own country and other countries, and the path of the progress of peace opened still more.

Whatever and to whatever extent changes pertaining to this kind of progress or civilization have come in the human kingdom on the basis of pleasure and pain, certainly represent wonderful and beautiful picture of the evolutionary process of Nature.

234

But even on the coming into being of this kind of progress in mankind and its gradually becoming civilized there has come no change in his fundamental nature of loving pleasure. By becoming lover of various kinds of new pleasures of his he has day by day become more of a pleasure-seeker. His pleasure-seeking has gone on increasing day by day. He has become more and more lover of the life of "eat, drink and be merry". His thirst for enjoyment has increased day by day.

With the growth of civilization whereas man's power increased in various ways and in comparison with savages or comparatively less civilized people, he became more and more powerful, with it his various kinds of loves of pleasures increased. Day by day he became greater lover of and slave to money and property, his children, his food and clothes, his name, his superiority, his domination over the weak, his government and imperial position and other enjoyments and their sources of satisfaction. So with the progress of his civilization various kinds of those evils were produced in him which were not found in his earlier state of uncivilized condition, e.g., hundreds of very rich persons who due to becoming on the one hand, lovers of pleasures and, on the other hand, on having stable incomes for their satisfaction, gave up work and took to a life of "eat, drink and be merry". On the one hand, again, these lacs of persons even though hard working and even on having true desire and capacity for earning their livelihood or work, could not get their livelihood or work through their hard labour and even on getting moans of livelihood or work, the money which they got for it, with that even daily necessities of theirs and of their family members were not fulfilled and so their dissatisfaction increased gradually. On the other hand, capitalists became desirous of taking more and more work from them in their factories etc., but remained indifferent to this sad state of theirs. The result of all this was that their mutual relations became very bitter and disquieting.

In order to satisfy their purposes connected with the temptation of governing and keeping imperial position and superiority, the desire of accepting and working on various kinds of intrigues and hypocritical policies increased.

In order to be called men of manners but having ill feelings for each other, the convention of meeting each other in a hypocritical manner was set up.

The law of purity connected with the relation between man and woman began to be violated and hundreds of young men and women of various countries began to believe their secret indulging in sexual pleasure even before marriage, proper and right and felt no harm of any kind in doing so.

Various kinds of absolutely false social distinctions were created on becoming gradually conscious of which various kinds of conflicts and revolutions took place between people of different countries.

Due to the practice of bad government of the ruling classes of various countries the feeling of mutual disbelief increased.

False and hypocritical policies increased in political matters.

By the increase of the pleasures of taste and hunting etc., the killing of various kinds of innocent, weak, and several kinds of serviceable animals increased.

On the creation of even small disharmony between husband and wife, by the increase of the temptation of sex-pleasures the method of giving up of each other i.e., taking or giving divorce from each other, has increased.

Many of the rulers of the various countries even on declaring themselves outwardly as protagonists of peace and even on signing peace treaties in relation to various countries, due to mutual disbelief in their hearts instead of decreasing armaments have tried to increase them.

In the people of those various countries in which there was awakened and increased the desire for getting such of their true or imaginary rights which the people of the other side were not prepared to grant them, low-hatred was produced in their hearts towards them. Those persons who in comparison with other hundreds of persons took very great part in exciting these low hatred of theirs and fanning the flames of that fire, became their leaders and their followers started giving them titles of very great honour and giving them very great respect by which their feeling of vanity went on waxing day by day, and by the increase in this hatred and the increase of vanity, in accordance with the laws of Nature, their perverted vision went on aggravating towards people of the other side. On the establishment of this perverted vision, they on the one hand, lost the power of seeing various kinds of shortcomings of their own and, on the other hand, their value increased in their eyes even against true facts. Due to this perverted vision the capacity to see the virtues of the people of the other side was lost and various kinds of falsehoods and hypocritically based actions were adopted towards them and the adoption of such various kinds of actions of falsehoods and hypocrisy were thought necessary and proper. Although with the development of various kinds of low-loves of pleasures, souls of the crores of persons went on becoming harder and harder and gradually darkness increased in them more and more, yet with the progress of science and with the increase of knowledge about the material things of Nature and about various kinds of energies of these things, various kinds of those other false beliefs disappeared, which were present in them before in the name of religion and whose disappearance was inevitable with the progress of science. But although on reaching this stage, these people felt compelled to give up various kinds of false faiths yet due to there being no true knowledge about religion, they began to grope in darkness and became even greedier and more slave to their low-loves than before. Several of such people became materialists and in this state became blind to and disbelievers of the truth of the fundamental and essential thing of their being i.e. their soul etc. etc.

Conclusion

(i) Before the emergency of Devatma, the whole of, mankind was full of spiritual darkness i.e., no human being in the human kingdom or even any of his so-called worshipful gods or goddesses or even any of his so-called guru, or rishi, or muni, or pir, or prophet, or jin, or thirthankar, or buddha etc., had any true knowledge of the organised existence of soul, its diseases, it degeneration and the true method of its salvation from its degeneration and dissolution and the necessity of the evolution of higher life in it and the true method of its acquisition.

Why wasn't it so? Because that sublime light ('Dev Jyoti') of Devatma through which alone such true knowledge could be gained, was not present in any one of them.

(ii) The above kind of true knowledge about soul and soul-life which is gained through sublime light of Devatma, that and that alone is true knowledge about true religion. Apart from it there is no other true knowledge about religion.

Therefore, due to being devoid of the true knowledge about religion, all men of this earth and all their worshipful gods and goddesses and all kinds of their so-called teachers of religions etc., were in a state of complete darkness even with regard to the true knowledge about religion.

Therefore, due to being devoid of the true knowledge about religion, all men of this earth and all their worshipful gods and goddesses and all kinds of their so-called teachers of the religions etc., were in the state of complete darkness even with regard to true knowledge about religion.

Due to this spiritual pitch darkness, crores of people of this earth were wrapped up in various kinds of extremely harmful and false beliefs in the name of religion.

Due to their being lovers of falsehood, crores of people of this earth not only believed in various kinds of false religious faiths, but besides being believers in those false faiths they, whenever necessary, made use of various kinds of falsehoods and moulded their conduct accordingly for earning money through their various professions, or for hiding some crime or sin or some fault of theirs, or of some shortcoming of theirs or for hiding some crime or sin or fault or shortcoming of some member of their family or other persons because of being bound up with them by some love of pleasure or for praising themselves or any of their things in order to get pleasure of the feeling of superiority, or for getting respect or position or fulfilling some such kind of political purpose for satisfying various kinds of feelings of hatred of theirs towards anyone else and for getting some other pleasure in various other mutual relationships.

(iii) Crores of people of this earth due to being wrapped up in their various kinds of false and extremely harmful beliefs in the name of religion believed in different worshipful beings.

These worshipful beings due to their being devoid of true `Dev Shakties' (sublime forces) and true knowledge of religion and being believed to be the embodiment of unreal powers as also for imparting various kinds of false and sinful teachings, were unfit to be regarded as worshipful beings.

In the same way, they offered worship to whomsoever they believed as their worshipful beings who were devoid of true sublime forces.

In that worship of theirs, the hymns and songs of theirs and reading and singing of praises about their worshipful beings were not true.

About their sins also they had no true knowledge.

Therefore they had various kinds of false beliefs about salvation from sins and in the name of religion they took to various kinds of improper and harmful or useless spiritual exercises and ceremonies and 'tap' and sacrifices and fasts ('vrat'), and pilgrimages etc.

Due to being lovers of their various kinds of low-loves of pleasures and being slaves to various kinds of low-hatred not only did they themselves indulge in various kinds of unjust thoughts and other actions in relation to various departments of Nature of their own accord but also by knowing them to be the teaching of this or that worshipful being committed various kinds of sinful actions on their sanction.

(iv) All the men, of this earth due to their having consciousness of pleasure and pain and having love of pleasure, naturally thought one or other kind of pleasure as the ideal of life, when in accordance with the true knowledge of soul no pleasure of any kind is the ideal of the being of man. Now that:

The whole of mankind was in a state of pitch darkness and ignorance with regard to true knowledge about soul and soul-life and crores of human beings were in the most harmful grip of the hundreds of kinds of false beliefs in the name of religion and besides this in their various relations, they acted on various kinds of falsehood, hypocrisy, deceit.

Motivated by their low-loves of pleasures and their consequent low-hatred whether in their mutual relation or in relation to the kingdoms lower to theirs, they indulged in various kinds of unjust thoughts and various kinds of unjust actions.

The various pleasure-giving but degrading actions of theirs to which they were subordinate due to being slaves to them, they were day by day going towards spiritual degeneration and death and they had no true consciousness about this spiritual degeneration of theirs, nor had they any desire in them for getting salvation from it, nor had they themselves the capacity to get salvation from such most sad and most helpless condition of theirs nor had they any true consciousness or any true desire of any kind of spiritual good.

Then, for bringing higher changes in this most dark, most ignorant, most degraded and most harmful state of mankind and for bringing into being absolutely new and blessed age, there was the necessity of the emergence of Devatma embodying in himself true and unique sublime forces. That Devatma embodying in himself those true and unique sublime forces is born and with his emergence there has begun that completely new age in mankind whose coming into being was inevitable in accordance with the process of evolution in Nature.

HIGHER CHANGES IN THE FOUR KINGDOMS THROUGH DEVATMA

Those kinds of higher changes, which have begun in human kingdom by the emergence of Devatma, could never come in it without the sublime influence of His true sublime forces. Therefore, in future also, in accordance with the laws of Nature, whatever kinds of higher changes in human kingdom are possible only through His 'sublime influences', for the further progress of its evolution, those higher changes or evolution will come through His `Dev Prabhavas' (sublime influences) and they are of this kind:—

(i) To the extent to which rays of that sublime light and power have entered in fit souls in accordance with their capacity, which sublime light and power have evolved by the evolution of true and unique sublime forces in Devatma, by them their souls have been illumined, and they, in that sublime light, have become capable of seeing various kinds of truths about the organised form of their soul and about various aspects of their soul-life and by realization of these truths they have got true knowledge about religion, which true knowledge they could never and from nowhere get without this sublime light of Devatma. And the various kinds of false beliefs about their souls which have disappeared by getting this true knowledge, those false beliefs also should never have disappeared without this sublime power of His.

This is the first kind of changes in the human kingdom which have come and which could come only through the emergence of Devatma. Therefore, in accordance with the immutable laws of Nature, in future also such higher change will come in fit souls of human kingdom only through His sublime light and power and never without them.

(ii) Fit souls, who on getting sublime light of Devatma have got the chance of realizing whatever of their unjust or bad actions in relation to any department of Nature as harmful for their soul and on getting rays of sublime power of His for whatever of these actions so much feeling of higher hatred is produced by which they, in accordance with the spiritual laws of Nature, have been able to give up those sinful or bad actions and to gain this true salvation also, has been possible only by getting the sublime influences of Devatma and therefore gained it. Whatever higher changes came in their souls by gaining this true salvation and thus they got the chance to be saved from infliction of those harms and pains, which harms they inflicted earlier on the different existences of different departments of Nature and which improper pain they themselves suffered, before coming of these higher changes. Such higher changes were possible in mankind only through getting the wonderful influences of Devatma and never without them. Therefore, in future also this kind of higher change will come only through the sublime influences of Devatma and never without them.

Beside this, those fit souls who on getting sublime light of Devatma and His sublime power i.e., His sublime influences felt, besides higher hatred, so much of higher pain for one or other sin or bad action of theirs towards any department of Nature, that motivated by it they got ready to do true reparation for one or other sin and in this way for doing true reparation of their respective sins, they, with sad hearts, returned money from their own pockets, to the harmed persons or to their heirs if the latter were dead, which money they had obtained through unjust actions of theirs and several of them returned it with interest and several others returned to the harmed persons, various kinds of misappropriated things of this kind. By such unique actions of theirs whereas on the one hand, they got true purity from those spiritual deformities of theirs which were produced in them by such kind of sins, and on the other hand the harmed persons or their heirs got back their lost money and their lost things and by it they got peace and higher pleasure. And when a person doing such reparation could not himself find the harmed person then he, instead of keeping that misappropriated money with himself, gave it for some good cause. Such unique and completely surprising higher spiritual changes also could never come in mankind without the emergence of Devatma. Therefore, in future also such kind of higher changes will come and can come in fit souls only through Dev Prabhavas of Devatma and never without them.

(iii) On getting the rays of sublime light of Devatma there has been awakening and evolution of such one or other kind of higher consciousness or higher feelings in fit souls whether in relation to various other kingdoms of Nature, by the motivation of which they by indulging in one or other kind of good thought or one or other kind of good action, got some help in increasing their spiritual constructive power. This awakening and evolution in human kingdom also was never possible without the emergence of Devatma. And in future also such kind of higher changes will

241

come in fit souls through the sublime influences of Devatma alone and never without them.

(iv) On attaining to those true and unique sublime-forces which appeared in seed form in Devatma and gradually evolved. He has true and complete love in His soul for whatever is good in relation to human, animal, plant, and material worlds of Nature and true and complete feeling of hatred for whatever is evil.

In the same way, in relation to every department of Nature whatever law or event is true and He has got knowledge about it, for that and that alone, He has complete love for believing it, for siding with it and for declaring and propagating it and contrary to it for every untruth or falsehood He has feeling of complete hatred and the feeling of complete enmity for destroying it. Therefore Devatma, by evolving these true sublime forces of His, has only goodness and truth-based relation with every existence of every kingdom of Nature and apart from it, He has with it no kind of relation of pleasure or that of hatred born of love of pleasure. The kind and extent of special consciousness of goodness and evil in relation to every department of Nature that He has, were not present in any of the so-called gods or goddesses or any founder of any of the so-called religions devoid of these true sublime forces. Therefore, on attaining to these special consciousnesses whatever special and completely new teachings in the form of injunctions and duties, in relation to all the four kingdoms of Nature, He has given for fit persons, those special and new teachings also they could not get from anywhere and from anyone else. By the study of these new injunctions and duties, fit persons of the human kingdoms on getting His sublime light, can see in accordance with their capacity the shortcomings in their souls in relation to various kingdoms of Nature, the knowledge of which shortcomings also could not be got from anywhere and by any method without His sublime light and without these teachings of His. Without getting this sublime light of His and without seeing truths of these teachings of His, no man at any time had ever got true knowledge and true consciousness about such shortcomings of his.

Again, on getting this very sublime power of Devatma, a fit soul, on seeing some such shortcomings of his, can feel higher hatred towards it and can become desirous of removing it; that higher hatred and that higher desire also could not be produced in him from anywhere and by any method without getting the sublime power of Devatma. Therefore, this kind of higher change also can come and will come in the future in fit souls, only through the sublime influences of Devatma and never without them.

Q. Do or can some higher changes come in the sub-human kingdom also as a fall out from the changes brought about in man, by the sublime influences of Devatma?

A. Certainly. When in a person, through the sublime influences of Devatma, consciousness is produced about some harmful or degrading action of his in relation to any of the lower kingdoms i.e. animal or vegetable kingdom or material objects, besides his own kingdom, or still more by the awakening of some higher consciousness or feeling, for doing some good is done to any of these kingdoms, then by every such higher change in him there is also a higher change produced in the kingdoms lower to his.

Therefore Devatma, who has appeared to bring higher changes in all the four kingdoms of Nature, sings the following stanza of the hymn connected with His supreme ideal in His daily spiritual exercises, by singing of which He spreads His sublime influences all around through His good wishes in accordance with the laws of Nature:

"Sakal vibhaagon mein Nature ke
Uchch gati prad parivartan ho;
Neech gati ho vinashat din-din
Shresht meil un mein utpann ho."

i.e. wherever and to whatever extent higher changes can come in every department of Nature through my sublime influences may those come, and to the extent some degrading activity can be destroyed, in every kingdom, may that be destroyed, and in this way as far as it is possible, may mutual sublime harmony or unity be produced in all the four kingdoms of Nature!